WEYERHAEUSER ENVIRONMENTAL BOOKS

WILLIAM CRONON, EDITOR

Weyerhaeuser Environmental Books explore
human relationships with natural environments
in all their variety and complexity. They seek
to cast new light on the ways that natural
systems affect human communities, the ways
that people affect the environments of which
they are a part, and the ways that different
cultural conceptions of nature profoundly
shape our sense of the world around us. A
complete listing of the books in the series
appears at the end of this book.

Drawing Lines in the Forest

CREATING WILDERNESS AREAS
IN THE PACIFIC NORTHWEST

Kevin R. Marsh

FOREWORD BY WILLIAM CRONON

UNIVERSITY OF WASHINGTON PRESS

Seattle and London

Drawing Lines in the Forest: Creating Wilderness Areas in the Pacific Northwest is published with the assistance of a grant from the Weyerhaeuser Environmental Books Endowment, established by the Weyerhaeuser Company Foundation, members of the Weyerhaeuser family, and Janet and Jack Creighton.

University of Washington Press
PO Box 50096, Seattle, WA 98145
www.washington.edu/uwpress

Library of Congress Cataloging-in-Publication Data
can be found at the back of this book.

The paper used in this publication is acid-free and 90 percent recycled from at least 50 percent post-consumer waste. It meets the minimum requirements of American National Standard for Information Sciences—Permanence of Paper for Printed Library Materials, ANSI z39.48–1984.∞○

CONTENTS

FOREWORD

God and the Devil Are in the Details

BY WILLIAM CRONON

I n the growing literature of American environmental history, few sub-
jects have generated livelier debate or richer scholarship than the origins and evolution of wilderness in the United States. Starting in 1967
with Roderick Nash's classic *Wilderness and the American Mind*, historians have traced the myriad roles that wilderness and the landscapes
to which this word has been attached have played in our national experience. We have had cultural and intellectual histories of why wilderness became so influential as a way Americans understood the special
qualities of their national landscape. We have had political and legal
histories of the policies, regulations, and laws that eventually culmi-
nated with the passage of the 1964 Wilderness Act. We have had biog-
raphies of writers, artists, activists, and politicians who were pivotal in
shaping American ideas of wilderness. And we have had social histories of the ways different human groups used and related to wilderness
landscapes in quite different ways, sometimes provoking conflicts that
even led to bloodshed. Indeed, some of the most important volumes in
this series—Paul Sutter's *Driven Wild*, Mark Harvey's *Wilderness Forever*, David Louter's *Windshield Wilderness*, and Thomas Dunlap's *Faith
in Nature*—all make strikingly original contributions to the history of
wilderness in the United States.

And yet despite this outpouring of historical writing, which might tempt one to imagine that there could be little new to discover about this subject, it is fair to say that no scholar has yet produced a study quite like Kevin R. Marsh's *Drawing Lines in the Forest: Creating Wilderness Areas in the Pacific Northwest*. At first glance, the book's approach might not seem very appealing: a closely argued local analysis of technical disputes about the boundaries of key wilderness areas in the Pacific Northwest from the 1950s through the 1980s. Since many readers in other parts of the country may never even have heard of some of the contested landscapes that are the focus of this book, it would be easy to conclude that its arguments are only of local interest, and that only scholarly specialists or nearby residents are likely to have the time or the inclination to work their way through what may seem likely to be a rather uninviting read for anyone else.

Such a reaction, however, would be both unfortunate and deeply misguided. In fact, *Drawing Lines in the Forest* offers insights that are relevant to all regions of the United States, and that arguably change the way we should think not just about wilderness, but about the much larger project of American land conservation in general. The seemingly simple but quite profound truth that makes Kevin Marsh's book so special is his recognition that *all land conservation is inherently local*. No matter how broad or abstract our ideas of land or wilderness might be, no matter how large or powerful the government agencies that oversee such places, no matter how far-reaching the economic forces or political pressures that influence the creation of a given wilderness area, in the end it all comes down to drawing very particular boundaries on very particular maps representing very particular lands relating to very particular communities and constituencies. There is nothing abstract about it, which means that if we really wish to understand the history of wilderness designation in the United States, we must finally study the subject at the local level.

When we declare that there are now more than 100 million acres of land in the American wilderness system—an area larger than the state of California—we convey both the scale of legally designated wilderness in the United States and the depth of our national commitment to protecting it. But there is nonetheless something disturbingly disembodied and lifeless about the phrase "100 million acres," because each of those acres exists at a very precise location, and each possesses its own peculiar attributes—geological, climatological, ecological, cultural, historical—that shaped the story of how it came to be designated as wilderness. Laws protecting wilderness areas are not passed in the abstract. They are the products of intricate negotiations among diverse parties with very divergent views about whether a given acre of land should or should not fall within the legal boundaries of wilderness. Government agencies like the Forest Service or the Bureau of Land Management have quite different institutional traditions concerning the degree of oversight and control they prefer to exercise over the lands they manage, and different parts of those agencies—and different employees within those different parts—by no means all think alike about where a proposed wilderness boundary might best be drawn. Ranchers and loggers and miners (to say nothing of ski resort developers and, in recent years, snowmobilers and off-road vehicle users) may all be inclined to think certain lands they care about should *not* be protected as wilderness—but they rarely hold this view about precisely the same acres. Even wilderness advocates are far from uniform in the priorities they assign to a given acre of land: a rock climber, for instance, may value very different qualities and experiences than a bird watcher or a whitewater canoeist or a professional ecologist.

The creation of wilderness, in other words, is a deeply political process involving myriad negotiations and compromises among a host of competing interests. Drawing a boundary on a map is hardly a simple act. Among the many virtues of this book is its ability to demonstrate just how subtle and complicated—and quite fascinating—the process of boundary drawing can be. But because Kevin Marsh uses the local history of wilderness designation in the Pacific Northwest as a way to understand the much broader national history of wilderness politics in the second half of the twentieth century, the importance of his study extends well beyond the political machinations and lobbying of various advocates for and against the wilderness areas whose histories he narrates. One of his most important claims is that a process initially controlled mainly by federal agencies became ever more open to public scrutiny and debate in the years leading up to and following the passage of the 1964 Wilderness Act. Early agency efforts to map potential wilderness were met by citizen efforts to draw quite different wilderness boundaries, and these in turn were met by industry representatives bringing still other maps to the negotiating table.

Marsh's narrative of this process is not a white-hat-black-hat story of heroic environmentalists confronting evil industrialists. One of his most important insights is that wilderness advocates and industrial interests shared a desire for defined boundaries so as to diminish uncertainty about what they could and could not count on doing in a given landscape. Defenders of wilderness wanted assurance that the lands they valued most could be removed forever from the threat of development—and those who wished to use portions of the public domain for economic purposes wanted assurance that they could invest capital in such development without fear of losing their investment to a subsequent extension of wilderness boundaries. To the extent that these two broad sets of interests could agree on the location of a wilderness boundary, they were both gaining a kind of certainty that was in many ways just as valuable as the actual acres involved. And the net result of an agreed-upon wilderness boundary was to constrain quite significantly the freedom of agency managers to change their minds about what could or could not happen on a given tract of land.

One of Kevin Marsh's most striking insights is that the resulting process of wilderness designation was essentially a form of land-use zoning, not all that different from the zoning systems that have been studied in much greater detail in major metropolitan areas. Rationalizing land use by imposing legal boundaries that partition economic and other forms of human activity across a spatial field regulated through the bureaucratic exercise of state power is among the defining features of modernism in the twentieth century. That the legal designation of wilderness is an expression of the same modernist impulse that sought to create homogeneous neighborhoods and functionally uniform commercial regions in the twentieth-century city may initially seem a surprising claim, but it is also hard to refute. Although it may seem odd that a landscape associated in many people's minds with primitivism and pristine nature should also be an expression of modernism, we will understand the complexities of modern wilderness and its protection far better if we grapple with these apparent contradictions—and recognize their deeper truths—than if we simply ignore them.

Because Kevin Marsh takes us close to the ground and asks us to look carefully at maps and boundaries of places many of us have never visited, he helps us understand important features of wilderness that are much harder to see when one looks only at wilderness on a national scale. He argues that recent scholarly debates about whether wilderness is or is not "pristine" are not especially helpful for understanding actual wilderness politics in the late twentieth century, because in fact real laws and real boundaries rarely turned on the question of whether land was or was not pristine. Instead, the designation of a given wilderness area had less to do with nature than with politics and history. If you wish to know why Americans care so much about wilderness, there are many other wonderful books you will surely want to read. But if you wish to know how Americans have actually made decisions about whether or not to protect a given acre as wilderness—and if you wish to understand the history of how and why such decisions have been differently made in different places over time—then this is the book you need to read. There are few more persuasive reminders that no matter how broad one's passion for protecting nature, in the down-to-earth, day-to-day work of accomplishing that lofty goal, God and the devil are always in the details.

ACKNOWLEDGMENTS

Although I have spent countless hours alone on this project, I have never been lonely in the process; my thoughts often wandered to the many people who have shaped my understanding of the Cascades, wilderness, and the study of history. Many of the questions pursued here arose during countless trips into the backcountry of the Cascades, often alone but most enjoyably with friends and family. I have climbed every step of the way with them in my thoughts.

Much of my personal experience with wilderness and the Cascades comes from my ten years working as a wilderness ranger for the Skykomish Ranger District. Although I reserve my strongest criticism in the following pages for the U.S. Forest Service, I am deeply grateful to the extraordinary individuals, particularly John Robinson and Katijo Willig, within the agency with whom I had the pleasure to work and who gave me the opportunity to know enough to write this book.

I thank my academic mentors for their great patience, guidance, and support. John E. Kicza, David Coon, and Laurie Mercier were very helpful, and I admire each of them as scholars and teachers. Paul Hirt has helped me through this project for many years, and his influence on my work is extensive. His input has made the final product far better than it otherwise could have been. He has taught me much about the process of writing history, and I am grateful to have him as a friend and mentor.

The greatest joy of my time as a graduate student at Washington State University was the lasting friendships that came from sharing several years of difficult work with other students. Many of my fellow WSU graduate students have seen various early stages of this book emerge over the years, and I want to especially thank Jeff Crane and the environmental history writing group that he initiated for their comments. Jeff, Andrew Duffin, Michael Egan, Sara Ewert, Greg Hall, Brenda Jackson, Mee-Ae Kim, Liza Rognas, and Steve Shay are all great friends and fine scholars. I'm glad to have played on their team.

I received research assistance from many archivists, but none more so than Cheryl Oakes at the Forest History Society. I am also grateful for the financial support of the Bell Fellowship, which sponsored my research there, and the Boeing Fellowship for Environmental Studies at WSU. Thanks also to Lauren Giebler for her careful archival research and to the Undergraduate Research Initiative at Boise State University, which funded her work.

The field of wilderness history continues to be rich with fine scholars. I owe many debts to those whose work I have tried to build on, but I am particularly grateful to the close readings that Paul Sutter and Michael McCloskey both offered on earlier drafts. I hope I have effectively absorbed enough of their fine advice.

Among the scholars I most admire is William Cronon, and I am deeply honored and grateful to him for generously including my work in the Weyerhaeuser book series that he edits. I am thrilled that the University of Washington Press decided to publish this work, and I thank Julidta Tarver, Beth Fuget, and Mary Ribesky for their support. Pam Bruton improved the book with her copyediting.

Among the pleasures of this project was the opportunity to conduct oral-history interviews with various influential individuals who appear in the following chapters. I thoroughly enjoyed the many hours of discussions—both formal and informal—with Polly Dyer, Brock Evans, Andy Kerr, Michael McCloskey, and Doug Scott. I greatly admire them for their knowledge and for the passion that they bring to issues of wilderness preservation. I thank them for taking time to meet with an unknown scholar, but far more so I am deeply grateful to them for their many years of service.

It is my great pride to have completed this book as a faculty member of the History Department at Idaho State University. It is a wonderful place to work. I both respect and enjoy my colleagues. They have all given me great opportunities, and I hope this book reflects positively on our institution.

My family is a wonderful influence and inspiration in everything I do, and this book is no exception. It is certainly a product of so much they have taught me. Aunt Dot took me to the Cascades at a young age and taught me to be attentive in their presence and to always bring rain gear. My parents have always offered great support and high standards, for which I am grateful. And Duncan and Tobin are role models I will forever be chasing.

It is certainly a satisfying feeling to have published a book on an important topic, but it pales in comparison with the joy of sharing life with my wife, Erika, and our son, Danil. They both enrich my life and work in inexpressible ways. I dedicate this book to them.

Drawing Lines in the Forest

INTRODUCTION

Bringing Wilderness History Back to the Land

There are places in the Cascade Mountains of Washington and Oregon where one can become immersed in a depth of isolation and solitude that is rare in our modern world. Within the dense forests that flourish on the rain-drenched western slopes of the range, hikers can lose themselves in "the forest primeval." Seekers of solitude praise the opportunity to become lost in time and space. Such a perspective is tempting in a place where the impact of humanity seems so distant and where an individual can be overcome with a sense of insignificance and humility, but it lacks any sense of history; it is timeless.

A surprising discovery abruptly awoke me from this ahistorical misconception several years ago at the end of a week-long excursion in the rugged, isolated, and densely vegetated valley of Camp Robber Creek in the Alpine Lakes Wilderness Area in the western Cascades of Washington State. I was conducting research on human impacts in the wilderness area for the U.S. Forest Service at the upper lakes of this drainage, where I had encountered no one and observed very few signs of human presence for the previous five days. In the lower reaches of the valley, just above where the creek empties into the East Fork Miller River, I broke out of the dense huckleberry brush, bloodied and bruised from pushing through miles of thick, woody undergrowth, and into a very

MAP 1. National Forest Wilderness Areas in the Cascade Range, Oregon and Washington. Map by Peter Morrison and Barry Lively.

small clearing under the forest canopy defined by the obvious outline of a square cabin. In the middle of this now-roofless home lay remnants of the domestic implements that belonged to the former occupant: pots, plates, utensils, and a collapsed cast-iron woodstove. I was still alone, but no longer was I isolated from human presence. The forest primeval had become the forest historic, an indisputable reminder that the rugged Cascade Range has been home to many people for a very long time and that our contemporary image of the range as temporary recreational retreat has been valid for only a very limited time.

The cabin along Camp Robber Creek raises many questions about both the history of the Cascades and wilderness throughout the United States. Among the most contentious struggles over American land use in the past fifty years has been the designation of wilderness areas on federal land. Although Forest Service employees Aldo Leopold and Arthur Carhart defined wilderness as a land use policy on national forests in the 1920s, the pivotal event in this struggle was the passage of the Wilderness Act of 1964. By prohibiting most mechanized transportation and industrial development, wilderness is the strictest classification of American land use.

The National Wilderness Preservation System is the collection of wilderness areas created by the Wilderness Act of 1964 and by individual wilderness bills passed during almost every Congress since then. As of 2006, the system contains nearly 107 million acres of land in 690 units managed by four federal agencies: the National Park Service, the U.S. Fish and Wildlife Service, the Bureau of Land Management (all under the Department of the Interior), and the U.S. Forest Service (of the Department of Agriculture). Prior to 1964, the Forest Service had its own system of protected areas, labeled "canoe area," "primitive area," "limited area," "scenic area," "wild area," and "wilderness area," with the distinctions usually based on size. From 1929 to 1964, the agency created, maintained, and managed these areas under its own administrative jurisdiction without congressional oversight.[1]

The word "wilderness" has an ancient etymology and a complex set of modern meanings.[2] The widespread use of "wilderness" as a vague reference to wild, undeveloped areas without human influence is historically inaccurate, since hardly any land is without human interaction, and it continues to create confusion for the general public and policy makers. In this book, all use of the noun "wilderness" refers precisely to those portions of public land that have been legally classified as wilderness areas, either by the Forest Service prior to 1964 or by Congress afterward.[3] (The one exception to this is the use of the term "de facto wilderness," beginning in chapter 3.) How and where those boundary decisions occurred on national forests and who participated are the central issues of the following chapters.

To many, such an obvious remnant of active human presence as the cabin along Camp Robber Creek contradicts a strongly developed mythology of wilderness as a place apart from humanity. People who have opposed wilderness designation for certain areas point to examples of development even less obtrusive than an old cabin to argue that a given site should be disqualified from protection as wilderness.[4] In recent years, many scholars who deconstruct the idea of wilderness might point to the cabin as an example that there is no such reality as a pristine wilderness unaffected by human influence and that to pursue such an idea in public policy is delusional and counterproductive.[5]

In the following case studies of debates over specific wilderness proposals after World War II, I find the existence of this cabin and countless other examples of human influence in the wilderness areas of the Cascades less problematic, because in the central core of the debates—defining wilderness boundaries—the mythology of a pristine wilderness was less important than environmental concerns over industrial logging practices and access to timber resources. In the years after World War II, most wilderness advocates and their opponents in the timber industry did not see a contradiction between an old cabin and wilderness. For them, "wilderness" was mainly a form of land use in which—in contrast to most areas in the national forests—road building, logging, and other forms of industrial development were not allowed.

Wilderness is a modern form of land use, one that, like other forms, has its own set of laws and regulations and also has an impact on the landscape. Creating and managing a wilderness area has an impact on the local environment, though one that is very different from the alternative options, which usually include road building and other development. One of the values of wilderness is that even though it is not a place of pure nature, it promotes biological diversity and ecological integrity more than any other land use option and supports a large economic sector in nonmotorized recreation.

When thinking historically, focusing on wilderness as a form of land use in specific places rather than as a vague and romantic ideology brings us back to the land and illuminates more constructively the historical and environmental significance of political disputes over wilderness areas. With this in mind, in the following chapters I will focus on debates over wilderness boundaries in specific places in Oregon and Washington from 1950 to 1984, identifying the central issues and participants, documenting how they changed over time, and tracing their influence on future land use in the Cascade Mountains.

I place this story in the Cascade Mountains of Oregon and Washington because the wilderness debates in this area have been continuous since 1950 and because several of these debates represent the most significant stages in the national history of wilderness since World War II. Although the following chapters present case studies in overlapping chronological order, the following geographical description of the range places each of the cases from south to north.

The Cascade Mountains create a thin band of rugged, spectacularly wrinkled geography from northern California to southern British Columbia.[6] It is the dominant geographical feature in the Pacific Northwest, a region often referred to as "Cascadia." In southern Oregon, the range sprawls across the landscape like a discarded towel, with a maze of deeply eroded river valleys. The ridges do not reach high elevations in this region, but the slopes are extremely steep and densely covered with a thick mat of brush and forests. Rich stands of Douglas fir dominate the vegetation here, providing valuable sources of timber even to this day. Partly due to the value of these forests to the timber industry, the wilderness areas in this part of the Cascades tend to be quite small. Although debated for decades, many of these were not established until 1984, after much effort on the part of wilderness advocates to protect these forests, such as those around Waldo Lake, with legislation.

The volcanic legacy of the Cascades is clear as one heads north toward the Three Sisters of central Oregon, site of the first major postwar wilderness debate in the Northwest and the topic of chapter 1. These relatively young volcanic cones rise to 10,000 feet and sit atop the "Old

Cascades," the broad, ancient lava flows that form the base of the Oregon Cascades. The Three Sisters support a series of glaciers, and their aprons of lava and pumice create a mostly treeless barrier around their bases. The Old Cascades, with their steep slopes and dense forests, spread far to the west, until they settle into the Willamette Valley. Drier forests of ponderosa pine and lodgepole pine reach up shorter slopes from the east out of the Deschutes River basin. Chapter 1 emphasizes that all these lower forests, especially on the west side, were the focus of wilderness debates beginning in the 1950s, and chapter 5 examines how much the Three Sisters debate and its participants had changed after 1968.

A little way to the north, Mount Jefferson, standing alone and taller and older than the Three Sisters, is a towering, glaciated presence, the most intimidating of all the peaks of the Oregon Cascades. It sits on a narrow bench, and the lower, western forested valleys delve in nearly to its base. At the northwest foot of the mountain lies Jefferson Park, perhaps the most photographed and most popular backcountry recreation site in the Oregon mountains. Although Jefferson Park is the most visible symbol of the Mount Jefferson Wilderness Area, the debate over the area's boundaries focused on the valley forests below the alpine zone, as chapter 3 documents. This chapter also discusses the Forest Service's use of a definition of "pure wilderness" ("the purity doctrine") in its attempt to limit the amount of timber Congress would protect in this area.

From the north bank of the Columbia River, the Washington Cascades rise until they reach the climax of the entire range along the border with Canada. Mount Rainier is a dominating presence in the Northwest, visible from long distances and an elegant and powerful symbol for Washington State. In 1899, shortly after the creation of Crater Lake National Park, Mount Rainier became protected under national-park status. Congress had given much of central Washington to the Northern Pacific Railroad in the nineteenth century, which later passed it on to timber companies. The federal government traded public lands in other states to consolidate ownership for Mount Rainier National Park and transferred acreage from the Pacific Forest Reserve to the national park, setting a precedent for later heated disputes over jurisdiction of Cascade forests between the Forest Service and the National Park Service, as we shall see in chapter 2.[7]

North from Snoqualmie Pass, the Cascades rise in increasingly shattered crescendos, a granite landscape scoured by glaciers down to heavily forested valley floors just a few hundred feet above sea level. The ridge tops, at 8,000–9,000 feet, drop off into dizzying vertical space down to the valley bottoms. Fur trader Alexander Ross, who made his way from east to west across this region in 1814, recalled, "A more difficult route to travel never fell to man's lot."[8] These are "the American Alps" and the broad setting for chapters 2 and 4. Although the monumental alpine scenery allowed wilderness advocates in the 1960s to generate support for the creation of the North Cascades National Park, the focus of their concerns once again lay in the valley forests. The park campaign served as an important tool for them to limit logging and challenge the authority of the Forest Service. Later wilderness debates of the 1970s and 1980s, documented in chapters 4 and 6, questioned the status of forests left out of the North Cascades National Park in 1968.

The southern end of the northern Cascades region is marked by a high, alpine plateau covered with hundreds of lakes. Photos of this Alpine Lakes country grace many calendars and coffee tables. Like spokes from an axle, deep, heavily forested valleys radiate out from its alpine core. Chapter 4 demonstrates how controversy over where to draw wilderness boundaries in these forests elicited a new level of public participation that greatly reshaped the nature of all future wilderness debates.

The economic focus in the mountains has been on the low- to middle-elevation forests of the western slopes, especially since the development of industrial logging in the late nineteenth century. The massive stands of Douglas fir, western hemlock, and western red cedar have attracted investors throughout the world and have inspired poetic descriptions of their grandeur. In 1869, Samuel Wilkeson, reconnoitering proposed routes for the Northern Pacific Railroad through the Cascades in Washington, wrote glowingly about the potential resources of the region and the riches that would be opened up for exploitation by the forthcoming railroad. "But of all the marvels, and all the beauties, and all the majesties of this region," he exclaimed, "these forests of giant trees are chief." He described "forests in which you cannot ride a horse . . . forests into which you cannot see, and which are almost dark under a bright midday sun . . . ; surpassing the woods of all the rest of the globe in the size, quantity, and quality of the timber."[9]

Most of the low-elevation, coastal forests that Wilkeson described no longer existed by the mid–twentieth century. Private timber companies and settlers had claimed the best lands and most valuable forests in the nineteenth century and proceeded to cut timber rapidly through the mid–twentieth century. The most valuable sources of timber came from these private lands outside, and at lower elevations than, the national forests.[10] The national forests represent the middle and higher elevation zones of the Northwest, and the timber on their lower slopes and valleys became the staple supply for the region's forest industry only after World War II. These forested valleys have since served as the main arena for debates over the proper use of public lands in the region and where to determine the boundaries of protected wilderness. It was with respect to these valleys that the most important and contentious decisions were made on where to draw lines in the forest.

Historians of the United States recognize World War II as a transforming watershed for all aspects of American life, and historian Samuel Hays has documented how environmental politics underwent remarkable change in the immediate postwar years as well. The wilderness issues were no different, but it is important to recognize that all sides of the debate changed in ways that set the stage for heightened conflict. This is not simply a history of an emerging environmental movement; the roles of the timber industry and federal foresters as active players in wilderness debates also changed greatly during these years.[11]

The U.S. Forest Service clearly shifted its priorities toward increased extraction of timber from the national forests in the years following World War II. An era of stewardship of the nation's forests gave way to an emphasis on rapid extraction of timber resources as part of broader federal strategies to promote economic growth during the Cold War. Private timber companies had exhausted most of their supply before the war, and now federal foresters enthusiastically stepped forward to meet the growing demand. Their prior dedication to wilderness protection clearly took a backseat to timber sale and road construction programs during these years, as evidenced in their slogans of "multiple use" and "intensive management." The Douglas fir forests of the Cascades became the leading source for this boom in timber supply.[12]

The postwar era also witnessed an increase in outdoor recreation and in political support for environmental protection, including concern for undeveloped sites. In direct response to increased development on public lands, this growing environmental movement organized to promote passage of a national wilderness bill in order to remove from the Forest Service its previously autonomous authority to decide the fate of wildlands under its jurisdiction.[13] Debates over forestlands in the Cascades provided critical impetus for the creation and expansion of the American wilderness system in the succeeding decades. For this reason alone, a study of Northwest wilderness debates is important for understanding wilderness history throughout the nation.

Its advocates saw wilderness designation as an important and effective tool to limit logging on public lands. Brock Evans, one of the leading architects of Northwest wilderness campaigns in the 1960s and 1970s, recalls, "The issues are not really wilderness purity and the legalism of the Wilderness Act or any of those things. The struggles always were over logging first."[14] Often they described the results of their efforts as akin to municipal zoning ordinances; as political methods of establishing land use boundaries, wilderness designation and zoning ordinances have many similarities. Conservationists used other tools as well, such as creating a national park (where logging is not allowed) out of Forest Service land in Washington State in the 1960s and turning to lawsuits to protect endangered-species habitat after Congress restricted wilderness debates in the mid-1980s. But wilderness advocates continued to favor wilderness designation over other options, because after 1964, when the Wilderness Act was passed, it was more permanent than legal injunctions and more effective in preventing development than other land use designations, such as national parks.

Their opponents in the timber industry valued wilderness decisions as an important opportunity to secure access to reliable timber supplies, and, like environmental groups during this era, industry coalitions organized on an increasingly national scale to lobby for their interests. I wish to emphasize throughout this work that their role is not that of the simple opponent; they are very much responsible for the passage of various wilderness laws and the resulting boundaries on the land. Those in the timber industry employed wilderness designation as a tool to define specific boundaries, outside of which they hoped to count on a more reliable supply of timber from public land. Without the wilderness boundary, the fate of large areas of roadless forestlands often remained in limbo, with timber sales increasingly challenged by environmental lawsuits beginning in the late 1960s. Drawing boundaries that left valuable forests outside protected areas was as important as putting trees in the wilderness. A. W. Greeley, assistant chief of the Forest Service, expressed this interpretation clearly after Congress created the Mount Jefferson Wilderness Area in Oregon in 1968: "We construe the passage of the Mt. Jefferson Wilderness Act as an expression of Congressional intent that the lands outside the Mt. Jefferson Wilderness area should be managed for uses other than wilderness."[15]

Both sides of the debate were influential, as evidenced by the impressive growth in acreage of protected land under the Wilderness Act and the simultaneous transformation of the majority of old-growth forests on public lands into industrial tree farms. One lesson that I suggest from this history is that designating wilderness in the Northwest benefited both preservation and logging interests.

If there is a clear loser in this story, it is the bureaucratic autonomy of the Forest Service. In the 1950s, the agency had complete control over setting wilderness boundaries; neither the timber industry nor conservationists seemed to have much leeway in influencing those decisions. By the 1970s, however, the Forest Service had in many cases the least control of any major player in the debates. As the influence of the federal bureaucracy declined, both the industry and wilderness advocates consistently improved their organizational structures and ability to shape debates in Congress, which itself asserted absolute authority in establishing or changing wilderness boundaries after 1964.

One result of these changes that I wish to emphasize is that by the 1970s the debates became far more open to broad public participation than they had been in the 1950s. Historian Paul Sutter has noted in his study of the prewar founding of the modern wilderness movement, "Prior to World War II, wilderness politics were insular; after the war they became increasingly popular."[16] More precisely, I believe that this process, which began after the war, accelerated greatly after passage of the Wilderness Act. The public had limited access to and influence with the Forest Service, but after 1964, when Congress assumed the authority to define wilderness boundaries, the public had more influence over the outcomes of the debates through their congressional representatives. This is one of the most significant, though neglected, legacies of the Wilderness Act nationwide, and much of this development was a product of the conflicts that erupted over logging in the Cascades.

Rather than being a closed and elitist process, as critics have often portrayed it, these political conflicts over public land encouraged countless citizens to become more involved in decisions over their own resources, thus challenging the previously exclusive authority of the Forest Service in these matters. Since the 1960s, the question of wilderness is among the issues that have elicited the greatest public input to government decision making in American history. This is not a story of political elitism, nor is it solely a heroic tale of a growing grassroots political movement for wilderness overcoming the obstacles of powerful industrial interests. Rather, it is a story that demonstrates the growing complexity of the political process in the postwar era and the much broader public participation in that process. Environmental historian Nancy Langston's observation about resource disputes in the Malheur Lake basin of eastern Oregon applies clearly to wilderness debates: "conflicts disrupted the hold of narrow orthodoxies on resource management."[17]

The story of how American citizens chose to define pockets of landscape across the country as wilderness areas is a critical element in the political and environmental history of twentieth-century America, particularly the latter half of that century. Many scholars have illuminated significant parts of this story, focusing most commonly on the shifting ideologies within American culture that generated support for wilderness protection and on the national political movements and their leaders, which galvanized broad political approval for passage of the Wilderness Act of 1964. Far fewer have studied the wilderness movement since 1964.[18]

In the following contribution to this ongoing discussion of wilderness, I seek to root my study of wilderness history in the land itself, where debates over designating wilderness have always focused. Wilderness debates after World War II have most often occurred in the context of specific places and specific resources in the American landscape.[19] Those places and people's varying relationships with those lands and resources are the source of the conflict and consensus that characterize these vital land use debates, and nowhere is that more evident than the lines we have drawn in the forest and on the ground. After nearly forty years of lobbying for wilderness areas, Doug Scott recently noted, "The imperative in preserving wilderness is to draw lines—and draw them firmly."[20] Wilderness boundaries are both the crux of these debates and their most significant legacy.

I have had the distinct pleasure of crossing over wilderness boundaries more times than I could ever recall. Through ten summers as a wilderness ranger for the Mount Baker–Snoqualmie National Forest in the central Washington Cascades, I helped to manage federal wilderness areas. In the Cascades, the experience of crossing wilderness boundaries almost always takes place in a forest, and the intersection can be too subtle to notice. Differences in landscape or land use patterns often are not radically or immediately apparent upon crossing this legal threshold, and most travelers are unaware of the exact location of the line. On a well-traveled route, a simple lettered sign of white oak mounted to a tree is the only immediate (and usually approximate) indicator of the wilderness boundary on lands administered by the Forest Service. Nature does not recognize those boundaries; thus when left substantially undeveloped, a wilderness boundary is nothing more than a wooden sign on a tree, slowly decomposing in the dampness of the forest. As Robert Frost wrote in his 1918 poem "Mending Wall," "Something there is that doesn't love a wall." That "something" is nature.[21]

Nonetheless, boundaries matter. In this case, they separate two distinct and incompatible realms of human land use. Most national-forest land lies outside the boundaries of wilderness areas and has been developed for resource extraction and motorized recreation. Within wilderness areas, such development is banned to save space for the range of nonmotorized and nonextractive uses and to, according to the Wilderness Act, provide "outstanding opportunities for solitude."[22] Though quite distinct, both sides of the line reflect human decisions and values. Historian William Cronon observed this in his landmark study of land use in colonial New England: "The choice is not between two landscapes, one with and one without a human influence; it is between two human ways of living, two ways of belonging to an ecosystem."[23]

Wilderness boundaries also matter because the process of defining them is a distinctly human endeavor that deeply shapes—and is shaped by—

our history. This is true for all the borders, walls, fences, frontiers, lines, and boundaries that humans impose on the landscape. Referring to Frost's "Mending Wall," legal scholar Eric Freyfogle suggests an additional meaning for its most famous line, "Good fences make good neighbors." The poem tells the story of two New England neighbors who meet every year in the spring to repair portions of their adjoining stone wall that "the frozen-ground-swell of winter" has brought down. Nature, Frost suggests, does not recognize the wall as a boundary. Humans do recognize the wall, however, and "good fences make good neighbors" has become a proverb to justify individual property rights. Freyfogle, though, asks us to think about the cooperative process of building and repairing that wall rather than the divisive presence of the wall as a barrier. Good fences make good neighbors because a solid, strong fence requires neighborly cooperation in maintaining communal property lines.[24]

I think it is valuable to apply this analysis to wilderness boundaries as they have been built and maintained over the past fifty years, although the story of wilderness is far more complex. Wilderness and nonwilderness lands on the national forests represent different patterns of land use. The boundaries themselves, however, are a joint product of competing interest groups, far more than is explained by the traditional interpretation that preservation was imposed upon public lands by the Sierra Club and the Wilderness Society.[25] The process is in some ways a dialectical one. The thesis is represented by the corporate use of the national forests for timber extraction, which dominated Forest Service efforts beginning in the 1940s. By the 1950s, an antithesis of wilderness preservation for those same forests emerged as an effective political opposition.

The modern wilderness system and particularly its boundary lines are the synthesis of these two political and economic forces. This is not to say that the work has been done in amity and friendship but simply that it has not been one-sided, and it never will be. In the Cascades, the timber industry has had a powerful influence over where those boundaries lie. In the history of Cascade wilderness, the proverbial neighbors have done far more than just repair walls; they have moved them, taken them down, and built new ones around different areas.

The drawing of lines around wilderness areas also illuminates significant historical conflicts in the history of the American West. According to Patricia Nelson Limerick, one of the leading interpreters of the West, "Western history is a story structured by the drawing of lines and the marking of borders."[26] Competing imperial land grabs, nations, Indian reservations, private land, mining claims, homestead claims, railroad land grants, forest reserves, and territories, states, counties, and municipalities are all important examples of land designation in western history.

The process of drawing wilderness boundaries is part of a long legacy of human decisions shaping the Cascades. The mountains have their own myriad mix of boundaries dividing flora, fauna, climate, and water flow, but on top of these, humans have long instituted their own distinct political and economic lines. Native American villages and families staked out distinct territories to divide up the resources of the Cascades. Because they signified different management practices, these human-imposed boundaries had major implications for land and resources.[27] Later, American control and development of the Pacific Northwest in the nineteenth century focused on distinguishing social, political, and economic boundaries. Various federal treaties with Northwest Indian tribes in 1854 and 1855 and land distribution acts such as the Northern Pacific Railroad Land Grant of 1864 and the Oregon Land Donation Act of 1850 all relied on drawing property boundaries to promote development of the region as part of a growing United States.[28]

By the 1890s, growing concern over the abuse of land distribution laws by timber companies and the desire to protect timber and watersheds in the Cascades led to the establishment of the forest reserves. These new boundaries, established by the president under the authority of the General Revision Act of 1891, placed much of the upper elevations of the Cascade Range off limits to private ownership at the turn of the century. In the words of historian Paul W. Gates, this law was a "turning point in public land policy."[29] Creation of the forest reserves set the stage for more than a century of debates over the proper management of public lands.

Boundaries drawn in the Cascades in the 1890s have deeply shaped the course of land use since that time by permanently establishing public lands. In response to local petitions, in 1893 President Grover Cleveland created the Cascade Forest Reserve, which encompassed most of the Oregon Cascade Range, from Mount Hood in the north to Crater Lake National Park in the south, nearly 5 million acres.[30] In the Washington Cascades, President Cleveland established the Pacific Forest Reserve around Mount Rainier the same year, and on George Washington's birthday in 1897, he created the 3.6-million-acre Washington Forest Reserve and expanded the Pacific Forest Reserve into the 2.2-million-acre Mount Rainier Reserve. The Forest Service was created in 1905 under the Department of Agriculture, and the forest reserves were renamed national forests two years later.[31] The increasing scarcity of resources such as timber in the late twentieth century and the growing value of preservation and tourism throughout the century, accelerating after World War II, created another major shift in land use in the United States. The designation of federal lands as wilderness areas under the Wilderness Act of 1964, protecting them from industrial development, is part of this long history of land use patterns.

Particularly in the West, land has been gilded with a surplus of expectations as the basic source of an ongoing faith in national and individual opportunity.[32] Wilderness, too, has been asked to carry more than its share of expectations. In many cases of rhetorical flourish, wilderness advocates promoted wilderness preservation "as a panacea of the nation's ills," as "part of the geography of hope," and as one last place to experience the true individual freedom of an earlier, frontier era.[33] In response, opponents accused wilderness laws of locking up the public's land and thereby limiting individual initiative.[34]

Just as opponents exaggerate its threats, often it seems that advocates have asked or demanded too much of wilderness; it cannot solve our national problems. Activists have repeatedly used the rhetoric of a romanticized wilderness, falsely free from all human impact, to generate public sympathy for their cause. The works of many nineteenth-century landscape artists promoted this mythology, as did various exhibit-format photography books published to support specific wilderness campaigns in the Cascades and elsewhere. In turn, the timber industry and the Forest Service often rested their cases on old myths of the yeoman lumberjack or the altruistic, professional forester. Looking beyond the rhetoric, however, we see that wilderness is more than just an idea; it is a form of land use. Wilderness boundaries separate two dominant visions of how people should use certain forested regions of the Cascades: resource extraction or preservation.

The lost cabin along Camp Robber Creek is not an isolated story.

Human occupants and visitors have used most of the Cascade Range for several thousand years. As is the case elsewhere on Earth, the history of the Cascades is the story of a dynamic relationship between people and their environment over time. Their patterns of use have left a legacy of their passing on the land and in the vegetation. In some places, that use is more obvious than in other places.

It is not surprising that the impacts of the lonely cabin dweller on Camp Robber Creek are far more difficult to discover and less obvious than those of the large mining and railroad community that existed downstream near the mouth of Miller River at the time the cabin was occupied. Between the two sites, less than a mile from the old cabin, a logging road built by the Forest Service before 1970 ends in a clear-cut, which now serves as a crowded trailhead on weekends for hundreds of hikers, mainly from the Puget Sound metropolitan area, visiting the Alpine Lakes Wilderness. The road and its corresponding clear-cuts on one side of the wilderness boundary are distinctly different from the existing traces of land use around the remains of the old cabin inside the wilderness area.

By removing romantic notions of wilderness ideology and focusing instead on the land and the lines we have imposed upon it, one might risk draining the wilderness story of its moral fervor and grand visions. In discussing the role of boundaries in western history, Limerick identified a key challenge: "If Hollywood wanted to capture the emotional center of Western history, its movies would be about real estate. . . . Moviemakers would have to find some cinematic way in which proliferating lines on a map could keep the audience rapt."[35] If Hollywood did choose to portray some of the stories told in the following pages, the cinematography would not be a problem; these are some of the most magnificent landscapes in North America. The narrative tension of the story should also not be a problem. Partly it flows from the passion with which people have valued these lands, often with competing, incompatible visions. It also comes from the heated, increasingly democratic process that allows growing numbers to get involved in the decision-making process on public lands. And a lot rides on the outcome, for these are not abstract debates. The resulting boundaries will determine vast differences in the land itself and the way people use that land for generations to come.

1 THE THREE SISTERS, 1950–1964

The valley of Horse Creek lies in the central Cascade Mountains of western Oregon. National-forest logging roads snake their way up the west side of the northward flowing creek, and a variety of clear-cut logging units break up the dense forest canopy of evergreen trees. These roads leave State Highway 126 near the town of McKenzie Bridge, where Horse Creek drains from the south into the McKenzie River. Horse Creek valley is typical of countless low-elevation valleys in the Willamette National Forest, where an extensive system of roads, built over the past five decades, facilitates the extraction of valuable trees for softwood lumber and provides access to forested areas for a variety of recreational users. Trails lead from the roads into the heavily used Three Sisters Wilderness Area.

Horse Creek valley does not stand out for its land use patterns; one can find similar valleys of intensive forestry throughout Oregon. It does not gather the attention of many travelers passing by the mouth of Horse Creek on Highway 126; its views and scenic attractions are overshadowed by other nearby magnets for recreation. It does not inspire fierce debate over the future of land use in Oregon; once an area is logged, such debates move on to more pristine, unlogged valleys where ancient forests remain intact. But once it did.

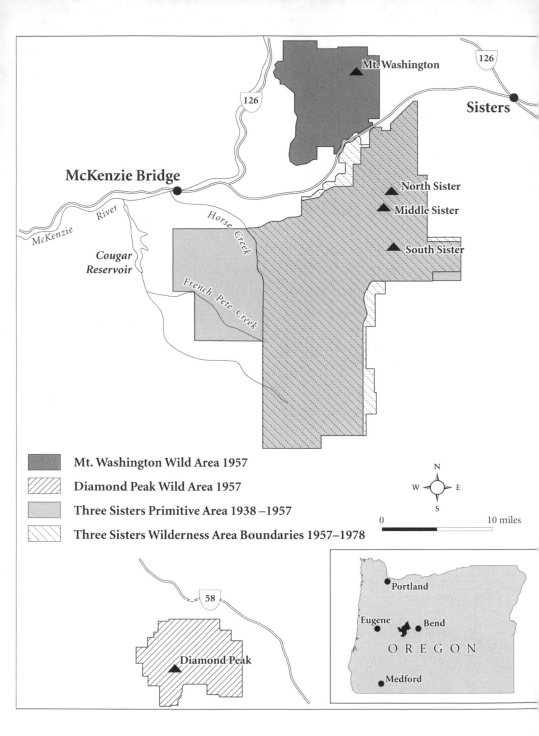

MAP. 2. The Three Sisters, Oregon. Map by Peter Morrison and Barry Levely.

In the mid-1950s, Horse Creek was the center of an increasingly national debate over logging and preservation that would have far-reaching implications throughout the Cascades and across the country. In the wake of the small ripples caused by these debates over a single drainage and the broader tides of social and political change in the decades following World War II, public use and perception of national forests up and down the Cascades would be altered forever. The social values imposed on these lands would change, as would the land itself, depending on which set of values won out in shaping national-forest policy. In the case of Horse Creek, and many other similar sites throughout the Cascades, the values of wildlands, scientific investigation, clean water, and nonmotorized recreation competed with the values of resource extraction, timber management, motorized recreation, and local jobs in debates over whether or not to open such a drainage to road building and logging. The focal point of this political battle of the mid-1950s was the question of where the Forest Service should draw the boundaries of its proposed Three Sisters Wilderness Area.

In 1950, the Northwest Regional Office of the Forest Service, in Portland, Oregon, notified leaders of local alpine clubs and chambers of commerce of its desire to redefine the boundaries of the Three Sisters Primitive Area, which the agency established in 1937. Forest Service officials wanted to reduce the size of the protected area and open up 53,000 acres to logging. In exchange, they offered to create three new high-elevation "wild areas" and to upgrade the primitive area to a "wilderness area," with greater protections from development. Under their proposal, Horse Creek would serve as the new western boundary of the Three Sisters Wilderness Area. All formerly protected forests west of the creek would be open to logging.

The initial response was low key, but many agreed to accompany agency personnel on a fact-finding auto tour around the perimeter of the primitive area. Members of the Eugene Natural History Society, including Ruth Onthank, were not satisfied with this auto trip, however, and they requested a pack trip into the area of Horse Creek and its neighboring ridges and valleys the following summer. In July 1951, four employees from the regional office in Portland and one local ranger from the McKenzie Bridge Ranger District hosted the backcountry tour, which was joined by representatives of the Federation of Western Outdoor Clubs, the Mazamas from Portland, the Obsidians of Eugene, and the Portland Chamber of Commerce. In addition, Professor Robert Storm, of the zoology department at Oregon State College in Corvallis, and Dr. Ruth Hopson, a professor of biology with Portland State College, joined the gathering. These two scholars and Ruth Onthank represented the Eugene Natural History Society. From Moose, Wyoming, came Olaus Murie, director of the Wilderness Society, invited by Ruth Hopson.[1]

The response of these participants to the Forest Service's proposal for the Three Sisters was mixed, but most acquiesced in the change. Only Ruth Onthank and Ruth Hopson of the Eugene Natural History Society strongly opposed any reduction of the primitive area.[2] In agreeing to exclude commercially valuable forests from the wilderness area, others in the group reflected the common belief that wilderness should be defined solely according to its recreational value. The Forest Service strongly promoted this view of wilderness as an alpine recreation zone by emphasizing that they were replacing the low-elevation forests with an even larger acreage of high country in the new wild areas along the Cascade Crest. The position that only areas of "rock and ice" could be called wilderness would increasingly draw fire from the conservation community, but in 1951, many on all sides took it for granted. Even Olaus Murie agreed that the new high-elevation wild areas "more than compensate for the proposed elimination." Disheartened by the lack of unity among the conservationists, Murie felt a need to compromise. "It would be unwise to hold out only on the principle of not eliminating wilderness territory anywhere," he concluded. "Accordingly, I felt that it was best to agree to eliminate most of the western block, even to making Horse Creek the boundary if necessary. . . . I am confident that we can hold the line at Horse Creek."[3]

The Forest Service left the 1951 tour of the area with a sense that opposition to their plan would be minimal, that conservationists would be appeased by the exchange of alpine wild areas for the 53,000 forested acres west of Horse Creek. Thus, they expressed shock at the opposition they faced once they formally announced their plan in 1954.[4]

Such surprise on the part of forest officials may seem naïve to us now, but we must remember that rapid changes in environmental politics were taking place throughout the country. It is important to understand that both resource managers and citizen conservationists were changing in ways that ruptured their previous alliances. Conservationists within the Forest Service had established the outlines for wilderness preservation before the war, but the agency's definition of wilderness began to diverge markedly from that of many citizens. In the 1950s nowhere was this new division more apparent than in the debates over the fate of Horse Creek valley.

As commercial development of the national forests accelerated in the first half of the twentieth century, a growing desire to preserve some areas from road building and logging arose among the ranks of the Forest Service. Aldo Leopold laid the groundwork that led his agency to create the Gila Wilderness in New Mexico in 1924. Arthur Carhart successfully voided agency plans for a road around Trappers Lake, Colorado, in 1920. In Idaho, Elers Koch suggested a hands-off approach toward forest fires on the Clearwater National Forest in the 1930s.[5] By 1929, the Forest Service began to institutionalize wilderness as a land use designation by creating the L-20 Regulations. These standards allowed the chief of the Forest Service to create "primitive areas" on the national forests, which limited, but did not eliminate, industrial use of these sites.[6]

Pushed by the boundless energy of Bob Marshall, cofounder of the Wilderness Society and Forest Service recreation planner in the 1930s, and by the threats of losing land and authority to the National Park Service, the Forest Service upgraded its wilderness designation rules by creating the U Regulations in 1939.[7] As head of the national Division of Recreation and Lands for the Forest Service, Marshall pushed hard for enhanced protection of primitive areas and preservation of roadless lands that had no official protective status. He urged foresters to protect pristine areas "before some damn fool chamber of commerce or some nonsensical organizer of unemployed demands a useless highway to provide work and a market for hotdogs and gasoline." For Marshall and many other wilderness proponents, as historian Paul Sutter has noted, roads were the biggest threat to the areas they valued.[8]

Under the U Regulations, the secretary of agriculture could declare selected areas over 100,000 acres in size as "wilderness" and certain undeveloped parcels under 100,000 acres as "wild areas." The regulations for wild and wilderness areas were stricter than those governing the primitive areas; road building and logging would not be allowed, as they often were in primitive areas.[9] Decisions on new wilderness or wild areas had to come from the cabinet level—that is, from the secretary of agriculture—and creating or changing a wilderness or a wild area required public hearings. Decisions would not be as arbitrary as they presumably were under the less restrictive L-20 Regulations.

The chief of the Forest Service created the Three Sisters Primitive Area in 1937 under the L-20 Regulations. The initial designation contained 191,108 acres of high-elevation terrain. It was a direct response to studies conducted in the 1930s on whether to create a national park in the Oregon Cascades, a source of motivation that fueled many Forest Service preservation efforts at the time.[10] The following year, Bob Marshall successfully pushed for an addition of 55,620 acres of low-elevation forest along the western boundary of the original primitive area. This addition included the valley of Horse Creek and several other heavily forested tributaries to the McKenzie River, including French Pete Creek, which would become the focus of heated debate and public protests from 1968 to 1978.[11]

The Forest Service would later argue that these boundaries set in the 1930s were not meant to be permanent. Acting Secretary of Agriculture True Morse claimed in 1957 that primitive area boundaries "were often delineated rather loosely on maps . . . pending further study as to their primary public value."[12] By some accounts, Marshall expanded primitive areas throughout the West in a very haphazard fashion, drawing rough boundaries on maps. His desire to protect low-elevation forests in the Northwest was very clear, however. During his travels to the region in 1938 he explored much of the area and proposed many low-elevation additions to protected areas in both Oregon and Washington. He certainly did not see such boundaries as temporary.[13]

Marshall's addition west of Horse Creek stood out from the rest of the Three Sisters Primitive Area because of its lower elevation and thick forests. The terrain of deep valleys and steep ridges is very rugged. As Horse Creek flows past the boundary of the primitive area, it is at an elevation of 1,900 feet. Farther west, along the westernmost edge of the area, East Fork, Rebel Creek, Walker Creek, and French Pete Creek all flow into the South Fork McKenzie River at less than 2,000 feet.

The ridges dividing each of these valleys reach up to over 5,000 feet. In western Oregon the most productive timberlands are at lower elevations, and for the Willamette National Forest and the Three Sisters region, the lands Marshall protected represent the lower range of altitude and the higher range of timber productivity.[14]

Geologically, too, this area is distinct from the higher portions of the Three Sisters. It is part of the outer shoulder of the Old Cascades, the broad lava flows that form the base of the Oregon Cascades. On top of this foundation stand the newer lava flows, volcanoes, and alpine terrain of the high Cascades. Bob Marshall felt it was ecologically important that the Forest Service protect portions of both areas.[15]

Leopold and Marshall helped to define the meaning of wilderness for national policy before World War II, but in the 1950s a more powerful force shaping the debate over Oregon wilderness was the enormous increase in timber sales and logging on the national forests. Much of the incentive for the national wilderness movement and the campaign to pass the Wilderness Act came from the dramatic increase of resource extraction on public lands in the postwar years. Although historians of the environmental movement place much emphasis on the efforts to prevent the construction of large federal dams in the arid West at places such as Dinosaur National Monument, the Grand Canyon, and Hell's Canyon, concern in the Cascades focused on timber harvests in national forests.[16]

Just as it profoundly shaped so many other aspects of Northwest history, World War II marked a watershed of change for wilderness and the timber industry. Prior to the war, most timber came from private lands owned by corporations such as Weyerhaeuser. Production peaked on these lands in the 1920s, after which these companies faced both lethargic markets during the Great Depression and scarce supplies, having already cut much of their timber. After the war, the federal government's role as a supplier of timber greatly increased. In the Willamette National Forest both the sale of timber and the volume of timber cut more than quadrupled between 1945 and 1955, and these figures continued to rise significantly in the following decades.[17]

The Forest Service planned to redesignate primitive areas under the new U Regulations before the war; however, Marshall's death in 1939 and the onset of World War II delayed such action. After the war, reclassification of these lands continued, but now it occurred in the context of dramatically increased demands for commercial timber production. To fuel its growing role as a provider of timber, the Forest Service sought to maximize production by making all forests open to the timber sale program.[18] Thus, in 1954, when the agency proposed reclassifying the Three Sisters Primitive Area under the stronger protection of wilderness area, it removed from within the old boundary 53,000 acres of commercial timberlands west of Horse Creek. This was most of the land that the chief of the Forest Service had added in 1938 at Marshall's urging. In exchange, the Forest Service offered to create two new wild areas in high-elevation sites at Diamond Peak and Mount Washington.[19] The agency argued that the excluded lands west of Horse Creek had no recreational or scenic value and that they were needed to alleviate a timber supply shortage in Lane County.[20]

With the tremendous self-confidence that permeated the Forest Service by midcentury, agency personnel proclaimed that they were both "improving" wilderness by adding the Mount Washington and Diamond Peak Wild Areas and by building an access road up Horse Creek and at the same time also providing for the resource needs of the local economy. Forest Service officials and foresters celebrated their ability to satisfy both sides of this controversial issue as a clear example of the benefits of "multiple use" as their guiding philosophy.[21] They portrayed their proposed Horse Creek boundary as a compromise position, claiming it was a middle ground between moving the new boundary even farther east to Separation Ridge and retaining all of the Horse Creek drainage in the wilderness area.

Yet they made these claims after very little consultation with citizen and industry groups. Local hiking clubs and conservationists as well as the local timber industry had very little influence on this decision. The regional officers of the Forest Service later admitted that they had not gained the support of any segment of the population when they announced their intent. In a staff meeting on 26 April 1955, they noted that the timber industry itself did not get involved in the issue until several months after the proposal was publicized, which strongly undermined the agency's claim that the timber along Horse Creek was needed for the local economy. They were left as the provocateurs when they wanted to portray themselves as the objective mediator between competing interests.[22]

Discussions over the fate of the Three Sisters were a formative crucible for various people and organizations as they represented their interests in the area. The Forest Service officials who met in April 1955 tried to prevent future problems of communication and public relations after their meeting, but they were not successful. In addition, the timber industry coalitions began to develop a coordinated response to defend their interests (mainly continued access to timber from public lands) in the wilderness debates.[23] The most remarkable development, however, would occur within the conservation community; a loose-knit collection of hikers, scientists, and social liberals would evolve over the next few decades into a powerful grassroots movement in Oregon and across the country.

Since the 1951 informational tour, conservationists had unified and strengthened their opposition to the Forest Service plan to reduce the primitive area. Ruth Onthank, her husband, Karl Onthank, Ruth Hopson, and other local activists helped to gather local hiking-club members, scientists, and conservationists to form the Friends of the Three Sisters Wilderness in 1954 "to defend the area and call for a boundary at Horsepasture Mountain south along Ollalie Ridge." This would ensure that the entire Horse Creek drainage was preserved in the new wilderness area.[24] Karl and Ruth Onthank promoted the need for a new organization, campaigned for new members, and hosted the initial meeting in their Eugene home. Karl Onthank, who served as dean of students at the University of Oregon, described the leadership of the Friends as "mostly scientists who know something of our Cascade Mountains and are interested in seeing a little [of] them preserved for future enjoyment in their natural state and for scientific study."[25] The Friends of the Three Sisters established a model for later site-specific, grassroots activism that historian Samuel Hays would call "the key to the success of wilderness action."[26]

Wilderness advocates were no longer appeased by the addition of two new high-elevation areas in exchange for the forests west of Horse Creek. These areas around Mount Washington and Diamond Peak were already protected as limited areas (a land management designation in the national forests that was less stringent than wilderness and unique to Forest Service Region 6 in Oregon and Washington), and they faced few threats from logging, mining, or road building. The Friends of the Three Sisters focused instead on the loss of the low-elevation forests from administrative protection. Karl Onthank objected strenuously to the agency's plan to "remove the timber from existing wilderness areas, create new areas in the barren high country which no one wants—yet—and equate the acreage as evidence that the areas are equivalent."[27]

As required by the U Regulations, the Forest Service organized a public hearing on its proposal, to be held in Eugene on 16 February 1955, and the Friends of the Three Sisters took the lead in promoting and coordinating the prowilderness testimony. Longtime leaders in the Northwest conservation community spoke out against withdrawing the boundaries to Horse Creek; many now insisted that the boundaries not be altered at all. The Mazamas, the Obsidians, and other organizations, including the Oregon Federation of Garden Clubs, spoke out for retention of the entire primitive area as wilderness, despite their earlier acquiescence to the Forest Service plan.[28]

One of the more prominent opponents to any reduction in the size of the primitive area was the International Woodworkers of America (IWA), a branch of the Congress of Industrial Organizations (CIO). The international president, A. F. Hartung, learned indirectly about the Forest Service proposal, to which he expressed resentment. "We consider it unexplainable and unpleasant that the Forest Service has never seen fit to ask our particular segment of society as to whether we have any views on this subject," he complained. They did have strong views, which they brought to the hearing. They, too, expressed suspicion at the administrative fiat which determined the fate of primitive areas: "We have seen how the wilderness areas of other states have been gradually reduced to nothing, often through the use of subterfuge and outright corruption."[29]

The IWA's opposition reflected many of the concerns of other conservationists in Oregon. Maintaining recreational space, especially in the light of future population pressures, protecting native environments for scientific study, and making more efficient use of the existing public and private timberlands for lumber production were concerns frequently expressed. The union, Hartung wrote, was "interested in maintaining our recreational and flora and fauna study areas at the utmost scope plausible." "We are worried," he continued, "that the present privately-owned acreage is not being used properly in many instances, but that is no excuse for encroaching on the public's right to have a wilderness area large enough to be truly termed wilderness."[30]

Karl Onthank expressed similar concerns about efficiency, arguing that opening the western forests of the primitive area would not solve the timber industry's supply problems: "This industry will have to find other solutions, the first of which will doubtless be better utilization of the wood now cut, such as is already being done by the more efficient operators."[31] Howard Zahniser, executive secretary of the Wilderness Society, concurred: "Our hope in preserving areas of wilderness free from lumbering is dependent on our ability to achieve a prosperous lumbering industry based on sound timber management within the forests and woodlots outside the wilderness."[32]

Opponents to the Forest Service plan did not object to logging on principle, just as representatives of the industry did not oppose wilderness designation for high-elevation areas. Commercial logging was the dominant form of land use in the western Cascades, and conservationists in 1955 sought only to protect the lower forests within the existing Three Sisters Primitive Area for recreational and scientific uses. "The Willamette Forest prides itself upon producing more lumber dollars than any other national Forest," Ruth Onthank testified. "It has the untouched land and the scenery to make it superlative a[n]d possessing the most wilderness too. Why isn't it equally proud of that, and equally anxious to protect it?"[33]

Many who testified supported protection of the disputed areas west of Horse Creek for their value for scientific study. Forest ecology focused on timber production at the time, and most arguments for wilderness expressed recreational or aesthetic values until at least the 1970s. Nevertheless, a strong contingent of scientists from local universities pushed for an awareness of wilderness as a place for ecological research. Science professors Ruth Hopson, Sandy Tepfer, Dick Noyes, Jim Kezer, Bob Storm, and others were integral in developing the strategies to defend the areas around Horse Creek. Horse Creek divided the geologic region of the Old Cascades from the younger, higher volcanic zone of the New Cascades, and these scientists emphasized the unique biological and geological features of the lower Cascades west of Horse Creek.[34]

Their experiences watching Forest Service logging operations encroach on similar sites in the region prompted them to act. Bonita Miller, a biology professor at the University of Oregon, responded to proponents of clear-cutting, "While biologically and economically sound for timber cropping, the forest without all of its layers and habitats is just about as useful as a Ladino clover pasture for scientific study of all aspects of mature plant and animal communities, for observing the forest as it was and is in the absence of great disturbance, and for preserving wilderness conditions."[35] Professor Miller joined with colleagues from Oregon to appeal to the Forest Service to preserve the forests west of Horse Creek as wilderness and as a laboratory to study the land and life-forms of the Old Cascades.

Many conservationists were greatly pleased by the visibility of their community at the hearings, and Forest Service officials would later express surprise at the strength of their presence. Karl Onthank had been troubled by the earlier lack of unity among wilderness advocates, but he came away from the hearings pleased: "Finally, perhaps chiefly as a result of the Hearing rather than in advance of it, which would have been much better, we really did get together and presented a solid front and we have been much more successful."[36]

Since wilderness advocates arrived in much larger numbers than expected, the Forest Service extended the proceedings to the following day to accommodate all the speakers. Among those testifying on the second day was Howard Zahniser, executive secretary of the Wilderness Society. In his testimony, one can hear whispers of the language that he would incorporate into the Wilderness Act, which he was already drafting by 1955.[37] Reflecting his desire for federal wilderness legislation, he brought national concerns to the local question of Horse Creek: "I have come here to represent the national interest in this area that we citizens of all the other counties of the United States share with our fellow Americans in Lane County."[38] Zahniser's presence in Eugene demonstrates both the importance of the Three Sisters dispute to the national campaign for wilderness protection and the attempt by local representatives who sought to stop logging in the western portion of the Three Sisters Primitive Area to speak in a national voice, as well as a unified one. National leaders of the Sierra Club and the Wilderness Society became increasingly involved in the Three Sisters issue, and their publications spread concern over the potential reduction of the primitive area.

Bringing national attention to the controversy over the Three Sisters was central to the strategy of wilderness advocates; it was also a direct result of Forest Service decisions. Karl Onthank wrote to various people outside Oregon who might take an interest. After reading a letter to the editor of *Time* magazine in 1954, he wrote to the author of that letter in California explaining the Three Sisters debate and asking, "Perhaps you and some of the people you know could write a few letters. Since the argument for taking the heavily timbered portion out of the wilderness area is frankly defended on the basis of the need for more saw-logs by local operators, it is especially important to have it made very clear that it is not a local problem, but one of national interest."[39] Writing to another potential supporter from California, Onthank pleaded, "What is most needed now is a stream of letters to the Regional Forester and the National Forester [chief of the Forest Service] indicating that people want the area saved. Up to now they have heard mostly from the local lumbermen, particularly those who would like to get into the area."[40]

According to many accounts of the time, Onthank was right that Forest Service officials gave precedence to local concerns. In his 1953 study, James Gilligan concluded, "National forest wilderness area policy and regulations have not been sufficiently strong to override fundamental policies of land management primarily concerned with local economies." Less than a decade later, in his study of resource policies, Norman Wengert noted "an almost pathological emphasis on local factors, local development, local benefits, at the expense of a larger national view of the public interest."[41] To counter the focus on local economic concerns, residents advocating a limit to logging through wilderness designation sought to elicit national support. Although rhetorically emphasizing the local economy, the timber industry also employed similar tactics of creating national coalitions to promote its own interests in wilderness debates.

Reflecting growing national concern, the Sierra Club's David Brower became increasingly involved in the Three Sisters issue through correspondence with Karl Onthank and others and through appeals of his own. In 1956 he wrote to President Eisenhower's secretary of agriculture, Ezra Taft Benson, who was considering the Forest Service proposal for the new Three Sisters boundaries after the 1955 public hearings.

Benson's approval was needed for designation of any new wilderness areas under the U Regulations. "This is the first major decision on a wilderness matter that this administration has been called upon to make," Brower wrote. "The Nation's conservationists are deeply concerned." He asked that the boundaries of the primitive area be retained in the new designation. Brower also urged that the secretary delay any decisions to reduce the Three Sisters until a new national review board could assess the nation's supply and demand of recreational resources up to the year 2000. Sigurd Olson, of the Wilderness Society, approved of Brower's plea to Secretary Benson, commenting that "this makes sense and as a delaying action cannot be improved upon." Olson hailed the proposed review board, which would become the influential Outdoor Recreation Resources Review Commission, as being "as important as Echo Park," referring to the victorious campaign to stop federal dam construction in Dinosaur National Monument, Utah.[42]

Regardless of conservationists' increasing success in communicating their positions in ways that surprised and challenged the Forest Service, the Forest Service defined the terms of debate and wilderness advocates remained on the defensive. This situation characterized what Michael McCloskey, the first Northwest conservation representative for the Federation of Western Outdoor Clubs, identified as the first stage of the postwar wilderness movement. During this time, wilderness advocates were "fighting off attacks on areas already reserved," particularly national-forest primitive areas. This dominant pattern of the 1950s "embodied a limited view of the possibilities for conservation," he wrote in 1972. It "was a confession of weakness."[43]

The weaknesses were very apparent to leaders of the Three Sisters campaign. They fought a defensive battle to maintain existing boundaries and preserve 53,000 acres from logging, realizing that the realistic position was to accept a major loss and save only 12,000 acres west of Horse Creek. They struggled externally against the political power of both the Forest Service and the timber industry while they struggled internally to provide a cohesive, yet broad, front to present their positions. Years later Brock Evans, Mike McCloskey's second successor as Northwest conservation representative, recalled, "The long story of the efforts to save some of the remaining forests in the Oregon Cascades is a sad chronicle of too little too late, of disorganization among our people, of the power of the timber industry in that state."[44]

After he attended a meeting of the Executive Committee of the Pacific Northwest Chapter of the Sierra Club in 1956, Karl Onthank wrote to David Brower: "I am concerned by what seems to be a tendency, very natural, to fail to see the danger of carrying on negotiations with Forest Service officials without making very sure that all concerned are informed and have a voice. A sequence of such proceedings very nearly wrecked our Three Sisters efforts. Various people had talked with Forest Service officers and some at least had given them honest but erroneous impressions of the attitude of conservation groups." "The result," he concluded, "was that we fell way short of presenting a united front and our case was substantially weakened in consequence. . . . Our weakness is our disunity."[45] The difficulties involved in ensuring that as many people as possible join in the efforts to protect public forests while at the same time maintaining the unity of those efforts would not become apparent until a decade later when environmentalism had grown into a broad social movement, but in the 1950s Onthank and others had the luxury of neither.

By 1957, the Friends of the Three Sisters had lost the battle. The Forest Service defined Horse Creek as the new wilderness boundary, opening up the western half of the drainage to road building and timber harvesting. The decision frightened wilderness advocates across the country. Activists promoting broader protection of the forested valleys in the Glacier Peak region in the North Cascades of Washington State believed that "by 1955 the evidence was clear, that just as in the Three Sisters, the most the U.S. Forest Service had in mind was a 'wilderness on the rocks,' every commercially valuable tree excluded."[46]

The title of the Forest Service press release announcing their decision was "Three Sisters Action Adds 32,000 Acres to Oregon Wilderness."[47] Under their strict administrative definition of "wilderness," the Forest Service was correct in its arithmetic, but many in the growing wilderness movement clearly saw this as a loss of wildlands and sought ways to gain greater influence over such land use decisions. To them, wilderness legislation was a practical means to limit industrial development of public lands. Many discussed it openly as a type of zoning ordinance, a tool to prohibit "incompatible uses." By 1958 the Sierra Club had begun to push for a national land use classification system for the national forests based on municipal zoning traditions; wilderness was central to their zoning proposal. Charlotte Mauk, of the Sierra Club, said in 1954, "In our city and community planning we have developed a zoning concept. We don't build up industrial areas in our city parks, or set up carnivals in the restricted residential sections. We need to apply sound zoning principles to our nonurban areas, too."[48] The long battle over the boundaries of the Three Sisters Primitive Area in the mid-1950s galvanized those promoting zoning. In his testimony in Eugene in 1955, Howard Zahniser said, "Wilderness preservation in the national forests is possible only . . . by an application of what we might call the zoning principle." Wilderness zoning, he argued, would protect the widest range of values on national-forest land.[49]

The Three Sisters case became a rallying cry for the national wilderness movement. After their failure to protect the forests west of Horse Creek, wilderness advocates promoted a stronger, national ordinance for wilderness as a way to limit the Forest Service's control over administrative designations. Although increasing resource extraction on public lands fueled the wilderness preservation movement, it was the insecurity of administrative protection that led groups to push for statutory protection, a national system of wilderness established and defined by Congress rather than by land management agencies. The Forest Service decision to reduce the size of the Three Sisters Primitive Area confirmed the greatest fears of wilderness advocates and galvanized their efforts to push for a national wilderness system controlled by Congress.

Frustrated by their loss in 1957, Oregon conservationists turned to support the wilderness bill first introduced to Congress the previous year by Senator Hubert Humphrey of Minnesota. Karl Onthank wrote to his colleagues after the Three Sisters verdict, "The decision certainly points up the importance of passing a 'Wilderness Preservation Bill' which will give substantial and durable protection. If it is not passed we can take it for granted we will have this kind of battle on every one of the primitive and the limited areas found in Region 6." Without new national legislation removing wilderness decisions from administrative control, he believed the Forest Service "will do generally what has been done here."[50]

Oregon senators Richard Neuberger and Wayne Morse both objected to the Forest Service decision on Horse Creek, and they both responded by sponsoring the wilderness bill.[51] Neuberger, the junior senator, declared, "The decision emphasized the need for legislation which will give Congress authority to check such reduction in the future." The addition of two new wild areas along the Cascade Crest "does not alter the fact that the original Three Sisters Wilderness has been pared by 53,000 acres." Morse also called for congressional action to limit Forest Service authority in defining wilderness: "Those of us who oppose such action will have to do what we can in Congress to counteract such a decision, in order to protect the Three Sisters Wilderness area and to achieve a sound and predictable program for these areas throughout the country."[52]

Thus, the conflict over the forests west of Horse Creek was a pivotal moment in the wilderness movement nationwide. It was as much or more of a catalyst for the passage of the Wilderness Act of 1964 as the more famous battle over dam construction at Echo Park in Dinosaur National Monument, Utah.[53] In a 1961 letter to Senator Frank Church, floor leader of the debate over the Wilderness Act, Zahniser reminded the senator of the central role of the Three Sisters debate in shaping the campaign for national wilderness legislation: "For example, when the Three Sisters Primitive Area was reclassified Senator Richard Neuberger and Senator Wayne Morse strongly opposed the recommended elimination of some 50,000 acres (about 20 percent of the area). They were unable, however, to prevent this elimination, and this example strongly motivated their interest in the Wilderness Bill, in the original drafting of which Senator Neuberger had an important part. The intention was that in such an instance in the future the Congress would have a procedural way of preventing such administrative action to eliminate wilderness."[54] The Wilderness Act applied to all federal lands, but it focused on the national forests. The debate at Echo Park was over policies of development within the national-park system. When Congress moved in 1964 to check the unilateral power of the Forest Service to decide the fate of wilderness areas, the Three Sisters decision served as a model of administrative abuse of power.

Even some of the local media in Oregon who supported the final decision to open Horse Creek to logging objected to the process used by the Forest Service. These editorials criticized the unilateral nature of the administrative decision over wilderness. The *Redmond (OR) Spokesman* suggested two years earlier that if the Forest Service did not prioritize the protection of primitive areas, "then the job should be given to some department that does." The *Eugene (OR) Register-Guard* praised the Forest Service decision, but it expressed concern over "the ease with which such areas can be opened to logging." They concluded, "What is needed, it seems to us, is a national wilderness system."[55]

Timber sales began in the forests west of Horse Creek in 1964, and in September of that year President Lyndon Johnson signed into law the Wilderness Act, declaring the remaining Three Sisters Wilderness Area as part of the National Wilderness Preservation System and forever altering the process by which wilderness areas are created. Now the Forest Service no longer had the authority to change wilderness boundaries.

The Horse Creek issue of the 1950s foreshadowed a new era of debates over who would make decisions regarding management of public lands in the United States. Since the Progressive Era and the founding of the Forest Service in 1905, decisions over public forests rested in the hands of an elite group of professionals trained to manage forest resources in the public interest. Forest Service employees such as Arthur Carhart and Aldo Leopold were a driving force for conservation and wilderness preservation before World War II.[56] After the war, foresters' decisions increasingly prioritized resource extraction, while the resources themselves, including undeveloped forestlands, became scarcer. The debate over the Three Sisters indicated a significant shift in the environmental movement. To preserve wildlands, wilderness advocates turned against their former allies in land management agencies and sought to gain greater access to the decision-making process previously available only to a limited set of policy makers and scientists. One of the greatest legacies of the wilderness movement nationwide is the growing democratization of environmental politics, which opened up the policy process over public resources to millions of citizens. Forest Service opposition to wilderness campaigns over the next few decades rested as much on preserving the agency's established privilege of power as it did on the specific questions of resource management.[57]

After 1957, the Friends of the Three Sisters continued their efforts to reestablish protective status for the low-elevation forests west of the wilderness boundary. It was a running battle over the next decade, as the Forest Service extended roads and timber sales into many of the drainages west of Horse Creek. Karl Onthank foresaw the long time frame of wilderness debates. After the initial loss in 1957, he wrote, "It seems very important to maintain the attitude that this is just the first round of a battle which is bound to continue for a long time. And if we keep at it we will certainly win much of it in the long run, even though we may take some losses."[58]

2 THE NORTH CASCADES, 1956–1968

S imultaneous to releasing the secretary of agriculture's decision to remove the western forests from the protection of the Three Sisters Primitive Area in Oregon in February 1957, the regional office of the Forest Service announced its report and recommendations on designating wilderness in the Glacier Peak Limited Area in the North Cascades of Washington State. To Karl Onthank, the timing was not a coincidence but a clear attempt by the agency "to distract attention from the Three Sisters decision."[1] For Onthank, the two issues were clearly linked. Regarding the Three Sisters, he wrote, "The Forest Service rather obviously regards this as a test case. If it can get away with a substantial reduction here it will certainly attempt to do so elsewhere." Onthank recalled that a "chief representative" of the Forest Service regional office once asked whether wilderness advocates "preferred Glacier Peak or Three Sisters," insinuating that the agency would be willing to protect one or the other but not both.[2] Although initially seen from Oregon as an offshoot of the Three Sisters debate, over the course of the next decade a combative dispute over the forested valleys on all sides of Glacier Peak in the northern Washington Cascades would draw unprecedented attention from around the country. It became a national test of Forest Service management for values other than timber harvesting. Analyzing the national context, journalist Michael Frome wrote, "The ultimate showdown that convinced citizen conservationists that the Forest Service could not be trusted to preserve wilderness on the basis of administrative regulations came in the North Cascades."[3]

As in the Oregon Cascades, the political battles over setting wilderness boundaries in the North Cascades focused on the low-lying, heavily forested valleys. As one lumber executive from Chelan, Washington, wrote to a colleague early in the debate, "We are not opposing wilderness areas in principle, but only as far as they restrict the economic value of large volumes of merchantible [sic] timber."[4] The regional office of the Forest Service clearly identified this fundamental issue from the outset. Their 1957 land management study for Glacier Peak explained, "In determining the location of the wilderness area boundaries the forest manager must decide whether it is preferable to dedicate certain timber stands for wilderness preservation, or . . . for the systematic harvesting of the timber."[5]

Buck Creek, Downey Creek, and the long valley of the Suiattle River on the north and west sides of Glacier Peak held impressive and valuable stands of old-growth Douglas fir, the most valuable species in the softwood lumber market and the graceful signature tree of the region's ancient forests. These glacially carved valleys with broad, flat floors and steep walls funnel rain clouds far into the heart of the mountains, where they release over one hundred inches of rain annually. There grow the classic temperate rain forests of the western Cascades. The rivers are fed by melting glaciers and the slow melting of the enormous winter snowpack. The White Chuck, the Sauk, the Skagit, the Cascade, and many other rivers all had served as major transportation corridors into the mountains to and from the Puget Sound region for several thousand years.[6]

East from the Cascade summits flow a number of drier, yet similarly spectacular valleys that support rich stands of pine and fir. The eastern slopes of the North Cascades contain valuable timber, which played a significant role in the political debates over Forest Service land use in the region. The White River, the Chiwawa River, Railroad Creek, Early Winters Creek, Phelps Creek, and Agnes Creek all served as battlegrounds over where to draw the boundaries between logging and preservation east of the Cascade Crest.

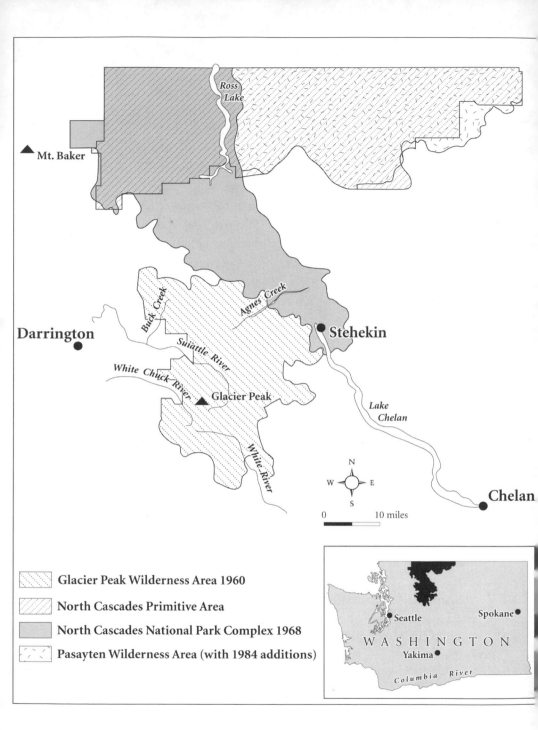

Ross
Lake

▲ Mt. Baker

Darrington

Buck Creek

Agnes Creek

Suiattle River

● Stehekin

White Chuck River

▲ Glacier Peak

White River

Lake
Chelan

N
W ✦ E
S

0   10 miles

● Chelan

Glacier Peak Wilderness Area 1960

North Cascades Primitive Area

North Cascades National Park Complex 1968

Pasayten Wilderness Area (with 1984 additions)

● Seattle   Spokane ●

W A S H I N G T O N

Yakima ●

Columbia River

MAP 3. The North Cascades, Washington. Map by Peter Morrison and
Barry Levely.

Bob Marshall explored the Agnes Creek region in 1939, after his work on protecting the western forests of the Three Sisters Primitive Area the year before. He believed strongly that the area should be included in a large Glacier Peak Wilderness Area, under his recently approved U Regulations.[7] The chief of the Forest Service, Ferdinand Silcox, supported the boundaries suggested by Marshall, but the plan did not receive approval from the secretary of agriculture. Marshall's proposal called for including nearly 800,000 acres within a wilderness area. Citing concerns over mineral rights and state development plans for a highway across the North Cascades, the agency rejected Marshall's boundaries. Chief Silcox approved a Glacier Peak Limited Area of only 350,000 acres in 1940, a year after Marshall's death.[8] Agnes Creek and the other major forested valleys east and west of Glacier Peak remained outside this protected area.

After World War II, threats to the forests of Agnes Creek and other valleys from planned Forest Service timber sales and roads sparked a revived effort from conservationists to establish wilderness boundaries around the extended Glacier Peak region. Studies to reclassify the limited area to wilderness area status began in 1951, but they proceeded at a pace painfully slow to wilderness advocates. The limited area designation was unique to the national forests of Oregon and Washington, a status the regional office unofficially called "stop, look, and listen" or "wait and see." As a land use category, it offered significantly less protection than wilderness or primitive areas did. For conservationists it was "a peculiar classification that seemed to suggest there were too many commercial trees not yet ready to be harvested." The assistant regional forester claimed they were not ready to classify these areas for recreation or wilderness.[9] Delays in the Forest Service study did not slow down timber sales, road building, and logging operations in the lower valleys, but they did prevent any efforts to protect those forests as part of an expanded Glacier Peak Wilderness Area. Michael Frome explains, "these [studies] were dragged out or delayed, while logging proceeded in valleys that conservationists felt deserved inclusion in any permanently protected area."[10]

In 1955, Grant McConnell, a young professor of political science at the University of California, Berkeley, returned to his family's cabin near the small town of Stehekin and found signs of pending Forest Service timber sales in the area. The thought of logging roads and clear-cuts in the Agnes Creek valley horrified him. He was well aware of the agency's proposal for the Three Sisters, and he feared the same fate awaited the lower forests of the Glacier Peak region. McConnell recalled, "I came back to Berkeley in a panic, realizing the Forest Service was ready to clearcut all the forests of the North Cascades. I managed to interest Dave Brower and got the Sierra Club Conservation Committee to put the area on its agenda, but only pretty low on the list, what with Dinosaur's [National Monument] fate unsettled and other big fights going on. The problem was that the North Cascades were so little known."[11]

That same summer a small group from the Seattle Mountaineers alpine club traveled through the eastern portion of the Glacier Peak Limited Area to learn more for themselves so that they could more effectively lobby the Forest Service for wilderness protection. Philip and Laura Zalesky and Polly Dyer hiked up from the old mining camp of Holden and several days later down the Agnes Creek valley to Stehekin. Although they did not meet McConnell directly on that visit, while there they did learn of his concerns and efforts.[12]

McConnell joined with Philip and Laura Zalesky, Dyer, and many others from Washington and Oregon to get the question of how to manage the forests of the North Cascades on a national agenda. This quickly became a guiding strategy of wilderness advocates, who hoped to generate political pressure on the Forest Service. As one headline in the national *Sierra Club Bulletin* asked, "Will we discover the Northern Cascades in time?"[13]

In an effort to gain broader political support and to most effectively influence the decisions of the Forest Service, a coalition of concerned organizations and individuals gathered in Portland in 1957 to coordinate their response to the initial Forest Service proposal. There they founded the North Cascades Conservation Council (NCCC). The regional office of the Forest Service declined an invitation to appoint a representative to join the organization. The NCCC, under the leadership of Philip Zalesky and Patrick Goldsworthy, proved to be a central player in the debate over the North Cascades during the following decade.[14]

Conservationists felt pressed by a series of agency actions to open undeveloped forests to logging, which accelerated after the Three Sisters decision in 1957. The original Forest Service announcement of intent for a Glacier Peak Wilderness Area in 1957 frightened wilderness advocates, because it denied protected status to the low-elevation valleys. David Brower, executive director of the Sierra Club, angrily labeled these areas "the missing million," referring to the roughly one million acres of national-forest land in the North Cascades not protected by the agency's proposal for wilderness.[15]

The agency did not hide its intent to open forests outside protected areas to the timber sale program. In 1959, the Forest Service published its final proposal for the Glacier Peak Wilderness Area, which was open to public comment. Maps that accompanied the plan clearly showed the deep indentations into the wilderness area from all sides, demonstrating the clear efforts of the Forest Service to exclude richly forested valleys from wilderness consideration.[16] From the west, an arm of unprotected land reached over eleven miles up the Suiattle River valley. Kennedy Hot Springs, a primitive camping area along the White Chuck River southwest of Glacier Peak six miles from the closest road, would be open to car camping under the plan, which called for road construction up each of the surrounding valleys. Wilderness advocates quickly dubbed the Forest Service's plan "the starfish proposal," a policy that confined the wilderness "to tentacle-like ridges of rock and snow, of 'wilderness on the rocks,' with the intervening valleys devoted to commercial development."[17] Throughout the entire debate over management of the North Cascades, these valley forests would remain the crux of the issue, what Brock Evans called the "heart and soul" of the controversy.[18]

The Forest Service proposal reinforced the experience of conservationists in the Three Sisters Wilderness Area and led to increased support for a wilderness bill in Congress that would take these decisions out of the hands of the Department of Agriculture. In a 1958 article McConnell wrote, "This part of the search for a decision in the public interest can only be carried out by the people themselves. As with war and the generals, this aspect of administration is too important to be left to the administrators."[19]

Representatives of the timber industry also immediately responded with objections to the Forest Service proposals of 1957 and 1959. The agency plan suggested increasing the size of the original Glacier Peak Limited

Area by about 75,000 acres, an enlargement of 20 percent. Although the Forest Service expanded the timber volume open to logging by increasing the percentage of high, alpine terrain in the proposed wilderness, mill owners and industry lobbyists fought against the precedent of increasing the acreage of designated wilderness. George Wall, the president of the Chelan Box and Manufacturing Company in Chelan, Washington, wrote, "The first major thing we are doing is trying to combat the U.S.F.S. on general principles. If we don't they will use the Glacier Peak Wilderness as a pattern to determine the policy on future decisions affecting wilderness areas." Wall became an active leader in the campaign to reduce the acreage proposed, and his company bought the timber in the Stehekin Valley, the proposed sale of which had provoked McConnell's outrage back in 1955.[20]

Although he expressed concern over the general principles of wilderness protection for the forests, Wall also responded with specific changes to the boundaries. In a letter to Herbert Stone, the regional forester, he requested "the Forest Service to revise its preliminary boundary of the proposed Glacier Peak Wilderness Area so as to exclude an additional mile or so of the Flat Creek drainage and the rest of the main body of the Agnes Creek drainage."[21]

Economic opportunities for local communities, active management of resources, and building roads for access to mountain recreation were each common arguments employed by Wall and others who sought to limit wilderness acreage to the higher elevations. In addition, the timber industry tried to characterize the designation of public lands as wilderness as support for a single, exclusive form of use. Henry Clepper, the executive secretary of the Society of American Foresters (SAF), described the designation of wilderness as an effort "to lock up vast areas of national forests exclusively for the preferred use of certain minority recreationists."[22]

This rhetoric reinforced the Forest Service's emphasis on "multiple use," which was the dominant concept in American forestry by the 1950s and the clearest ideological rival to wilderness preservation in the postwar era. Professional foresters cited "multiple use" as a dictum of truth. As the Forest Service and the timber community defined it, "multiple use" referred to the management of forest resources to gain the greatest benefit while serving the widest array of interests. Gifford Pinchot's motto in founding the Forest Service in 1905, "the greatest good for the greatest number," was a forerunner to the concept of multiple use, which had become widely used by the 1930s. Wilderness preservation was just one of the uses included in the doctrine of multiple use in Forest Service planning since the first wilderness and primitive area designations in the 1920s. In the Multiple Use and Sustained Yield Act of 1960, Congress clearly included wilderness within the definition of "multiple use." Government and private foresters, however, used the concept as a justification for timber harvest in areas previously or potentially set aside as wilderness. It was their most important rhetorical weapon. They easily and often criticized wilderness as a "single-use" designation; Clepper's comment above is a clear example of this rhetorical strategy.[23]

The Forest Service employed the concept of multiple use in trying to fend off the National Park Service, which sought to acquire national-forest land of highly scenic or recreational value. According to Paul Hirt, the leading historian of the national forests in the postwar era, "Rather than a clear management policy, it [multiple use] seemed to be a defense against Park Service incursions and a rationale for maintaining agency management discretion."[24]

Congress had created many national parks from Forest Service lands. In 1899 Mount Rainier National Park took land from the Rainier Forest Reserve, and Congress created Olympic National Park in 1938 from a national monument managed by the Olympic National Forest. The Forest Service fiercely defended its turf in these battles over jurisdiction.[25] Since timber harvesting, mining, and hunting were prohibited within national parks, the Forest Service protected its jurisdiction by labeling National Park Service management as single use or "single-purpose." As with wilderness areas, national parks have a wide range of uses for a diverse set of interest groups, but foresters called them exclusionary to assist in fighting off acquisition of their land.[26] They employed this same tactic against wilderness proposals in forested areas on the Mount Baker and the Wenatchee National Forests around Glacier Peak.

The extensive effort employed by the Forest Service to defend its interests based on multiple use and to distinguish its role from that of the National Park Service may help to explain why it provided less support for wilderness in the 1950s and 1960s than it had before the war.

Certainly the booming demand for timber on public lands during these years was the driving engine of change in the agency's policy, but the way it employed the concept of multiple use gave tremendous leverage to those interest groups who sought to prioritize making public timber available for commercial extraction. Ralph Hodges, of the National Lumber Manufacturers Association, the primary national lobbying arm of the timber industry, explained his view to a fellow forester in 1959:

> The national parks were created by the government for play, preservation and aesthetic purposes. On the other hand, the national forests were created for the purpose of producing timber and water. . . . We hesitate to see national park objectives applied to the national forests. We think any change in national forest management from one of production to one of purposeful non-production should be limited to those areas where the foreseeable economic potential is low and the aesthetic potential is high.[27]

"Multiple use" became an important rhetorical tool for those who pushed the agency to release more timber for commercial use.

Advocates for a limited, high-elevation wilderness in the timber industry and local chambers of commerce sought to portray themselves as representing local economic concerns, but they did so with an increasingly regional and national infrastructure. In this, their response was similar to that of the wilderness advocates who created a locally based coalition in the NCCC but who increasingly turned to national organizations for support, especially as Congress took control of the debates in later years. The Industrial Forestry Association (IFA), a regional consortium of forest products companies in western Oregon and western Washington, quickly became an outspoken opponent of the Forest Service plan for the Glacier Peak area in 1959. In the public hearings held by the Forest Service in Bellingham, Washington, in October and in written comments and maps, the IFA asked that over 42,000 acres of forest in several valleys west of Glacier Peak be removed from the wilderness proposal, a reduction of 10 percent. Regarding the valleys of Buck Creek, Downey Creek, the Suiattle River, the North Fork Sauk River, and other streams, the IFA argued "that if these areas are managed under multiple use, the needs of the public will be better served, than if they are included in a single-use wilderness withdrawal."[28]

The Western Pine Association played a similar role, lobbying against wilderness protection for valleys on the east slopes of the North Cascades, where rich stands of pine predominated. J. D. Bronson, president of Western Pine, explained that, while "we are in accord with the principle of setting aside wilderness areas, . . . we disapprove of including within wilderness areas unusually and unnecessarily large segments of productive crop lands such as commercial timberlands." They, too, proposed new boundaries "considered mainly on the basis of timber management needs." Their proposal aimed to reduce the wilderness by an additional 40,000 acres on the east side of the Cascades.[29]

The fight over the North Cascades also motivated the timber industry and professional foresters to organize a national defense of their interests. Within the SAF, the largest and most influential professional forestry organization in the United States, a debate arose over whether or not to become more directly involved in political issues.[30] Although the SAF had long acted in political circles, it did so with an air of professional detachment, believing that the profession of forestry should remain separate from and above political turmoil. Most Forest Service leaders were also SAF members.

Leaders of the SAF weighed in on the best methods to cultivate and use their political influence. A. W. Nelson wrote, "Since the Society embodies the largest single pool of talent in the rural, nonagricultural field, the policies which Society members might develop with respect to the problems confronting the nation in the use of these land resources ought to carry considerable weight among those who make the decisions in the political area."[31] Bernard Orell, of the Weyerhaeuser Corporation, put it more aggressively:

> It seems to me an empty and futile undertaking for our profession to strive for improvement in the five basic fields of forestry we emphasize so strongly in education and as basis for membership in the Society and then to sit back and say we will not get involved in controversial policy matters. It was this very same attitude on the part of the German business people and industrialists that let Hitler rise to power and crush them ultimately.[32]

Orell's colleague at Weyerhaeuser, Jay Gruenfeld, appealing to the international context of the Cold War, added, "With this economic cold war in mind I'm sure Mr. Khrushchev would like to see the entire Cascades range plus the Sierras put into one huge wilderness area."[33]

The SAF increasingly began to enter the political fray, which reflected a growing trend of broad political organizing among those who sought to maintain commercial access to the forests for timber. The National Lumber Manufacturers Association, which later changed its name to the National Forest Products Association (NFPA), organized much of the national political campaign as the main lobbying arm for the timber industry.

In addition to the support of regional and national industry organizations and lobbying groups, concerned business owners recruited the support of members of Congress. George Wall and others convinced Washington State's two senators to support and reiterate industry criticisms of the Forest Service proposal. In a joint letter to the chief of the Forest Service, Richard McArdle, Senators Warren Magnuson and Henry M. Jackson wrote:

> Undoubtedly your agency, as our offices, has received the suggestion that areas below 3,500 feet in elevation lying both in the south fork of Agnes Creek and the Flat Creek Drainage area in Eastern Washington and the Seattle [Suiattle] area of Western Washington be removed from the Wilderness area planned and remain instead under the Forest Service sustained yield program. We would respectfully urge that this possibility be given the most thorough exploration at hearings contemplated in view of the importance of our lumbering industry to the economic well being of our state.[34]

If their inability to distinguish between the wilderness valley of the Suiattle River deep in the Cascades and the region's largest city on the shores of Puget Sound is any indication, the senators and other leaders on the national stage knew very little about the North Cascades, but they were likely well aware that a boundary at 3,500 feet in elevation would eliminate from wilderness protection nearly the entire extent of the merchantable forests in these valleys.

The senators' position, however, turned out to have increasing influence as the North Cascades became the focus of a national discussion and congressional debate through the 1960s. Jackson himself would turn from his initial support of the timber industry and become the leading figure in pushing for preservation as he learned more about the issues. Gaining the support of influential politicians was a high priority, but in order to gain broader political support, interest groups on both side of the debate—but particularly wilderness advocates—increasingly began to take their positions to a national audience, to dissolve the mists that shrouded the forests and the conflicting values over their use.

Among the ranks of North Cascades wilderness activists in the late 1950s, a common strategy emerged to publicize the area and the major issues of land use at stake. Drawing regional and national attention to the dramatic alpine terrain and the forests of the surrounding valleys became central to their efforts to limit logging in those valleys. The isolation and extremely rugged terrain of the region made it unique and had long protected the area from the transforming power of industrial development, but these characteristics also kept it hidden from a broader appreciation. As Supreme Court justice and life-long explorer of the Cascade Range William O. Douglas wrote in 1960, "The Glacier Peak area is so little known it has few friends. Those bent on exploiting it, therefore, have a great advantage. They hope to perfect their plans before the public is aware of the great treasure that is there."[35]

The strategy of greater publicity was not unique to the fight over the North Cascades; activists sought to attract attention to the scenic and scientific values of forests throughout the Northwest. In Eugene after the Horse Creek decision, Ruth Onthank organized exhibitions of photography by Ansel Adams, Ray Atkeson, and others that celebrated wild landscapes in the Northwest. With help from Michael McCloskey and Frances Newsom, she coordinated the selection of photographs of the Cascades that were shown in various public places in the state in 1961. She used pictures of the forests west of Horse Creek in Oregon and the valleys of the North Cascades taken by David Simons over the course of several trips into the mountains from 1956 to 1959.[36] Before his sudden death in 1960 at the age of twenty-four, Simons came to exemplify the emphasis on publicizing the campaign to preserve forests in the North Cascades.

The winter following Grant McConnell's 1955 summer trip to Stehekin, Simons, a young student from Springfield, Oregon, responded to McConnell's call for help and dropped by McConnell's office at the urging of Karl Onthank. Simons had arrived in Berkeley as a student in 1954. In Oregon, he had been a member of the Obsidians hiking club in Eugene, where he met Onthank, who became a mentor to him. From California and back home during the summers, Simons became an active participant and letter writer in the debates over the forests of the Three Sisters Primitive Area. Since high school he had studied the art of photography, and in 1955 he enrolled in a workshop conducted by Ansel Adams. Wilderness debates were not new to Simons when he arrived in McConnell's office, but he knew nothing about the North Cascades. Within two years, however, he would become one of the experts on the region, widely sharing his convictions that the area deserved the broadest possible protection and pushing wilderness advocates toward a more aggressive strategy to achieve that protection.[37]

McConnell asked Simons to spend the following summer exploring and photographing the North Cascades in order to attract public attention to the region. David Brower scratched together funds from the Sierra Club for food and equipment, and McConnell offered his house in Stehekin as a base camp for Simons's travels. Simons took a wealth of photographs that summer, which appeared in several journals and publications in later years, but perhaps more significantly, the experience converted Simons to complete devotion to the cause of a large wilderness in the North Cascades. He wrote back to Karl Onthank in Eugene that in national importance and his own personal judgment the Three Sisters case paled in comparison to the stakes farther north. Onthank continued to defend the Three Sisters at the front lines of the wilderness battle, but he did nothing to discourage Simons's passion. Simons wrote from Berkeley to the elder activist in the spring of 1957 as he prepared for a second season in the North Cascades, "This is truly a *national* problem, of even greater importance than the fight over Dinosaur National Monument."[38]

The Sierra Club also tried to increase awareness among its own membership, sponsoring three trips in 1956 into the North Cascades as part of the club's annual national schedule of outings. The tradition of organized outings had been a mainstay of the annual calendar for alpine clubs like the Sierra Club, the Mazamas, and the Mountaineers since John Muir led such hikes in the late nineteenth century. The Sierra Club Conservation Committee, under the leadership of Doctor Edgar Wayburn, of California, sought to have participants in the outings contribute to a detailed study of the wilderness resources of the North Cascades and be prepared to further publicize the region as a recreation area with the added authority of "having been there."[39] McConnell urged people to visit areas under dispute, not just study the maps. "The mountain public," he wrote in 1958, "no less than the administrators who participate in the decisions which are soon to be made have a special obligation to the nation to discover and to assess the values of this long-forgotten world."[40]

The Wilderness Society joined in this effort to publicize the North Cascades by holding the annual meeting of its board of directors at Stehekin in 1958, and that same year David Brower made a film about the region. *Wilderness Alps of Stehekin* toured the country as an eloquent and inspiring call for protection of the area. After each showing, organizers would pass out to the audience information pamphlets and guides for writing letters to Congress and the Forest Service. Patrick Goldsworthy remembered Brower's film as an "*extremely* useful vehicle" for promoting the campaign of the NCCC.[41]

Books also became a common tool in Northwest wilderness debates at this time, following the model set by *This Is Dinosaur*, which effectively generated support for the opposition to building a dam at Dinosaur National Monument. In Oregon, Karl Onthank had advocated a similar strategy for publicizing the case for wilderness in the Three Sisters.[42] Harvey Manning wrote the text for the first large-format photography book on the North Cascades. Published in 1964 by the Mountaineers, *The North Cascades* featured photographs by Tom Miller in an effort to promote the arguments and sentiments for protecting much of the area from logging. The following year, the Sierra Club published a larger work, *The Wild Cascades: Forgotten Parkland*, also written by Harvey Manning, but with a wider range of photographs from various contributors, including Ansel Adams, Philip Hyde, and David Simons, and poetry from Theodore Roethke. The book was part of the Sierra Club Exhibit-Format Series, edited by David Brower. *Wild Cascades* was dedicated to the memory of David Simons, who died in 1960 of hepatitis at Fort Bragg, North Carolina, where he was stationed in the army. If only people knew about these areas, went the rationale, public outcry would certainly save them from logging. Every member of Congress received copies of the book, and it would serve as a model for promoting later efforts to create wilderness areas.[43]

Yet the battle for public opinion was a limited tool, especially in the era before the Wilderness Act, and wilderness advocates became more aggressive in proposing land use classifications in the North Cascades than they had been in the Three Sisters. In response to the 1957 Forest Service proposal for the Glacier Peak area, they soon turned their focus to removing much of the area from the control of the Forest Service and placing it into the hands of the National Park Service. In 1958 the NCCC focused on this new goal of creating a national park rather than fighting the Forest Service over its own wilderness designation.

Proposing that Congress transfer the land from Forest Service jurisdiction to the National Park Service was a well-honed political tool by then; it was also a powerful and aggressive tool that frightened the Forest Service and the Department of Agriculture.[44] The expanding timber sale program on the national forests after World War II brought new urgency to this old strategy. To many conservationists in the Northwest, the lesson from the Three Sisters battle was that the Forest Service could not or would not commit itself to adequately protect wilderness in forested areas, and the agency's proposals for the Glacier Peak region in 1957 and 1959 confirmed this suspicion. One scholarly study from 1953 predicted the growing frustration: "It seems clear that preservation of large wilderness areas within national forests is not compatible with basic Forest Service policy."[45] David Simons wrote, "The primeval forest magnificence, the very essence of the Cascades, has small chance of survival outside of the National Park system. . . . That is the real issue." John Osseward, of the Wilderness Society, argued that transferring land to the National Park Service was "the only remaining recourse."[46]

Proving to the public that the North Cascades as a whole was compatible with National Park Service standards was another hurdle that park proponents had to overcome, though not a difficult one. The standards for land to qualify for a national park were changing in the early 1960s, but the North Cascades easily fit both old and new criteria. Since their inception in the nineteenth century, the national parks were celebrated as scenic monuments of the American landscape. As park activist and Wilderness Society cofounder Robert Sterling Yard wrote, they were "the Exposition of the Scenic Supremacy of the United States."[47] The national sympathy for scenic monuments, historian Alfred Runte has shown, lay at the heart of efforts to maintain and expand the national-park system. Anyone who had seen the North Cascades never questioned their monumental character. "Here is scenic grandeur that unquestionably belongs in our national gallery of natural beauty," wrote a federal committee assigned to study the area.[48] By the early 1960s, however, a growing desire to establish parks to preserve large areas for their ecological characteristics challenged the old emphasis on monumentalism. And since the fundamental concern behind the original park proposal for the North Cascades was to preserve the low-elevation forests from the Forest Service timber sale program, the area fit well into the new ecological rationale for the national-park system.[49]

David Brower and others saw two potential benefits from pursuing Park Service status for the Glacier Peak region. First, a successful campaign would remove the threat of logging from the forested valleys and mining in the surrounding high country. National parks could limit mining claims on their lands far more effectively than the Forest Service could, and most logging is prohibited within national parks. Even within a wilderness area, the Forest Service could not stop development of mining claims.[50] Second, the threat of losing jurisdiction might move the Forest Service to scale back its own timber sale agenda and offer increased wilderness protection to improve public relations and maintain control over the land. Many believed that studies in the 1930s for new national parks in Oregon and Washington, including the North Cascades, had provoked increased commitment on the part of the Forest Service to preservation within primitive areas. Bob Marshall had successfully campaigned for increased wilderness acreage throughout the country and in the Cascades using concurrent Park Service studies for leverage.[51]

There were also many in the conservation community, however, who resisted such a shift away from their previously diplomatic relations with Forest Service personnel, and they perceived a national-park campaign as too radical. The NCCC board of directors narrowly approved the new park strategy by a three-to-two vote in 1958. Some worried that a movement to create a national park out of Forest Service land would jeopardize or drain energy and resources from the existing campaign for national wilderness legislation, which was the priority for many conservation organizations across the country at the time. The Mazamas argued against the park plan, complaining that its proponents "are in effect lining up with interests who want no more wilderness areas established of *any* kind."[52]

Many also did not trust the National Park Service, which had embarked on an aggressive plan for road and tourist developments within the parks. Bob Marshall expressed this concern for the North Cascades as early as 1938, in response to a specific park proposal of a year earlier. "If this area should be made a park," he wrote, "it would have roads extended into its heart."[53] The first president of the NCCC, Philip Zalesky, worried that given "the development tendencies of the Washington congressional delegation, I suspect that the wilderness aspects of the bill would be compromised out of the bill" in any future legislation to create a park in the North Cascades.[54] David Brower, however, compared the strategy to a gun "pointed at the Forest Service's temple."[55] It was a risky maneuver, but growing frustration with the Forest Service over Horse Creek and the North Cascades had pushed him and others to take this more aggressive stance.

The changes in Forest Service policies after World War II are essential in understanding this fundamental shift in the strategy of wilderness advocates. In the interwar era, building roads, campgrounds, and other developed recreation sites generated the biggest fears of Bob Marshall's generation of activists, and the National Park Service was the more aggressive road builder and tourism promoter of the two agencies. When the Forest Service embarked on its logging boom, however, shifting land to Park Service jurisdiction became far more palatable because logging had become the biggest threat to conservation on public lands.

David Simons, who was too young to remember a Forest Service supportive of wilderness, was instrumental in persuading many to support the strategy of using the Park Service to fight the policies of its rival. In 1958, Brower distributed a report that Simons wrote based on his previous two summers exploring and documenting the North Cascades. In *The Need for Scenic Resource Conservation in the Northern Cascades of Washington* Simons outlined his observations of the country and his concerns over Forest Service management there. He concluded the thirty-six-page document with a call for creation of a national park surrounding the Glacier Peak region and bordering the North Cascades

Primitive Area, which had been established in 1931 along the U.S.-Canada border north of the Skagit River.[56]

Simons's arguments helped to persuade many who were reluctant. Polly Dyer, a founding member of the NCCC, recalls, "I favored the U.S. Forest Service, thinking a good, strong Wilderness Bill would solve our problems. But after reading Dave's brief, I decided a national park was our only option."[57] David Brower wrote a note to Dyer atop her copy of Simons's proposal: "Two Dave's can't be wrong."[58] By 1960, all the efforts to increase awareness of the North Cascades—the exhibit-format photography books, the film *Wilderness Alps of Stehekin*, and other aspects of the campaign—focused on the goal of creating a national park.

Yet all of these efforts gained little immediate headway. In 1960, the secretary of agriculture approved the final boundaries of the Glacier Peak Wilderness Area under the agency's U Regulations. Secretary E. L. Peterson signed the order on 6 September, which increased the Forest Service's earlier proposed wilderness by over 35,000 acres to a total of nearly 450,000 acres. Peterson's statement suggests that he was responding to the growing support for wilderness protection of the valley corridors and perhaps to threats of a national park: "In general, the consensus was that the corridors were too numerous and too deep. Prominently mentioned in this regard were the Suiattle, Agnes Creek, Phelps Creek, White Chuck, and the White River corridors which cut into the proposed wilderness for five to nine miles."[59]

Again, the high-elevation areas were not under significant dispute in the wilderness debates. The secretary's additions occurred in the Suiattle River, Agnes Creek, and Phelps Creek valleys, although other valleys, including those of the White Chuck River and the White River, remained nearly entirely outside the wilderness boundary and open to timber harvesting. These latter two valleys and the fact that most of the lower Suiattle drainage, including the tributaries of Buck Creek and Downey Creek, remained unprotected gave very little for conservationists to cheer about.[60] Therefore, they continued to campaign for a national park. Even when the Glacier Peak Wilderness Area became part of the National Wilderness Preservation System under the Wilderness Act of 1964, a national park in the North Cascades remained a top agenda item for conservationists.

The efforts to put the North Cascades on a national agenda and the resulting tensions that developed between the National Park Service of the Department of the Interior and the U.S. Forest Service of the Department of Agriculture began to pay dividends for conservationists at the same time that the conservationists lost ground in the Cascade forests themselves. Having finalized their administrative decision on the Glacier Peak Wilderness Area, the Forest Service continued with its timber sale agendas for the Mount Baker and the Wenatchee National Forests. They extended roads farther up several valleys where conservationists sought further study for potential wilderness or national-park designations. Congressman Thomas Pelly, on behalf of wilderness advocates, requested a moratorium on road construction and timber sales in the greater North Cascades region, a plea the Forest Service rejected. In defense of its current policies, the agency cited the completed study and decision on the Glacier Peak Wilderness Area and a High Mountain Policy for the Cascades, approved in 1961. This latter set of guidelines arose in response to criticism from conservationists, but the result was a new policy that affirmed limited development in the high-altitude regions of the Cascades but did not include the lower valleys, which "were the crux of the conflict." The issue was closed, according to the assistant secretary of agriculture, and he told Congressman Pelly that the Forest Service intended to continue with an additional two hundred miles of planned road construction in the area.[61]

Thomas Pelly's support in Congress was one important way in which the campaign for a national park gained greater acceptance. Pelly introduced legislation in 1961 and 1962 to establish a study team to assess the potential for a park in the region, and the proposal received support from the new administration of John F. Kennedy. The Kennedy administration sought to dispel some of the growing tensions between the Departments of the Interior and Agriculture fostered by public advocacy for creating parks in the North Cascades and other places in the country. An important agreement emerged between Orville L. Freeman, secretary of agriculture, and Stewart L. Udall, secretary of the interior, to develop "a new era of cooperation" in managing their lands for recreation. Both sides promised not to institute unilateral efforts to change the jurisdiction of federal lands, thus eliminating the potential for study of the North Cascades by the National Park Service alone. However, they did agree that "a joint study should be made of Federal lands in the North Cascade Mountains of Washington to determine the management and administration of those lands that will best serve the public interest." Known widely as the "Treaty of the Potomac," this agreement created a joint North Cascades Study Team in 1963 that brought the issue of designating a national park to the highest levels of the federal government. In response, the NCCC revealed a detailed proposal, authored by Michael McCloskey, for a national park in the Glacier Peak region in 1963.[62]

The 1963 NCCC proposal for a national park reflected a consistent priority of wilderness advocates throughout the nation to push for a wide-ranging, comprehensive approach to land use planning. Before the Forest Service defined even its preliminary proposal for the Glacier Peak Limited Area, Grant McConnell wrote, "The area's problems are complex and will not be readily solved by the simple declaration of a Glacier Peak Wilderness Area. . . . A wilderness area is an excellent device, but something more is needed to meet the policy requirements of the entire region. Some combination of policies is essential. Such a combination can be developed only through more extensive study and through zoning."[63] David Simons added, "The region is unquestionably so magnificent that we cannot afford to look only at one area or one aspect of its conservation; we must consider complete zoning of the entire northern range as our ideal goal."[64] Toward this end, wilderness proposals often included calls for more efficient use of timber resources in areas where roads and clear-cuts already existed and in the regional lumber and pulp mills. The North Cascades Study Team did take a broad look at the entire region, a stretch of over 150 miles, north to south, encompassing over seven million acres, but in the end their legislative proposals focused rather narrowly on the northern sections, north of Stevens Pass. When Congress acted on their proposals beginning in 1967, the area under question narrowed even further.[65]

The study team released its report in 1965. The report proposed a park to cover most of the high-elevation terrain between the Canadian border and the Glacier Peak Wilderness Area to the south. In addition, it proposed expanding the Forest Service's Glacier Peak Wilderness Area to include more of the low-elevation forests of the Suiattle and White Chuck River valleys. A new Pasayten Wilderness Area on the Okanogan

National Forest would cover 500,000 acres east of the new park. And the report recommended new wilderness areas to the south of Glacier Peak: Alpine Lakes, Enchantment, and Mount Aix. These three areas were high, alpine terrain, and their boundaries as proposed by the North Cascades Study Team would allow the Forest Service to open timber sales and road construction in the forests of the Alpine Lakes and Cougar Lakes Limited Areas where logging previously was restricted. This was designed as a compromise to compensate the Forest Service for the park farther north.[66]

Congressional action focused exclusively on land north of Glacier Peak, thus putting off decisions on land use in the Alpine Lakes and Cougar Lakes Limited Areas. The Senate passed this narrower bill in November 1967. Opposition in the House of Representatives was resolved the following year after Senator Jackson used political leverage to release a study of water development on the Colorado River to appease Representative Wayne Aspinall of Colorado, the major House opponent to most wilderness legislation. The final votes in both houses were overwhelmingly in favor. In 1968 President Johnson signed the bill creating the North Cascades National Park, Ross Lake National Recreation Area, and Lake Chelan National Recreation Area. Congress also used its authority under the Wilderness Act to create the Pasayten Wilderness Area and expand the Glacier Peak Wilderness Area by including more of the forests along the Suiattle and White Chuck Rivers.[67]

Ironically, the creation of the joint North Cascades Study Team and the congressional hearings that followed removed the national-park plan from the hands of conservationists at the same time that it gave those organizations the national exposure they had long sought. President Johnson spoke to Congress about the need for a national park in the North Cascades in 1967, and Senator Jackson, powerful chair of the Senate Committee on Interior and Insular Affairs, made it a personal mission to create a park. Creation of the joint study team also served to revise the fundamental questions of the debate from a dispute between wilderness and industrial logging to a simpler question of federal jurisdiction: Park Service or Forest Service. According to the leading scholarly assessment of the creation of the North Cascades National Park, "The team failed to address the issues which generated the controversy to begin with. . . . In the final analysis, the battle over the North

Cascades became a jurisdictional fight between two powerful federal agencies."[68]

In 1968, Brock Evans, the new Northwest conservation representative for the Sierra Club, criticized a series of articles on the park issue published in the *Journal of Forestry* for ignoring the voices of wilderness advocates: "The impression left with the reader is that the primary issue is over which agency shall manage the wilderness and scenic beauty of the North Cascades, and that the viewpoint of the conservation organizations out here who have fought for the area for so long has no merit."[69] Conservationists' concerns focused on whether or not the forests of the lower valleys would be open to industrial logging. Proposing a national park was viewed as a means to preserve those valleys. Their opponents in the timber industry sought with equal effort to maintain access to the timber supply within those forests. The final result was a political compromise that preserved mostly high, alpine terrain and a few very prominent examples of the lower forests in a national park and Forest Service wilderness areas in exchange for releasing most of the forested lands to timber harvesting.

The political process created a national park that the study team described as containing "the most breathtakingly beautiful and spectacular mountain scenery in the 48 contiguous States," but it did not solve the most fundamental disputes over competing values.[70] Although Congress embarrassed the Forest Service by creating the North Cascades National Park complex and in doing so removed 671,000 acres from Forest Service control, the valuable forests of the lower valleys remained within the national forests and outside wilderness boundaries, and thus open to timber sales. Conservationists got their park, but they achieved protection for relatively few acres of the prized old-growth forests. Allan Sommarstrom, of the University of Washington, noted, "The units mentioned by the legislation had their outside boundaries shaped by the timber industry as a minimum of commercial timber was included [in the park and wilderness areas]."[71] Michael McCloskey, who went on to succeed David Brower as executive director of the Sierra Club, commented in 1968 that the boundaries were "far short of what we know they should be."[72]

Decisions of the North Cascades Study Team and acts of Congress demonstrated the new political strength of conservation organizations and provided a spectacular national park that arose from their daring vision of ten years earlier. Although in many ways these results seemed hollow victories for wilderness advocates at the time, they set an enormous precedent for altering Forest Service policy, in addition to "saving some of the key places," such as Agnes Creek.[73] Sitting at a small café breakfast table, Brock Evans told me, "In the end, I would have supported a national park the size of this table just to make the political point that we had the political power to take land from the all-powerful Forest Service." For Evans and others, the symbolic precedent of defeating the Forest Service was critical. And it was the beginning of significant changes to come. Brower told Evans at the time, "That's the train that's leaving the station. Get on that train."[74]

3 MOUNT JEFFERSON, 1961–1968

The Whitewater Creek valley reaches far into the Cascades, extending low-elevation Douglas fir forests nearly to the base of Mount Jefferson, the second tallest peak in Oregon. The valley pushes an incision so deeply into the Cascade Range that the high-elevation Mount Jefferson Primitive Area was pinched into a narrow belt between these valley forests on the west and the Warm Springs Indian Reservation on the east. The Confederated Tribes of the Warm Springs own and manage the forestlands east of the Cascade Crest under treaty rights established in 1855. The Cascade Forest Reserve, created in 1893, bordered the reservation on three sides. Unlike the Three Sisters Primitive Area as expanded in 1938, the Mount Jefferson Primitive Area, established in 1933, did not include much valuable timber. Very few parts of the area were below 3,500 feet in elevation, where the Douglas fir forests begin to merge into the subalpine forests of less commercial value.

Since the crux of wilderness debates in the Northwest focused mainly on valleys below 3,500 feet, the creation of the Mount Jefferson Wilderness Area out of the old primitive area focused on whether to protect from logging some of the lower forests outside the original boundaries. In the early 1960s, conservationists petitioned for an

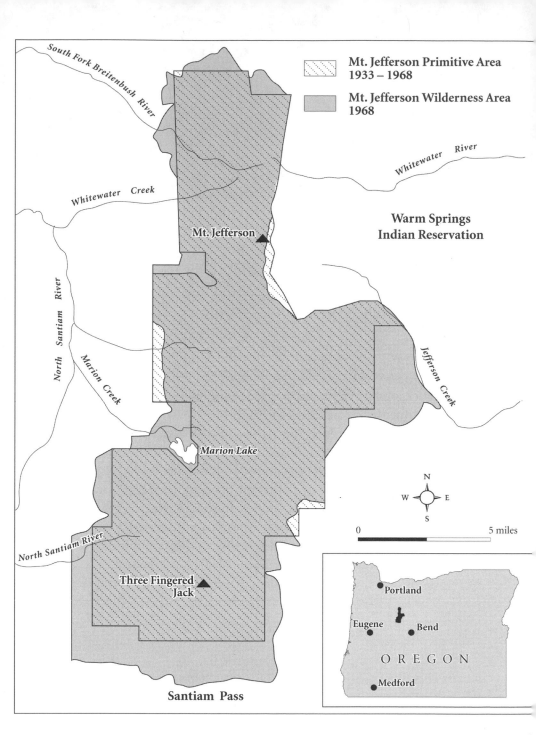

Legend:

Mt. Jefferson Primitive Area
1933 – 1968

Mt. Jefferson Wilderness Area
1968

South Fork Breitenbush River

Whitewater River

Whitewater Creek

Mt. Jefferson ▲

Warm Springs
Indian Reservation

North Santiam River

Marion Creek

Jefferson Creek

Marion Lake

North Santiam River

Three Fingered
Jack ▲

Santiam Pass

N
W E
S

0   5 miles

Portland

Eugene   Bend

O R E G O N

Medford

MAP 4. Mount Jefferson, Oregon. Map by Peter Morrison and Barry Levely.

extension of the existing boundaries, a position that Michael McCloskey, the initial coordinator of the Mount Jefferson campaign, later suggested was a shift to a more aggressive strategy than the earlier, conservative defense of the existing boundaries of the Three Sisters Primitive Area in the mid-1950s.[1] In 1963, the Forest Service agreed to expand the boundaries outward east and south, adding more acreage to the protected area, but it stopped short of including the forests of the western valleys. In fact, the new boundaries would reduce the protection offered these lower forests, releasing lower-elevation forests contained in the existing primitive area and opening them up to the timber sale program. By 1962, as the debate over proposed new wilderness boundaries continued, the Forest Service built a road and sold timber deep in the Whitewater Valley, close to the boundary of the primitive area.

As logging and road building worked their way up into the middle elevations of the national forests (roughly 1,500–3,500 feet in elevation) to satisfy the growing appetite for timber in the postwar years, conservationists increasingly drew attention to the diminishing undeveloped forested regions pinched between these ascending forces of development and the boundaries of the high-elevation protected areas. Wilderness advocates pointed to these unprotected roadless areas as an important resource for the rapidly growing interest in nonmotorized recreation beginning in the 1950s. The logging industry also sought to secure access to these lands for future timber supply. Increasingly, the attention from all sides focused on wildlands outside the existing boundaries of formally protected areas: the "de facto wilderness." The Mount Jefferson debates reflected this changing aspect of wilderness debates throughout the country after passage of the Wilderness Act in 1964. The Mount Jefferson Wilderness Area has not garnered much attention from historians and others concerned with wilderness in the United States, but the Mount Jefferson debates are important because they demonstrate a new emphasis on de facto wilderness lands and on struggles over the definition of "wilderness."

The process to redesignate the Mount Jefferson Primitive Area had begun by 1961, when the Forest Service invited citizen proposals to assist in their reassessment, as required under the U Regulations. The Obsidians, a Eugene hiking club, joined five other groups, including the Oregon Cascades Conservation Council, to submit a proposal to increase the size of the area, expanding the current boundaries westward to protect the lower-elevation valleys and provide an extended buffer zone to reduce foot and horse traffic in the fragile high-altitude areas.[2] The thirty-eight-page plan written by Northwest conservation representative Michael McCloskey called for the secretary of agriculture to designate a Mount Jefferson Wilderness Area of 117,000 acres.

The existing primitive area encompassed 85,000 acres, a long, narrow alpine strip straddling the crest of the Cascades from Santiam Pass to the North Fork of the Breitenbush River. At its narrowest spot, it reached only three miles from east to west, from Mount Jefferson to Woodpecker Ridge above Whitewater Creek.[3] An assortment of alpine lakes and spectacular views of Mount Jefferson and the area's relatively easy access made the Mount Jefferson region among the most popular backcountry recreation sites in Oregon. Even though it was a relatively small area, no wilderness area, wild area, or primitive area on national-forest lands in the Oregon Cascades saw larger numbers of visitors by 1960.[4]

In the fall of 1963, the Forest Service released its own proposal for the new Mount Jefferson Wilderness Area and scheduled a period for public comment the following year. The Forest Service proposed an increase in the total acreage of the protected area but eliminated some of the forests along the western boundary with merchantable timber. This was the same strategy used in creating the Glacier Peak Wilderness Area in 1959–60: the acreage of the protected area increased but the volume of commercial timber protected from harvest decreased. Around Mount Jefferson, the Forest Service added acres in the high-elevation forests and lava fields near Santiam Pass on the south end of the primitive area. These were not areas with valuable commercial resources; thus, placing them within the proposed wilderness boundary did not generate much controversy. Rather, the debate again focused on whether or not to include big trees in the wilderness area; the focal point was the low-elevation forests on the west side of the primitive area.

The conflicts over Mount Jefferson, just like the Horse Creek battle and the North Cascades fight, are classic examples of the fundamental role of big trees in the debates over wilderness designations in the Northwest. Preserving the high-elevation alpine and subalpine regions for recreation was rarely challenged. After listening to public testimony on the Mount Jefferson proposal, Robert Smith reported in the *Portland Oregonian*, the state's largest newspaper, "There was no opposition to creation of the Mt. Jefferson Wilderness Area as such. This area has for many years been a primitive area, a designation being abandoned. The conflict centers entirely on boundaries."[5]

In the course of the Mount Jefferson debate, the general mood of cordial relations between conservationists and foresters that had predominated since the Progressive Era faced severe challenge as agency road-building operations expanded into previously undeveloped forests—the de facto wilderness—bordering the primitive area. In 1962, the Forest Service built a road deep into the Whitewater Creek valley to access a few timber sale units there, a move that infuriated conservationists as a blatant obstacle to any efforts to expand the boundaries of the Mount Jefferson Wilderness Area into these disputed forests. They had hoped to include those lands at least into a broader discussion of land use planning. The agency argued that it was simply carrying out its timber management plans for the area, but the road bypassed several miles of forests to reach timber sale units placed at the farthest reaches of the valley. Over the following few years, the Willamette National Forest continued to offer additional timber sales in the upper valley.[6] The road very clearly served two purposes: supplying timber for the local economy and, after 1964, blocking Congress from considering the area for wilderness designation because it could no longer be considered undeveloped.

The latter purpose intensely frustrated conservationists, who were increasingly feeling betrayed by the Forest Service nationwide. "The story of the Whitewater is one of the sorriest in recent resource history," wrote Rodger Pegues, McCloskey's successor as Northwest conservation representative, in a 1966 report. "There is good reason to believe that the Forest Service invaded this valley with roads and logging to preclude the valley's being considered for preservation as wilderness. Perhaps this was not a conscious intention, but the Forest Service has given every appearance of being satisfied with that result."[7] Holway Jones, librarian and wilderness activist from Eugene, documented several dozen logging contracts sold by the Forest Service since 1961 within the area conservationists proposed that year for wilderness status. "This would seem to indicate a definite attempt on the part of the Forest Service to preclude much de facto wilderness along the western fringe of the Primitive Area from any further consideration in dedicated wilderness," he concluded. To this day, conservationists harbor a bitter resentment against what they have always held was a deliberate attempt by the Forest Service to undermine the debate over these forestlands.[8]

As part of an ongoing effort to delay additional Forest Service timber sales in the areas surrounding primitive areas such as Mount Jefferson, McCloskey drafted a proposed federal law in 1962 to require public hearings prior to any timber sales and logging activity within two miles of a wilderness area or national park.[9] As with previous and later proposals to limit the Forest Service timber sale program outside wilderness boundaries, this did not become reality. The Forest Service and the timber industry reacted quickly and decisively to eliminate any such restrictive buffer zones around wilderness areas.

The Forest Service held public hearings on its Mount Jefferson Wilderness proposal in Salem in June 1964, but the process was put on hold after the Wilderness Act passed in September of that year. The new law immediately incorporated existing Forest Service wilderness and wild areas, such as the Three Sisters Wilderness Area (as reduced in 1957) and the Glacier Peak Wilderness Area, into the National Wilderness Preservation System. If the Forest Service chief had approved the agency's 1963 proposal for a Mount Jefferson Wilderness Area of 96,944 acres, that too would have become part of the wilderness system automatically. Instead, it remained a primitive area, and the Forest Service no longer had the authorization to change that status without the consent of Congress. The Wilderness Act required the Forest Service to assess all its existing primitive areas for possible designation as wilderness and submit recommendations to Congress within ten years. Following that mandate, the Forest Service reexamined the Mount Jefferson area, the first primitive area in the Cascades to undergo review under the requirements of the Wilderness Act.[10]

The secretary of agriculture during these years, Orville Freeman, argued in 1972 that, ironically, the Wilderness Act slowed down the creation of wilderness areas because of these "procedural and legislative requirements" imposed on the Forest Service.[11] Whether he correctly identified the irony or not, he missed the point and long-term significance of the Wilderness Act. It was not an effort to accelerate the creation of wilderness areas; it was a direct attempt to slow down or stop the erosion of wildlands at the hands of Forest Service chiefs and agriculture secretaries, who had the power to move boundaries and sell harvest rights to the timber of de facto wilderness lands that were not protected, as had been done on several million acres of national forest from 1961 to 1964. The agency's roads and clear-cuts deep in the White-water Creek valley were powerful examples of why wilderness activists focused so much energy on codifying a wilderness system created and maintained by Congress. In the long run, contrary to Secretary Free-man's interpretation, the Wilderness Act resulted in a massive increase in the acreage of land protected as wilderness in the United States.

In the process of composing a plan for Congress to consider, in 1966 the Forest Service reintroduced its own previous proposal for the Mount Jefferson Wilderness Area and again invited public comments.[12] The agency slightly reduced its 1963 proposal; it suggested similar boundaries around an area of 95,450 acres. Oregon conservationists expanded by 7 percent their proposal of 1961 and 1963 and requested protection of 125,000 acres. They asked for additional lands along Whitewater Creek, where roads and timber sales had moved up the val-ley while the wilderness boundaries remained under debate. Before preparing its formal proposal for Congress to consider, the Forest Ser-vice held a public hearing in Salem in 1966. Oral testimony dramati-cally favored the larger conservationist proposal to extend the boundaries farther down the western slopes, but the final recommendation that the Forest Service sent to Congress varied little from its original plan.[13]

The Forest Service did not attempt to hide its opinion that valuable forestlands should be kept out of wilderness areas. Herbert Stone, the regional forester for Region 6, covering Oregon and Washington, justified the agency's proposal to remove portions from the western edge of the Mount Jefferson Primitive Area due to the "excellent stands of commercial timber."[14] The significant additions the agency did propose were mainly high-elevation areas on the south and east sides of the existing primitive area. North of the Santiam Pass highway, they added 5,447 acres of alpine forest, which held relatively little value as a source of timber. Lava flows took up most of the 3,970 acres added in the Candle Creek drainage.[15] Many of these additions were not areas of dispute, nor was there a strong disagreement over their value. The lower forested areas were the center of the debate. As Brock Evans wrote at the time, "It is this forest—the semi rain forest of giant, low elevation Douglas Fir, Cedar, and Hemlock—which is the focal point of all wilderness controversies in the Mount Jefferson area and elsewhere in the Northwest."[16]

Conservationists' objections to the agency plan reflected concerns over the aesthetic and recreational values at four specific sites along the perimeter of the proposed wilderness area. They expressed concern that logging roads would encroach up to the boundaries of what remained a very narrow strip of protected area, just as had happened in the Whitewater Creek valley.[17] The Forest Service's proposed expansion of 10,000 acres did not widen the primitive area in its narrowest and most heavily used portion; in fact, it slightly narrowed this area because it removed forests along Woodpecker Ridge above Whitewater Creek.

At public hearings, wilderness advocates expressed their concerns that timber harvests and access roads would encroach on their enjoyment of the area for recreation.[18] Eleanor Heller had spent twenty-nine years hiking, climbing, and skiing in the Mount Jefferson region before she testified in support of an expanded wilderness area. "To hike between Jefferson Park and Pamelia Lake," she stated, "was once a true wilderness experience. . . . Now, on the same kind of hike, one's attention is diverted by the sight of clear cuts. Obviously, more buffer zone is needed west of Mt. Jefferson." Twelve-year-old Jon Krakauer testified in Salem in 1966 that he wanted the wilderness area to include the lower valleys. "As you walk into Jefferson Park, you shouldn't have to pass through an ugly area," he said.[19]

In addition to expanding wilderness acreage, many conservationists once again pushed for a more efficient use of timber resources in areas outside wilderness to relieve pressure on the forests within de facto wilderness. Wilderness advocates were careful not to argue against logging in principle—just as the industry did not publicly oppose the idea of wilderness—but they did challenge where and how logging should occur on public lands. They argued that the demands for timber could be satisfied by developed lands—both private and public—in the foothills, if only those lands were used more effectively and if lumber mills and other processing facilities reduced waste. They refused to believe the Forest Service and timber lobbyists who argued in 1968 that a shortage of supply pushed timber sales into higher-elevation areas near the boundaries of the Mount Jefferson Primitive Area.

Conservationists had long held that more efficient utilization of these lower-elevation lands would reduce the pressures to log the less-productive forests on public lands surrounding wilderness areas. Lloyd Tupling, of the Sierra Club, commented that the 28,000 additional acres requested in his group's proposal for the Mount Jefferson Wilderness Area was insignificant compared to an estimated 300,000 acres in western Oregon that "is not producing timber as it should."[20] Karl Onthank, who called for more efficient forestry in his 1955 statements against reduction of the Three Sisters Primitive Area, claimed in testimony on the Mount Jefferson issue that the great challenge to foresters "is to grow wood of desired quality on sites adapted to low cost harvesting and transportation. It is not to grow stumpage on every and any acre of forest land."[21]

Likely because the proposed Mount Jefferson Wilderness Area did not include a very large area or significant volume of commercial timber and because both Forest Service and conservationist plans placed no limits on forestry management outside the wilderness, there was a relative lack of concerted, public opposition on the part of the timber industry in Oregon. After McCloskey's failed 1962 draft legislation to create buffer zones, the wilderness proposals did not incorporate any language to limit timber harvests in the surrounding forests. Both the Forest Service and the timber industry opposed the conservationists' larger wilderness area that would include parts of the Whitewater Creek valley, but industry representatives did not submit a separate proposal of their own. They seemed satisfied with the Forest Service's proposed boundaries. Preserving the subalpine forests and the higher alpine meadows and glaciers was not a threat to them. When testifying in favor of more protection at a congressional hearing in Washington, DC, in 1968, some conservationists were quite surprised that the industry offered no opposition to the Forest Service proposal.[22] But of all the primitive areas, wild areas, and wilderness areas on national-forest lands in Oregon, only one had less "productive timber" by acre than Mount Jefferson (and not coincidentally, this area had the largest acreage of "barren" alpine terrain).[23]

Expanding wilderness protection into more valuable, lower-elevation forests, however, carried too much additional cost to the industry and might push Willamette National Forest officials to recalculate the forest's level of annual timber harvesting. The conservationists' proposal would reduce the available timber supply to the local economy by eleven million board feet annually, Oregon Senator Mark Hatfield claimed, and "serious economic hardship could result if the available timber supply was reduced by that amount." His senior colleague, Wayne Morse, also favored the Forest Service plan, under which "there will be little change in the present annual allowable cut for the Willamette, Deschutes, and Mt. Hood National Forests." Morse concluded of the Forest Service proposal, "A good job has been done in blending economic and aesthetic and intangible factors, with the least possible impact on the vitally important lumber industry." To add the forested areas proposed by conservationists would result in the loss of six hundred jobs in the local economy, regional forester Herbert Stone claimed.[24]

A consortium of small logging and lumber companies in the area had persuaded their senators that the costs of putting an extra 30,000 acres of forest off limits to logging were too high. Large corporations were not as concerned with access to these stands of public timber because most of their supply came from their own land. In 1968, a boom in the export of raw logs, mainly to Japan, reduced the supply of logs for small mills in Oregon. Large corporations who owned their own timber profited from this boost in foreign demand, but the smaller companies and mills that relied on timber sales from the national forests struggled to compete in this market. Given the reduced supply of logs, they pushed harder for increasing the supply of timber from public land.[25] In this economic atmosphere, adding the valuable forests of Whitewater Creek to the wilderness, regardless of their minimal economic contribution, was not politically acceptable to Oregon's congressional delegation. As a result, the Mount Jefferson Wilderness Area, as approved by Congress in 1968, did not include the Whitewater Valley.

The Confederated Tribes of the Warm Springs, whose reservation bordered the primitive area on the east, expressed their own opposition to both wilderness proposals. They were concerned over access to specific resources in a small, precise area. Many American Indian tribes expressed opposition to federal wilderness on their own lands as an affront to their sovereignty, but for the Warm Springs, the proposed Mount Jefferson

Wilderness Area revived frustrations generated from an earlier boundary dispute in the late nineteenth century.[26]

North from the summit of Mount Jefferson, two competing survey lines defined the boundary of the Warm Springs Reservation. In 1894, Congress recognized the easternmost of these two lines, disregarding the original boundary line of the reservation as agreed to in 1887. This action removed 61,000 acres, known as the McQuinn Strip, from the reservation. Federal courts later recognized the unjust expropriation of this area and ruled that in lieu of returning the land the tribe was entitled to compensation from Forest Service timber receipts generated by timber sales within the McQuinn Strip. Congress agreed to this in 1948.[27]

Almost all of the disputed land was well north of the Mount Jefferson area, but a narrow slice spreading from the summit of Mount Jefferson made up the southern segment of the McQuinn Strip. Placing this portion of the strip within the wilderness would eliminate any money from future timber sales there, leaving the tribes with less compensation for their lost land. Since most of the section had been part of the primitive area since the 1930s, they had not received any funds up to that point; the conflict was over potential future payments.

The tribes continued to lobby for a return of the entire McQuinn Strip, but until that happened they spoke out against efforts that undermined their rights to compensation. In the decade following creation of the Mount Jefferson Wilderness Area, the Forest Service remained the last obstacle to legislation to return the McQuinn Strip to the Warm Springs. As we have seen in the North Cascades, the agency aggressively opposed efforts to remove land from its jurisdiction. In 1972 Congress did return all of the McQuinn Strip to the tribe except the small portion then within the Mount Jefferson Wilderness Area.[28]

The argument over boundaries was fought not only over competing values placed on the forests surrounding the primitive area but also over competing definitions of wilderness. The history of the Mount Jefferson Wilderness Area demonstrates one of the key methods by which the Forest Service sought to oppose wilderness designation by Congress. Although the Forest Service in its post-1964 review of primitive areas "committed itself to impeccable compliance with the letter of the law," according to one conservationist, it challenged the intent and spirit of the Wilderness Act in order to defend its own interests.[29]

The Forest Service proudly portrayed itself as the keeper of the original wilderness preservation tradition in the twentieth century. They opposed the Wilderness Act partly because they genuinely felt that there was no need for a duplicate system, partly because of possessive pride, and partly to maintain their management autonomy. Hamilton Pyles, deputy chief of the Forest Service from 1962 to 1966, remembered, "My initial reaction [to the Wilderness Act] was that we, the forest service, were the initiators of this whole concept. We had established a wilderness system within the national forests by secretarial regulation and at that time didn't see the necessity of setting up a separate system."[30]

The agency promoted a set of standards for wilderness based on ideals of a pristine landscape free of all human influence. While much of the motivation for its strict definition of wilderness was based on heartfelt idealism, which can still be seen today in many aspects of Forest Service wilderness management policies, foresters used their idealized standards to carefully segregate the "pristine" and picturesque alpine areas from the managed commercial forests of the lowlands. They also argued that accepting some lands that were not seemingly pristine diluted the quality of the entire wilderness system. Secretary of Agriculture Orville Freeman reflected this common view in a 1967 speech: "If development already exists in one unit of the Wilderness System, it is harder to keep development out of others." This "purity doctrine," as it became known among its critics, was a key element of the Forest Service's attempt to limit the size of the Mount Jefferson Wilderness Area.[31]

The Forest Service felt strongly that developed lands or areas with roads should not qualify for wilderness status. Herbert Stone singled out the Whitewater Valley at the 1966 public hearing on the wilderness proposal by declaring that "the existing road is not compatible with wilderness."[32] Many in Congress and in the wilderness movement agreed that roads destroyed the pristine nature of the landscape and thereby disqualified the area from protection, but only the Forest Service stuck to a rigidly purist definition of wilderness in support of its positions in various wilderness debates.

Wilderness advocates, on the other hand, asked that the road and logging units in the Whitewater Valley be included in the new wilderness area and allowed to revert to a forested state. Sanford Tepfer, a veteran of the battle over Horse Creek ten years earlier, argued that the road up the Whitewater Valley made access to Jefferson Park too easy. Challenging the Forest Service's strict definition of wilderness, he testified, "This road should be closed and the valley allowed to return to wilderness."[33] Stewart Brandborg, of the Wilderness Society, added a national voice to this campaign: "The Forest Service commitment of some of the contiguous lands to commercial logging in the period (since 1961) when reclassification studies were underway should not go unchallenged. But this administrative action, undesirable as it has been, should not preclude needed extension of the Wilderness Area boundaries."[34] Many wilderness advocates felt that to give in on the Whitewater Creek road would only serve to reward the Forest Service for its actions. Employing a far more pragmatic interpretation of the Wilderness Act, they asked that the road be dug up and allowed to return to a forested state within the boundaries of the new wilderness area.

Many conservationists hesitated to campaign for admitting roads and clear-cuts into the wilderness for some of the same reasons stated by the Forest Service, but the opportunity to add additional forested areas to the wilderness won out. "Ordinarily such uses would preclude the consideration of the affected areas as dedicated wilderness," Brandborg admitted. Others disagreed. "There is ample precedent of inclusion of the existing road within the Mount Jefferson Wilderness," the Sierra Club testified to Congress in 1968.[35]

Areas with roads and other human impacts had been included in the National Wilderness Preservation System since its inception in 1964, and congressional intent seemed clear that such areas qualify for wilderness protection. As Frank Church, senator from Idaho and the Senate floor leader in passing the Wilderness Act in 1964, said about the purity doctrine in 1973: "Nothing could be more contrary to the meaning and intent of the Wilderness Act. The effect of such an interpretation would be to automatically disqualify almost everything, for few if any lands on this continent—or any other—have escaped man's imprint to some degree."[36]

When Congress created the Mount Jefferson Wilderness Area in 1968, the Whitewater Valley was not within its final boundaries, but the value of the timber during a time of tight supply for the region was the dominant reason, not the preexistence of the road. Although a victory for the Forest Service, it was not a congressional endorsement of the agency's purity doctrine.

Although the Forest Service did win its battle in Congress to keep large stands of commercial timber on the west side of the primitive area out of the new Mount Jefferson Wilderness Area in 1968, its attempt to keep Marion Lake out of the wilderness based on the purity argument failed. Marion Lake, on the southwest side of Mount Jefferson, had become a popular boating lake by the 1960s, complete with boathouses and motorized craft. Up to two hundred boats were stored at the lake. A logging road came within one mile of the lake from the west, and a trail provided access from the road. The Forest Service wilderness proposal of 1963 called for establishing a scenic area, under the U Regulations, which would allow for continued use as a developed recreation site. The boundaries would create a sharp 3,000-acre indentation into the wilderness area surrounding the lake on three sides. The agency argued that the existing use of motorized equipment and the presence of nonwilderness facilities disqualified the area for wilderness.

Many examples could be found of Forest Service policies that accepted nonconforming uses, such as airplanes or motorboats, within areas it managed as wilderness, and the Marion Lake basin did not contain a remarkable source of timber or other resources for the agency. This was a symbolic battle, one of many in the years after 1964, in which the Forest Service sought to maintain control over the definition of wilderness on its land. It had lost the power to designate wilderness, but the purity doctrine was an attempt to take the lead in defining what lands Congress should and should not label as wilderness.

To preserve the forests below the outlet of the lake and to expand the width of the primitive area at its narrowest belt, each conservationist proposal for a new wilderness area since 1961 called for inclusion of the lake. Rodger Pegues, of the Sierra Club, wrote in 1966, "It is absolutely essential that Marion Lake be included within the wilderness. The Forest Service proposal to place the area in scenic-area status offers no long-range promise for the future of the lake and its surrounding lands. Motor boats are used on the lake, but are a permissible non-conforming use of the wilderness."[37]

Although many would call for a slow phaseout of motorboat permits, wilderness advocates did not view motorized use of the lake as a disqualifying factor for wilderness designation. They regarded the motorboats as "a temporary non-conforming use," which should be phased out over the course of a few decades. Congress agreed and rejected the purity doctrine when it included Marion Lake in the new Mount Jefferson Wilderness Area in 1968.[38]

Yet the Forest Service continued to follow its own strict definition of wilderness purity in forming management plans for Marion Lake, which refueled the debate over wilderness boundaries in the Mount Jefferson area even after Congress designated the area as wilderness. The agency moved immediately to order boat owners to remove all motorized craft from the lake the following year, which understandably angered those who had come to enjoy their regular visits to the lake. These constituents, led by Alva Morris, of Salem, began a campaign to have the lake removed from the wilderness area by Congress. They successfully put pressure on Senator Hatfield to introduce legislation in 1969 to redraw the boundaries of the Mount Jefferson Wilderness Area.[39]

Conservationists quickly pointed out to Hatfield that the source of the conflict was not wilderness legislation but the agency's purity doctrine. The Senate committee report on the Mount Jefferson Wilderness Area bill did include language instructing the agency to remove all existing facilities, including picnic tables, water pumps, and fireplaces. The report did not give a time line for removal of these facilities, however, and Senator Hatfield soon turned his anger toward the Forest Service. Nine years later, Congress amended the language of the Senate committee report: "In its report on the Mt. Jefferson Wilderness established in 1968, the committee made specific reference to certain installations at Marion Lake. . . . That report may have contributed to some misunderstanding. To assure clarity on these issues, the committee wishes to reemphasize that hand water pumps, rustic fire rings, and sanitary facilities (including privies, pit or vault toilets) may be provided and maintained in wilderness areas."[40] Although the issue of primitive privies may seem like an unlikely crux for political debate, the fight over the definition of wilderness and the purity doctrine did often hinge on such details. Eventually, the issue waned as Hatfield and other members of Congress rejected the Forest Service's ideological approach to determining qualifications for wilderness.

Creation of the Mount Jefferson Wilderness Area demonstrated the limited role of an ideology of pure nature in the wilderness debates. Certainly the Forest Service was not alone in defining wilderness as a place of absolute pristine beauty. Such an idea has a long tradition in American intellectual history, and prowilderness rhetoric in films and books often exploited this sentiment for political gain. However, the political decisions over the boundaries of the Mount Jefferson Wilderness Area demonstrate that economic and material concerns over the land and resources and the pressure that various citizen interest groups bring to bear on Congress are the most influential forces shaping wilderness boundaries. This is true for other wilderness debates as well. As demonstrated in arguments over the management of Marion Lake after Congress added it to the wilderness area, however, debates over the definition of wilderness have not ended. They continue in various forms in the political arena and are quite prominent in recent scholarship on wilderness. Nevertheless, the boundary decisions made by Congress have rested far more on material concerns since 1968.[41]

The Mount Jefferson controversy hinted at changes that would come to predominate in wilderness debates beginning in the 1970s. That is, it focused on undeveloped forestlands outside existing protected-area boundaries, the de facto wilderness areas. A major issue was how much of the contiguous lands along the periphery of the existing protected area to include in the new wilderness designation. But what about the much larger areas, many millions of acres, that had neither seen industrial development nor been offered secure, official protection by the Forest Service? After 1968, debates turned to these roadless lands, and to this day the forests of these undeveloped areas are the crux of land use conflicts in the national forests. In the Pacific Northwest, the first and most significant of these debates centered on the Alpine Lakes region of the central Washington Cascades.

4 THE ALPINE LAKES, 1958–1976

The remains of the cabin along Camp Robber Creek remind a hiker lucky enough to stumble upon them of an earlier form of land use in the Alpine Lakes region when solitary miners and trappers in the early twentieth century sought to extract marketable commodities for profit. Their cumulative impact on the landscape was small, but in the decades after World War II industrial logging followed in their wake, displacing such small-scale forms of land use, bringing roads and clear-cuts up the Miller River valley, and significantly altering the local ecosystem.

Immediately downstream of the cabin site one of the most popular hiking trails in Washington State passes by, funneling several hundred hikers along the East Fork Miller River to Lake Dorothy on any given summer weekend. These crowds along the trail and at various camping and picnicking sites along the lakeshore reflect the dominant form of land use in the Alpine Lakes region today: recreation. Located in the central Washington Cascades, the Alpine Lakes offer the closest backcountry mountain recreation for residents of metropolitan Seattle. This plateau of polished granite is studded with several hundred lakes, from which radiate a number of deep, forested valleys.

The Miller River drainage was not part of the Alpine Lakes Limited

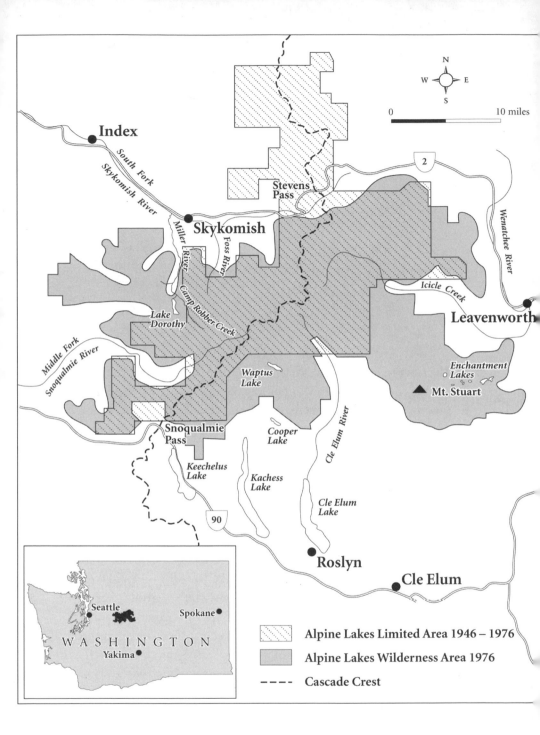

N
W ⊕ E
S

0   10 miles

Index

South Fork Skykomish River

Stevens Pass

Miller River

Foss River

Skykomish

2

Wenatchee River

Icicle Creek

Leavenworth

Camp Robber Creek

Lake Dorothy

Middle Fork Snoqualmie River

Waptus Lake

Enchantment Lakes

▲ Mt. Stuart

Cle Elum River

Snoqualmie Pass

Cooper Lake

Keechelus Lake

Kachess Lake

Cle Elum Lake

90

Roslyn

Cle Elum

Seattle   Spokane

W A S H I N G T O N

Yakima

Alpine Lakes Limited Area 1946–1976

Alpine Lakes Wilderness Area 1976

Cascade Crest

MAP 5. The Alpine Lakes, Washington. Map by Peter Morrison and Barry Levely.

Area, created in 1946, and thus had no protective zoning to limit resource use in the area. In the years after World War II, the Forest Service planned a pattern of land use for this area that emphasized timber extraction and developed, roadside recreation. Managers of the Snoqualmie National Forest sought to build a road up the valley to Lake Dorothy, then over the low saddle which separates the lake from the neighboring basin to the south, which holds Deer, Bear, and Snoqualmie Lakes. Their road would then follow the Taylor River down to the Middle Fork Snoqualmie River and the town of North Bend.[1]

Although developed recreation was a strong selling point for this proposed road project, the timber in the lower valleys did not escape the eyes of Forest Service timber sale planners. The forests surrounding the cabin site and the trail to Lake Dorothy represented the rich stands of conifer forests that made the Northwest coast the richest timber supply in the United States. By 1970, the Snoqualmie National Forest had built logging roads up the valleys of the Miller River, with clear-cuts only one-half mile away from the old cabin along Camp Robber Creek. The wilderness campaign in the Alpine Lakes began as a reaction against the policy that gave preference to logging in the lower valleys of de facto wilderness such as the Miller River and became an important part of a larger movement to wrest control of land use decisions away from the unilateral power of the Forest Service and into the more open forum of Congress.

The Alpine Lakes debate was similar to the earlier conflicts in that it focused on the forests of the lower valleys radiating from the alpine plateau at the core of the area, but it was new in that the Forest Service lost control over the terms of the debate. This was a citizen-inspired initiative; by the 1970s, the U.S. Forest Service no longer controlled the issue. Because the debate focused entirely on de facto wilderness, Congress took the lead in making decisions on wilderness boundaries, inspiring a more extensive and aggressive grassroots lobbying campaign from all sides and a more democratic and participatory political process in drawing wilderness boundaries.[2]

The campaign to protect the valley forests of the Alpine Lakes region within a wilderness area began in the late 1950s in direct response to Forest Service timber sales. The conservationists who created the North

Cascades Conservation Council (NCCC) in 1957 included the Alpine Lakes region in their efforts to stem the tide of logging on the national forests. They focused on a small area near Cooper Lake, across the mountains from Lake Dorothy. The Wenatchee National Forest planned to develop timber sales around Cooper Lake near the resort community of Salmon La Sac in the Cle Elum River drainage south of the Alpine Lakes Limited Area by 1960.[3]

The Forest Service's consistent defense that all its planned roads for the region remained outside the boundaries of the Alpine Lakes Limited Area did not find a sympathetic audience among the region's wilderness advocates. They sought to preserve portions of the forests in de facto wilderness outside the limited area, and they did not have much faith in the level of protection offered under this administrative status.

The limited area was an informal designation, what regional Forest Service officials involved in the Cooper Lake controversy called "a 'stop-look-and-listen' approach."[4] A limited area did not have the same protective status as a wilderness or primitive area under Forest Service management. Although few roads existed in the Alpine Lakes Limited Area, permission for new construction was needed only from the regional forester, as Herbert Stone demonstrated in at least three cases in the Alpine Lakes in the 1960s when he approved roads for mining and timber harvests.[5] Because of the weak status of the limited area designation and their failing trust in Forest Service administrative authority, conservationists sought to promote the area for wilderness or national-park considerations.[6]

Objection to the agency's emphasis on the limited area stemmed from conservationists' demands to protect some forests below the high, alpine country, and through the course of the Alpine Lakes debate this desire to preserve more than just "rock and ice" grew more clear. Just as in response to the Forest Service "starfish proposal" for the Glacier Peak Wilderness Area in 1959, wilderness advocates criticized the tendency in the Alpine Lakes to relegate protected areas for backcountry recreation to the high, alpine terrain where there would be no conflict with logging interests. Regional leadership of the agency clearly felt that lowland forests did not qualify; it was not the pristine and monumental landscape that they pictured in their view of wilderness. And as they

Middle elevation clearcuts dominate national forests in the Pacific Northwest with protected high country in the background. Defining wilderness boundaries focused around the process of dividing public lands between these two incompatible forms of land use. Western Ways, Inc. (Corvallis, OR) photo courtesy of the Forest History Society, Durham, NC.

A logging truck hauls timber out of the Gifford Pinchot National Forest
in the Washington Cascades, 1951. Road building and timber harvests
on public lands escalated sharply after World War II, leading towards
increasing conflicts with conservationists. Courtesy: U.S. Forest Service.

(*Facing page, top*) Logging on national forest land northwest of Mount
Rainier National Park in Washington State. The boundaries between Forest
Service land and national parks played a major role in the long-running
debate between logging and preservation in the Northwest through the twentieth century. Photo courtesy of the Forest History Society, Durham, NC.

(*Facing page, bottom*) An old sheepherder's cabin at White Pass in the North
Cascades sits on land that the Forest Service designated in 1961 as the Glacier
Peak Wilderness Area. A pure definition of "wilderness" might point to
this cabin as evidence that this area should not be eligible for protection.
However, wilderness debates historically focused on land use boundaries
in the heavily-forested lower valleys. The Forest Service later removed many
structures like this under their pure definition of wilderness. University of
Washington Libraries, Special Collections, UW25965z.

Logging expanded rapidly on the Willamette National Forest after World War II, as evidenced by these clearcuts in 1953. Courtesy: U.S. Forest Service.

This old-growth forest along the west bank of Horse Creek represented the central issue of the debate over the Three Sisters Wilderness in the 1940s. the Forest Service left this forest out of the wilderness area in 1957 and sold timber and built roads there in the 1960s and 1970s. David Simons took this photo in June 1959. Courtesy of the Bancroft Library, University of California, Berkeley. 1975.069:5

(*Facing page, bottom*) Organized trips into contested areas were an important tool for conservationists to increase public awareness of wild areas and threats to development. The Friends of the Three Sisters Wilderness, which sponsored this annual outing to Buck Meadows in July 1959, focused on the forests west of Horse Creek even after the USFS removed the area from the wilderness in 1957. When the Willamette National Forest proposed timber sales in the valley of nearby French Pete Creek in 1968, a large contingent of people familiar with the area organized in successful opposition to the plan. Courtesy of the Bancroft Library, University of California, Berkeley. 1975.069.28

District Ranger Ray Hornbeck, left, speaks with hikers from Portland on a trail in the newly established Three Sisters Wilderness Area, July 1957. Growing numbers of recreational users organized to oppose the Forest Service efforts to reduce the size of the Three Sisters Primitive Area from 1954 to 1957. Courtesy: U.S. Forest Service.

Hikers relax along the shores of Image Lake in the Glacier Peak Wilderness Area, August 1967. With the exception of mining claims, such as the proposed Kennecott operation on Miner's Ridge just west of this site, protection of the high alpine country was not usually in dispute. Courtesy: U.S. Forest Service.

(*Facing page, bottom*) A lone hiker stands among old-growth cedar and hemlock trees along the Cascade River in the Mount Baker National Forest, mid-twentieth century. Middle elevation forests such as these became the focal point for struggles to define the boundaries of the Glacier Peak Wilderness Area and the North Cascades National Park in the 1960s. Most of these forests along the Cascade River were left outside of the protective boundaries of the national park, when Congress created the park in 1968. University of Washington Libraries, Special Collections, UW26227z.

A hiker gazes across the valley of Agnes Creek at Dome Peak in the Glacier Peak Limited Area, 1938. The following year, Bob Marshall traveled through this area and campaigned for its protection under wilderness status. Forest Service administrators rejected his proposal and in 1946 included this region in the Glacier Peak Limited Area. Despite their efforts, the North Cascades Conservation Council could not include these peaks in the North Cascades National Park, when it was created in 1968. It remains part of the Glacier Peak Wilderness Area today. University of Washington Libraries, Special Collections, UW26330z.

Mount Jefferson stands above Russell Lake one year after the Forest Service
established the Mount Jefferson Primitive Area in 1933. Jefferson Park, in
foreground, was the focal point for backcountry recreation in the area.
Courtesy: U.S. Forest Service.

Hikers make their way from the Whitewater Creek valley into the Mount Jefferson Primitive Area, July 1968. Congress approved the Mount Jefferson Wilderness Area later that same year, rejecting calls to include the lower forests (to the hikers' right) within the protective boundaries. Courtesy: U.S. Forest Service.

National Park Service photographer M. Woodbridge Williams took this
photo on behalf of the North Cascades Study Team in 1963, looking south
towards the lakes of the upper West Fork of the Foss River in the Alpine
Lakes Limited Area. From left to right are Otter, Delta, Angeline, Big Heart,
Little Heart, Copper, and Malachite Lakes. Photograph, NOCA 11701, in
the collection of North Cascades National Park Service Complex. Courtesy
of the National Park Service.

Forest Service ranger Dick Woodcock surveys a clearcut in the Line Creek drainage in the eastern side of the Alpine Lakes, July 1957. The debate over preservation of the Alpine Lakes began in earnest that same year over other timber sales on the Wenatchee National Forest near Cooper Lake, south of this site. Courtesy: U.S. Forest Service.

(*Facing page*) The debates over proposed logging in the French Pete Creek valley beginning in the late 1960s reflected the increasing role of citizens and counterculture activists involved in public lands issues. On November 18, 1969, a crowd of up to 1,500 protesters marched from the University of Oregon to the supervisor's office of the Willamette National Forest in downtown Eugene, calling for a moratorium to logging. Photo by S. Frear, courtesy of the National Archives and Records Administration—Pacific Alaska Region.

Looking south across the drainage of French Pete Creek towards Diamond Peak, July 1958. David Simons took this photograph to document the forests that the Department of Agriculture removed from the Three Sisters Primitive Area in 1957. When the Willamette National Forest in 1968 announced plans to log this valley it became the focal point for wilderness debates in Oregon through the 1970s. The area in the photograph was added to the Three Sisters Wilderness in February 1978. Courtesy of the Bancroft Library, University of California, Berkeley. 1975.069.375

President Jimmy Carter signed the Endangered American Wilderness Act, including the French Pete addition to the Three Sisters Wilderness, into law February 24, 1978. At the signing ceremony, from left to right behind the president, are Senator Henry M. Jackson (WA); Tom Williams, counsel to the Senate Subcommittee on Public Lands; Representative Jim Weaver (OR); Nancy Showalter, a member of Weaver's staff; Senator Frank Church (ID); Fred Hutchison, a member of Church's staff; Representative Morris K. Udall (AZ); Doug Scott, Sierra Club Northwest Representative; and Representative Teno Roncalio (WY), chairman of the House Subcommittee on Public Lands. Courtesy: Jimmy Carter Library.

Off-road vehicles represent a rapidly growing user group influencing wilderness debates since the 1980s. This group of motorcyclists and jeep riders traveled the Natches Pass Trail near the proposed Cougar Lakes Wilderness Area in August 1976. Courtesy: U.S. Forest Service.

increasingly excluded wilderness protection from their definition of "multiple use," preservation lost out to timber production.

The response of wilderness advocates against such a definition of wilderness was clear early in the debate. After attending an informational presentation by the Wenatchee National Forest in May 1959 on its development plans for the Cooper Lake and Salmon La Sac region, the president of the Mountaineers, John Hazle, responded:

> One misunderstanding was evident at the meeting which we feel is of great importance and must be cleared up immediately. Several of the Forest Service personnel who spoke were clearly of the opinion that in segregating high, rocky, sparsely wooded and relatively inaccessible country for wilderness recreation, they were meeting the needs which we and other outdoors groups have expressed, and were doing their best to accommodate us. We appreciate such efforts very much. However, wilderness recreation is of far more importance in the lowland river valleys where the people use it constantly, afoot and on horseback. . . . Wilderness is for everyone, not just a few.[7]

Hazle's point was that wilderness should be made accessible to a wide range of users, not by building roads up the valleys to create shorter hikes to the high peaks and ridges, as the agency proposed, but by preserving portions of the low-elevation valleys themselves.

Both sides defended their position as most likely to provide wilderness accessibility to the public, and Hazle's argument is typical of those repeated throughout these debates in Oregon and Washington by proponents of expanded wilderness areas.[8] Their opponents often labeled their campaign for larger wilderness areas and undeveloped forestlands as elitist, because doing so would exclude all but the strongest from reaching the prized scenery and views of the high country. This argument was valid only if one agreed that visiting forested valleys did not qualify as a wilderness experience. This was not the position of wilderness advocates. John Warth, of the NCCC, lamented Forest Service timber sales in the low-elevation forests in the Cooper Lake region: "The lowland valleys, with their dense merchantable forests, are seldom considered predominantly of wilderness value—therefore roads, logging destruction, noise and conflict must prevail. Hence the efforts of organizations like the Sierra Club to save unspoiled some lowland wilderness areas where possible."[9]

Conservation organizations fought development plans through both publicity and administrative appeals. Advocates for wilderness protection used articles and photographs to publicize their concerns over the Alpine Lakes region to a broad regional and national audience, just as they were doing at that time for the North Cascades. Warth expressed a common goal and strategy of conservationists when he commented that "soon Cooper Lake may be one of the best-known lakes in the Northwest."[10] Coordinated by Michael McCloskey, Northwest conservation representative for the Federation of Western Outdoor Clubs, they also lodged numerous protests with the Forest Service over timber sales and road-building plans in nearly all the valleys surrounding the Alpine Lakes over the following decade and later.[11]

In most of these cases, the appeals were not successful; the Forest Service built its roads and sold timber-cutting rights in these valleys to regional logging companies. By 1962, the road extended beyond Cooper Lake and crested the ridge of Cooper Pass into the drainage of Lake Kachess, where the agency planned to link the new road with its road system to the west of Little Kachess Lake.

In the exchange of citizen appeals and agency defense of its policies, the Forest Service demonstrated the limits of citizen influence over its decisions during this era prior to passage of the Wilderness Act. While a lively and prolific exchange of letters passed between regional wilderness advocates and Forest Service officers regarding Cooper Lake and many other sites in the Cascades, the agency was never obligated to incorporate suggestions from any source of public input into its decision-making system. As seen in earlier case studies, agency personnel felt a great deal of pride in their position as the experts in all matters dealing with forestry, conservation, and wilderness preservation and especially as the self-proclaimed creators of the latter two concepts. Orville Freeman demonstrated this organizational conceit when he responded to John Warth in 1961, "The protection given this area [Alpine Lakes] and others is an example of the foresight and careful coordination for long-range needs, and is characteristic of the Agency which originated the concept of wilderness areas." He concluded, "After consideration of the facts available we do not plan to request the Forest Service to postpone the sale [at Cooper Pass]. Likewise, we are not requesting a public hearing."[12] The agency held public meetings and informal gatherings with concerned citizens regarding future logging and road construction around Cooper Lake in the late 1950s, but there is little evidence that input gathered at these meetings affected its plans in any significant way.

The response from conservationists was to become increasingly frustrated at what seemed to be an entrenched and isolated bureaucracy. The anger that stemmed from the agency's unilateral decision to reduce the size of the Three Sisters Primitive Area in 1957 was soon reinforced by decisions in favor of logging in places like Cooper Lake, feeding a growing desire for a Wilderness Act that would limit the power of the Forest Service.[13]

In May 1959, officials from the Wenatchee and Snoqualmie National Forests and the Northwest Regional Office of the Forest Service met in Wenatchee with six women and three men representing various conservation organizations to discuss land management plans for the Salmon La Sac country. John Hazle, president of the Mountaineers, initiated the meeting as an effort to further explain the requests from various organizations to delay timber sales and road construction in the Cooper River watershed until completion of the national Outdoor Recreation Resources Review Commission report and to learn more details of Forest Service planning for the region.[14] His follow-up letter to the regional forester expressed the ambivalent reaction of many who attended the meeting: "While the conference was not the two-way discussion we had hoped for, it was still of value in that we now understand many of your problems and have a good idea of your planning for this area." But, he lamented, "this conference did not afford an opportunity for discussion of our concepts of present and future needs in this area."[15] John Warth, who also attended, saw the meeting as merely an opportunity for the agency to present its plans and later wrote, "a public hearing has never been offered."[16]

A forester for the Snoqualmie National Forest described the meeting in arrogant, mocking tones. "Needless to say," he wrote to his supervisor, "note-taking and photographing of maps was religiously done by representatives present. The meeting was interesting, certainly educational and enlightening for all present. However, most of the outside group representatives had single-purpose use uppermost in their minds."[17] The official response from the regional office was more diplomatic. Herbert Stone replied to Hazle, "I am pleased that the Mountaineers were able to meet with [Forest Supervisor] Ken Blair and his staff to obtain a better knowledge of our processes in multiple-use planning." Yet a few months later he added, "We will proceed with our transportation and timber sale plan as we cannot permit further delay."[18]

Frustration on the part of wilderness advocates that the agency was not responding to their concerns preceded the meeting and continued to grow in the following years. Polly Dyer, a founding member of the NCCC and one of the six women in attendance at the meeting, expressed her disappointment to Wenatchee Forest Supervisor Ken Blair in a letter earlier that year that was sure to have offended his self-esteem as a professional forester. "We realize the problem of rationalizing the long term use of forest land for other than ultimate timber cropping with that for growing interest in the natural scene is a difficult one for the professional forester," she wrote. "I find myself wondering sometimes if perhaps a referee of some kind who has no obligation to put timber crops first might not be called in."[19] His response was predictably defensive: "The Department of Agriculture and the Forest Service has the responsibility for the administering of national forest lands and I feel that we would not be redeeming our responsibility if we asked someone to make our decisions for us."[20] The culture of the Forest Service fostered a righteous sense of loyalty to the agency and to the expertise of its professionals. Blair was very typical of forest rangers when he wrote that no one should make decisions for them. In their idealized vision of the agency and its mission, they believed that they made their decisions based only on professional judgment and long-term public interest, and above the political fray of interest groups.[21]

Taking another approach, conservationists requested the Forest Service to conduct polling among users of the area and residents of the local communities of Roslyn and Cle Elum. Many longtime visitors to the lakes, they claimed, were not aware of Forest Service logging plans for the area. Agency officials reacted quickly to what they perceived—correctly—as a challenge to their authority. Stone responded, "I cannot accept your request for a polling of opinion prior to a decision regarding management of land surrounding Cooper Lake. While the Forest Service always welcomes opinions and advice regarding our multiple-use management, we cannot base administrative decisions on the polling of opinion alone. I am sure you must realize that this method of deciding administrative policy matters would be cumbersome indeed."[22]

Despite the bitter controversy over Cooper Lake, the process of defining wilderness boundaries in the Alpine Lakes languished in the shadow of the North Cascades debate. Creating the North Cascades National Park and expanding the Glacier Peak Wilderness Area in 1968 intentionally left undecided the fate of the Alpine Lakes region. Whether or not there would be a wilderness area was never in question, however. The central core of several hundred lakes fed by glaciers hanging from sharp granite peaks, the remains of the Mount Stuart batholith, exhibited, according to the Forest Service, "all the elements necessary for wilderness."[23] Oregon forestry consultant Carl Newport later testified before Congress on the Alpine Lakes, "There seems to be no substantial disagreement over whether or not there should be a Wilderness. The major issues are the size of the Wilderness area and the management of the surrounding area."[24]

The question of boundaries could not be resolved in the 1960s, however. When the North Cascades Study Team convened in 1963, the Forest Service agreed to put off all decisions on the area covered by the study, including the Alpine Lakes and the Cougar Lakes country to the south, near Mount Rainier. After the study team released its recommendations in 1965, efforts to define wilderness boundaries in the North Cascades, from Stevens Pass to the Canadian border, took precedence in both congressional action and the energy of various citizen and industry interest groups. As Brock Evans said in 1968, the Alpine Lakes had become a "stepchild of the North Cascades."[25]

Specific boundary proposals for the Alpine Lakes initially came from a coalition of regional conservation groups. In 1963 the NCCC, the Mountaineers, the Mazamas, and the Federation of Western Outdoor Clubs submitted to the Forest Service an outline for a new wilderness area of roughly 300,000 acres, authored by Michael McCloskey. Although their proposal would protect the forests of the Salmon La Sac region, including the upper Cooper River watershed and the Lake Dorothy region, removing them from the potential timber supply of the national forests, they balanced this request by not opposing development for the forests in the Alpine Lakes Limited Area north of Stevens Pass. Thus, the groups claimed, "Little difference should be experienced by the lumber industry in the availability of timber from this general area as a result of this proposal."[26]

The Forest Service developed a confidential proposal that recommended two small, high-elevation wilderness areas and a scenic area of developed recreation and limited logging around Lake Dorothy. Their Alpine Lakes Wilderness Area would contain 164,000 acres. They proposed to also protect the dramatic terrain of the Stuart Range, the Lost World Plateau, and the Enchantment Lakes basin in a separate Enchantment Wilderness Area of 30,000 acres. This area to the northeast of the Salmon La Sac region, near the town of Leavenworth, Washington, had never been included within the limited area or any other protected status, but it had become a very popular site for hikers and climbers by the 1960s.

At the same time, the Wenatchee National Forest was extending roads and selling timber farther up the Icicle Creek drainage above Leavenworth. The forested corridor of Jack Creek separated the agency's two proposed wilderness areas. The Forest Service sought to build a logging road there. In addition to leaving the Lake Dorothy and Miller River areas open to development, the agency's proposal left out the lower sections of numerous other valley corridors on the edges of the alpine core. These were the main distinctions from the one citizen proposal.[27] The timber industry had not yet submitted a proposal.

While attention focused farther north, the Forest Service continued to plan timber sales in the forests surrounding the Alpine Lakes Limited Area. During the 1960s, it expanded road systems along Miller River, Foss River, Tonga Ridge, Icicle River—toward the Jack Creek corridor—and in the Cooper Pass region and areas north of Stevens Pass, in a region once proposed by Bob Marshall and Ferdinand Silcox as part of the Glacier Peak Wilderness Area. Brock Evans became involved in wilderness advocacy in 1965 after encountering clear-cut logging on national-forest lands he assumed were protected in the Alpine Lakes region.[28] After Congress created the North Cascades National

Park and the Pasayten Wilderness Area in 1968, the eyes of conservationists, the timber industry, and the Forest Service all turned toward the Alpine Lakes.

Passage of the Wilderness Act of 1964 completely derailed the process of competing proposals for the administrative designation of the Alpine Lakes, but unlike with the Mount Jefferson and other primitive area debates, there was no existing protocol for bringing an Alpine Lakes Wilderness proposal before Congress. The Wilderness Act gave specific instructions to the Forest Service to review all their primitive areas and submit a wilderness proposal to Congress within ten years, but for de facto wilderness lands, like the Alpine Lakes, the Wilderness Act provided few guidelines.

Early drafts of the act required that all new designations of wilderness begin with Forest Service proposals. Under this system, existing administrative wilderness and wild areas would become statutory wilderness, and new additions required only congressional approval of agency suggestions. Opponents to the wilderness bill felt that this would make additional designations too easy and that the role of Congress would be reduced to wielding a rubber stamp rather than acting as a critical reviewer. Wayne Aspinall, a congressman from Colorado and the bill's leading opponent, was concerned that the executive branch would have too much leeway under this system.[29] Congressman Aspinall played the central role in amending the Wilderness Act to appease his concerns. One result was a system of "affirmative action" under which Congress, not federal land agencies, proposed, debated and voted on new wilderness. This did make the process of adding wilderness after 1964 much more difficult. Correspondingly, removing wilderness from the system would be equally difficult, which was one of the primary goals of those who campaigned for the Wilderness Act.

Ironically, many wilderness advocates felt that Aspinall's amendment was actually a very positive step toward increased wilderness protection because it would fuel a grassroots citizen campaign to protect more public lands under the Wilderness Act. Howard Zahniser, the author of the act, spoke in Seattle just before he died in 1964: "It will be our undertaking—yours, especially, who live near these areas—to equip yourselves, to know these areas being reviewed, to prepare materials in cooperation with the land administrators, to appear at the hearings that will be held, to continue to support the establishment of this program."[30]

Hindsight demonstrated that the "affirmative action" clause of the act did generate a great increase in citizen influence over wilderness decisions. Stewart Brandborg, Zahniser's assistant and successor at the Wilderness Society, wrote in 1968 that Aspinall's amendment "has turned out to be a great liberating force in the conservation movement." It "has opened the way for a far more effective conservation movement, in which people in local areas must be involved in a series of drives for preservation of the wilderness they know."[31] The Alpine Lakes was a premier case in point.

The first example of a successful citizen initiative to preserve de facto wilderness (and to bring it into the National Wilderness Preservation System) occurred in Montana in the late 1960s. Cecil Garland, a hardware store owner from the small town of Lincoln, Montana, learned that the Forest Service planned to build roads and sell timber in the Scapegoat Roadless Area, which bordered the Bob Marshall Wilderness Area. He began to inquire into the details of the agency's plans and petitioned officials and political leaders for a reprieve.

Since the Wilderness Act gave Congress the sole authority to create or alter wilderness areas, Garland took his case to his representative and senators after Forest Service officials refused to alter their plans. The Lincoln Back Country Protection Association convened in 1964 and, with critical help from the Wilderness Society's Clifton Merritt, submitted proposed boundaries to Congress for a new wilderness in 1965. Montana's senators, Lee Metcalf and Mike Mansfield, both supported this claim and successfully overcame opposition from Wayne Aspinall and the Forest Service to create the Lincoln-Scapegoat Wilderness Area in 1972.[32] Shortly after Congress, led by Senate majority leader Mansfield, passed the bill, Aspinall stopped Garland, who had become a familiar face on Capitol Hill, and said, "Son, you've got one powerful senator."[33]

Over the next few years, the Forest Service increasingly lost control over the creation of wilderness areas. The regional forester in Montana, Neal Rahm, lamented at the time, "We have lost control and leadership in the sphere of Wilderness philosophy. . . . Why should a sporting goods and hardware dealer in Lincoln, Montana, designate the boundaries for the 240,000-acre Lincoln Back Country addition to the

Bob Marshall? . . . If lines are to be drawn, we should be drawing them."[34] The Alpine Lakes was the first de facto wilderness in the Cascades to be considered by Congress for formal designation as wilderness, and the fact that the issue came before Congress at all demonstrated the growing power of citizens and the diminishing role of the Forest Service in drawing wilderness boundaries.[35]

The Wilderness Act was not alone in providing avenues for increased public involvement in land use decisions. Certainly, the expansion of civil rights during the 1960s encouraged more open participation in the political system. The language used by wilderness advocates trying to generate public pressure on Congress to support new wilderness areas was often similar to the rhetoric of "participatory democracy" employed by the Students for a Democratic Society in 1962 and other social-reform organizations of the New Left. The Wilderness Act itself "set up the most advanced set of environmental study and public participation requirements in any law to that time."[36]

Opportunities for public participation and oversight of federal actions were also greatly expanded by the National Environmental Policy Act (NEPA), passed in 1969 under the leadership of Senator Henry M. Jackson, from Washington State. NEPA established the new requirement that environmental reviews had to be conducted for any federal policy or action that would cause significant impacts. Forest Service decisions to develop roadless areas for logging or recreation came under the guidelines requiring review of environmental impacts and greater public scrutiny. After 1969, citizen organizations filed lawsuits to challenge and delay agency development plans in the Alpine Lakes region.[37]

The Wilderness Act had opened the door for direct citizen involvement in creating wilderness proposals on de facto wildlands like the Alpine Lakes; to coordinate this effort a group of residents of communities from all sides of the proposed wilderness created the Alpine Lakes Protection Society (ALPS). On a cold, wet October day in 1968 at Hyas Lake, just north of Cooper Lake, the founders of ALPS gathered to create an organization that would focus all their efforts on this one area.[38] ALPS quickly began to compose an Alpine Lakes Wilderness bill for Congress to consider.

ALPS proposed a mixture of land designations comprising a core wilderness area surrounded by a national recreation area (NRA), which would place limitations on both public and private land use. Their goal was to prevent or limit logging, not just in the actual wilderness itself but in the surrounding areas, too. In their proposed NRA, clear-cuts on all lands would not exceed twenty-five acres.[39] This was not an arduous restriction on logging, especially on national-forest land, where twenty-five acres was a common size for clear-cuts and clear-cutting was not practiced until after World War II. On the private lands, which had few restrictions on cutting, this limitation was more severe. The timber industry and the Forest Service opposed any limit as an infringement on their management prerogative.

ALPS clearly saw its proposal for an Alpine Lakes Wilderness bill as a type of zoning ordinance. The core area, 364,000 acres, would be protected as wilderness. They proposed an outer buffer zone of 562,000 acres, in which the federal government would limit timber harvests. They pushed hard for an NRA because that legislation would allow for limits to be placed on private landowners. Congressman Lloyd Meeds, of Everett, their sponsor in the House of Representatives, suggested that it was also politically expedient. "I think that a National Recreation Area might be easier to pass in Congress than a Wilderness Area," he wrote to David Knibb.[40] Beyond the boundaries of the NRA would be the outermost zone, where industrial timber extraction could continue with few limitations. In the opinion of ALPS, wilderness designation would be one tool in zoning the entire region into a larger unit of planned management.

Increased citizen participation in the wilderness debates was by no means limited to wilderness advocates. Organizations within the timber industry also saw the Alpine Lakes as a watershed issue of tremendous importance to them. They mobilized their own national and regional organizations to challenge the proposals of ALPS and to promote their case for a policy in the region that would protect the existing natural-resource economy. Leaders of the Washington timber industry formed the Central Washington Cascades Study Team (CWCST) in 1971 in direct response to the political initiatives of ALPS. Guidance for creating CWCST came from political organizers and lobbyists in the National Forest Products Association (NFPA).

In laying out the preliminary framework for this new organization based on a model formulated by NFPA, Knox Marshall, of the Western Wood Products Association, stressed the importance of the Alpine Lakes to the industry: "At the outset, we agree that the current ALPS proposal could well be the most revolutionary and damaging to natural resource industries of any withdrawal case in recent years." It was "frightening," he concluded, because of the proposed restrictions on land use outside wilderness and the precedent that such legislation might set.[41] The particular limits on clear-cuts in the ALPS proposal were not severe enough to frighten Marshall and his colleagues, but the precedent of setting *any* limits on their logging operations did scare them.

Over the next five years, leaders of the timber industry and professional foresters formed an additional coalition to represent the political and economic interests of timber harvesting and developed recreation in the Alpine Lakes and to generate grassroots support for their cause. Whereas the CWCST represented leading companies in the timber industry, many of these same leaders realized the need to create a presence beyond the concerns of their own industry. They met in Portland in 1973 with members of the U.S. Ski Association and the Trailer Coach Association to lay the groundwork for a broader organization, the Alpine Lakes Coalition (ALC). ALC eventually included thirty-eight member organizations.[42]

Although their guidance in political strategy came from the NFPA, the point of the ALC was to provide a voice ostensibly independent of the timber industry, yet in support of its political positions. When ALC member spokesmen traveled to Washington to testify before Congress, the NFPA organized a luncheon to brief them on their presentations. Gus Kuehne, of the Industrial Forestry Association, insisted that "we arrange the session in a hotel room some distance from NFPA to avoid any appearance of industry direction of the meeting." CWCST members also worked under the direct guidance of NFPA organizers.[43] This is not to say that members of the ALC and CWCST were purely pawns to higher powers; they did have their own genuine interest in maintaining access to the Alpine Lakes region. As part of a growing grassroots coalition, however, they realized the value of presenting a coordinated front with their allies and obtaining the assistance of national lobbyists.

The ALPS and other local wilderness advocacy groups also worked within a larger effort increasingly coordinated by the Sierra Club. This was the intent of conservationists in Washington and Oregon in 1961 when they pooled their resources to hire Michael McCloskey as their full-time Northwest conservation representative.[44] National organizations provided the resources and expertise unavailable to local groups. Such organizing did not diminish from the genuinely grassroots nature of the groups on both sides of the issue, but the opponents of the conservationists certainly leapt at the opportunity to label the larger organizations as outsiders. For example, in congressional debates, timber industry representatives often referred to the bill introduced by ALPS as the "Sierra Club proposal."[45]

Interest groups on both sides embarked on similar strategies to propose a wilderness bill, lobby politicians, and publicize their views. The industry-sponsored coalitions submitted their own wilderness bill to Congress in 1973, which proposed two small, high-elevation wilderness areas. To generate support for their bill, they published reports and studies, lobbied politicians in national and state government, and generated letters to Congress from individuals who worked within the industry or who supported their position.[46] The "Legislative Plan" composed by NFPA lobbyists called for CWCST to ask their members to write letters to Congress "to bring grass-roots pressure to bear on the [congressional committee] members from industry and labor."[47] In turn, ALPS employed the well-established practice of publishing large-scale photography books to generate political support by publicizing the aesthetic values at stake. Brock Evans authored *The Alpine Lakes*, published by The Mountaineers in 1971. Every member of the relevant House and Senate committees received a copy, and at least one copy made it to the White House.[48]

Industry representatives did not fear or oppose the designation of wilderness in the Alpine Lakes, but they were very concerned about limits on their access to rich stands of timber in both private and public ownership all along the perimeter of the proposed wilderness area. Creating a wilderness area with legislation that included restrictive language for lands outside the wilderness boundary was a precedent that they were not willing to tolerate. Governor Dan Evans's state delegation studying the North Cascades in 1966 discussed a similar proposal, but

Bernard Orell, of the Weyerhaeuser Timber Company, objected, saying this would make the report "'highly controversial' a sure target of opposition by the forest products industry."[49] His prediction remained true a decade later.

The industry mustered its political strength to fight for legislation that was free of any restrictive language on land use along the perimeter of the wilderness. By 1975, its highest priority was to convince Congress to pass the industry's own wilderness bill. Failing that, a second objective was "to assure passage of amendments to the Meeds bill which would remove objectionable features."[50]

The Forest Service was the last organization to submit a proposal for an Alpine Lakes Wilderness. Congress and ALPS both petitioned the agency to accelerate finalization of its plans for the area. A common response from the Forest Service in such politically sensitive circumstances was that it needed more time to study the situation and the area. It claimed that the Alpine Lakes would have to wait until the agency completed all the national primitive area reviews in 1974, even though there were no primitive area reviews left to complete in Oregon and Washington. It also insisted on waiting until mineral surveys of the Alpine Lakes were complete. Representative Aspinall had made this an unwritten prerequisite for earlier wilderness bills, and the Forest Service interpreted his demands to mean that the surveys must be completed before any bill was presented. These surveys required two seasons of field research in 1972 and 1973. In a move that infuriated ALPS leaders and many in Congress, the agency refused to request mineral studies for any areas outside its own proposed wilderness boundaries.[51]

Another source of delay for the Forest Service in the early 1970s was its new Roadless Area Review and Evaluation (RARE). In 1967, the Forest Service embarked on a national effort to inventory all of its roadless lands in order to make final recommendations on their suitability for wilderness designation. After several years of delay and hundreds of public hearings, the agency completed the national inventory in 1972. In the Alpine Lakes region, the Forest Service identified five "wilderness study areas" that formed the basis for its wilderness proposal to Congress. Although the RARE process was, by court ruling and the admission of the Forest Service, legally insufficient under NEPA requirements, it was, historian Dennis Roth has said, "the most extensive public involvement effort ever undertaken by the Federal Government" to that time.[52]

Congressman Lloyd Meeds had successfully guided a compromise bill through the House Interior Committee by February 1976. He had persuaded ALPS to drop their NRA demand the previous summer and replace it with a more informal buffer zone. His new bill included 383,000 acres of wilderness. The entire state congressional delegation supported Meeds's bill except for Mike McCormick, whose district in central Washington contained the largest segment of the Alpine Lakes. Representative Harold "Bizz" Johnson, of California, as a member of the Interior Committee, introduced a competing bill on behalf of the timber industry that would have created a 342,000-acre wilderness with no provisions or restrictions on land use outside the boundaries—called a "clean bill" by timber lobbyists.[53]

That the industry was now supporting a bill that would designate far more acres as wilderness than Michael McCloskey suggested in the conservationists' 1963 proposal demonstrates how the debate changed over the course of those thirteen years. First, wilderness designation for an area like the Alpine Lakes had strong and broad political support. The industry never tried to object to wilderness designation on principle. Second, and perhaps more significantly, it demonstrates how the industry coalition was willing to accept more acreage as wilderness in exchange for more secure access to timber outside the boundaries of the wilderness area. When confronting the Meeds bill on the floor of the House in 1976, they certainly wanted to see a smaller wilderness area in the end, but this was literally the last item in their written list of legislative priorities. Their primary concern was to find a way to avoid both prescriptive language regulating land use in the forested perimeter and congressional oversight of the Forest Service timber program.[54] To achieve these ends, they were willing to give up more acres to the wilderness.

The national office of NFPA continued to coordinate visits to Washington, DC, of local representatives of CWCST and ALC to meet with members of Congress or testify at committee hearings. These industry representatives often appealed to House members to eliminate the language that might set a precedent that they would later regret. The president of the ALC, H. A. "Buzz" Chevara, warned Florida congressman James Haley, the chairman of the House Interior Committee, "Passage of the Meeds bill will establish statutory precedents such as limitation of economic activities in large areas including private land adjacent to the proposed Wilderness. I don't think you would want this in your own District."[55]

Meeds and others realized that additional compromise was needed if his bill was to pass in the House. Meeds served as a mediator between the two interest groups, who together hammered out new options. Bob Witter, of Weyerhaeuser, and Doug Scott, of the Sierra Club, established an agreement that laid the foundation for a new compromise bill that would create a wilderness of 393,000 acres and a surrounding "multiple-use management unit" of 527,000 acres, where the Forest Service could continue its timber program with limited oversight from Congress. The entire delegation unanimously supported this compromise, as did Governor Dan Evans.[56] Meeds later said, " 'Delicate' is almost too gentle a word to describe the compromise."[57]

To both sides, the incentive for compromise was clear. Wilderness advocates wanted to gain designation of a single, large wilderness area, and the timber industry sought to secure continued access to the timber supplies outside the boundary. Chevara explained that after the Meeds bill passed the House Interior Committee in February, "our backs were to the wall, so when Congressman Meeds offered to negotiate more wilderness acreage for a multiple use perimeter, it was in our best interests at that time to do so."[58]

Resolving boundaries and moving forward appealed to the timber industry, which was frustrated by the insecurity of its access to the forests of the Alpine Lakes region and its concern that it might lose even more if the debate wore on. Ralph Hodges, of the NFPA, worried, "Failure to enact a law this year would throw the issue wide open during the next Congress and the controversy would start anew." The compromise was, he added, "the best possible solution available to a controversy which has raged in the State of Washington and in the Congress since 1971."[59] The Senate Interior Committee passed the House bill unanimously, and the full Senate approved it in July, sending it to President Gerald Ford for his signature.

Conspicuously absent in the debates, now dominated by citizen interest groups, was the Forest Service. All sides increasingly left federal foresters out of the discussions. Within the agency and the Department of Agriculture arose a bitter resentment at being left behind. Testifying before the Senate Interior Committee in June 1976, the deputy assistant secretary of agriculture griped, "We wish to emphasize that neither this Department nor the Forest Service participated in developing the most recent language now referred to as a compromise." He objected to the amount of wilderness in the bill, 100,000 acres more than they had proposed. And all their careful studies have now gone to waste, he complained.[60] The lead editorial in the *Seattle Post-Intelligencer* on 9 July 1976 supported the bill and noted that "the Forest Service had its 'nose out of joint.'" "But Hell hath no fury," it observed, "like a government agency defending its prerogatives."[61]

When the Alpine Lakes Area Management Act went to the desk of President Ford, the Forest Service requested a veto. Both the timber industry, through NFPA, and the conservationists, through the Sierra Club, mobilized rapidly and in cooperation to fight the possible veto. The NFPA contacted its member organizations and friends on Capitol Hill to pressure the White House.[62] Governor Dan Evans, lobbying the president to sign the bill, handed Ford a copy of Brock Evans's 1971 book, *The Alpine Lakes*. Reportedly, Ford responded, "anywhere so beautiful should be preserved."[63] Still, the president waited several more days. Although a veto seemed imminent to most observers, the president signed the bill on the afternoon of 12 July 1976.

Timber industry leaders were grateful. The NFPA's Ralph Hodges expressed to the president his "deep appreciation" for "significant actions you have taken recently to ease the burdens of the forest products industries. . . . Your approval of the Alpine Lakes Wilderness measure, which reaffirmed the desirability and necessity for timber management in the lands surrounding the actual Wilderness Area, has established a highly desirable precedent which will reduce the unnecessary withdrawal of commercial forest lands."[64] One begins to wonder who were the losers and who were the winners.

Both sides felt that they had won, and both celebrated accordingly. Since deliberations on a compromise bill had begun in October 1975, ALPS and the Sierra Club were able to add nearly 17,000 acres to the wilderness area in the final bill. Included in that total were the "fight areas" that they had identified. The ALPS president at the time, David Knibb, recalled, "the 'fight areas' were those timbered valleys that we wanted in wilderness to prevent them from being logged. Tops on the list [was] Deception Creek on the west side."[65]

For its part, the timber industry avoided the legislative precedent of congressionally prescribed land use along the wilderness perimeter, and most of the valuable timber remained outside the boundary. Meeds explained during the Senate committee hearing, "The wilderness which passed the House is mainly non-commercial or inoperable commercial land, but there are a few areas containing stands of commercial timber. Jack Creek, Deception Creek, upper Icicle Creek, and Ingalls Creek are examples. I feel we have made a fair compromise, Mr. Chairman."[66]

Perhaps the loser is more obvious. The Forest Service, the agency that had defined wilderness as a land use category fifty years earlier and controlled all decisions over where to draw the lines until 1964, now seemed to have very little influence over the process. This perception could be deceptive when viewed on a broader scale, however. The Forest Service maintained control over land use decisions on the vast majority of its holdings in the Cascades (including within the Alpine Lakes region), and in the 1980s it would sharply accelerate its timber sale program on these lands. Thanks to the lobbying efforts of the industry, it also avoided an embarrassing precedent of strict congressional oversight of its management of non-wilderness lands. They had less influence over where to draw the lines, but outside wilderness, the Forest Service remained in control.[67]

Inside the wilderness boundaries at places such as the old cabin along Camp Robber Creek, the environment did not radically change. This in itself is of enormous significance. The remains of the cabin rot quietly in an undeveloped old-growth forest. The road and logging operations that the Forest Service had planned for this area would have dramatically altered the landscape. Drawing the boundary of the Alpine Lakes Wilderness to include the upper stretches of the East Fork Miller River and the entire length of its tributary Camp Robber Creek stopped the road where it sat in 1976. Regardless of one's judgment on this decision, the difference between the two competing land use options was significant.

Although the wilderness movement is often characterized as elitist, the Alpine Lakes debate demonstrates an important influence of the movement that in the long run was far from elitist. The movement to protect de facto wilderness and the increasingly organized political efforts on the part of both conservationists and resource industry coalitions and corporations changed the debate to a far more grassroots political discussion. The end result was to make wilderness politics more open to public participation through the political arena of Congress rather than the previously closed confines of Forest Service administrative decision making. In the 1950s, a very small number of people had any direct contact with and influence over the decision makers in the Department of Agriculture. By the 1970s, all citizens had some form of direct influence through their congressional representatives. The process became far more complicated in many ways and distant from the immediate locale of the actual areas in dispute, but it also became far more democratic. Another result of this change was that the social fabric and range of opinions within the wilderness movement became far more diverse. When attention returned to the forests west of Horse Creek in the Three Sisters region of Oregon during the 1970s, a very different group of people sought to conclude the debates begun by Karl and Ruth Onthank and other Oregon conservationists in the 1950s.

5 RETURNING FRENCH PETE TO THE THREE SISTERS WILDERNESS AREA, 1968–1978

B y the 1970s, the wilderness movement in the Northwest had come a long way from Karl and Ruth Onthank's living room in Eugene in 1954. The organizational structure and resources available to wilderness advocates and their influence on decisions regarding land use boundaries had expanded greatly over two decades. In addition, wilderness debates in the 1970s began to represent far more than just zoning and land use policies. They occurred within the context of significant cultural and social change, and young people involved in the cultural protests of the 1960s and 1970s latched onto the issue of wilderness as a battle against the status quo in politics and economic power. The growing influence and awareness of ecology beginning in the 1960s and heightening in the 1970s added greater significance and support to the wilderness campaigns.

The former emphasis on recreation and aesthetic values became only one of a host of concerns, which now included wildlife and fish habitat, endangered species, biological diversity, and watershed health. The often confusing mix of voices that supported additional protection for de facto wilderness was a direct product of the growing grassroots nature of the wilderness debates. Not only did citizens have greater access to the decision-making process, as seen with the Alpine Lakes debate, but

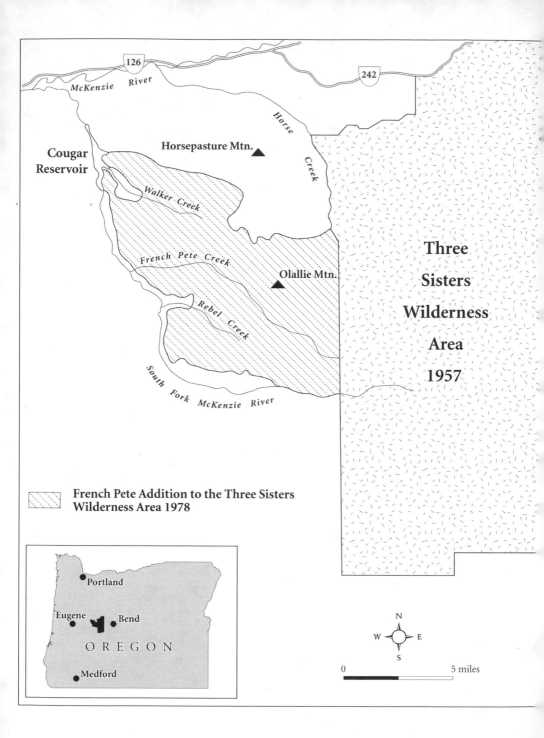

MAP 6. French Pete Creek, Oregon. Map by Peter Morrison and Barry Levely.

more citizens joined the efforts, bringing a more diverse set of interests, concerns, and strategies with them.

The extent to which the debate had changed by the 1970s is most apparent when it returns to focus on the forests west of Horse Creek in Oregon that had been the central concern of the Onthanks when they helped to form the Friends of the Three Sisters in 1954. Bob Marshall instigated the addition of this rugged country of the lower "Old Cascades" to the Three Sisters Primitive Area in 1938, and the Forest Service removed that protection in 1957. The agency began to build roads into the northern sections of this 53,000-acre parcel in the early 1960s, but by 1968, no roads had yet reached into the drainage of French Pete Creek. The Forest Service intended to log these areas, but greater citizen influence over wilderness decisions through Congress and a growing social movement of environmental concerns supported wilderness advocates in Oregon as they once again challenged the 1957 decision in the Three Sisters.

The French Pete debate demonstrates a significant change from earlier conflicts and from the concurrent discussion over the Alpine Lakes. For the first time, the area proposed for wilderness designation consisted solely of low- and mid-elevation areas with significant amounts of commercial timber. As a result, there was no support from the Forest Service or the timber industry for any wilderness designation. Each of the previous debates had established agreement on creating a wilderness area; disagreement focused only on the boundaries. In French Pete, the Forest Service and the timber industry stood firm on their insistence that none of this area should become wilderness, that "multiple-use" forestry should prevail.

To the growing environmental movement, French Pete became a battle cry for something greater: to determine whether any part of the timber base of the national forests could be put off limits to logging. Brock Evans, who coordinated the wilderness campaign in French Pete in its early years, wrote, "we would make the battle over this valley the 'Verdun' of our struggle with the industry in Oregon."[1] As a result, this debate was far more combative than earlier conflicts, and it laid the foundation upon which later high-profile disputes over forestry and wilderness in Oregon would be based.

French Pete had once been a very typical, anonymous forested valley draining the western slopes of the Cascades. At French Pete Creek's confluence with the South Fork of the McKenzie River, just upstream from the Cougar Lake Reservoir, the elevation is 1,900 feet. The highest reaches of the drainage top out at nearly 5,000 feet. The forests at the center of political debate were not unusual either in their size or their commercial value. Large fires had destroyed much of the timber in the 1800s. The trees, mostly Douglas fir, were relatively young, about one hundred years old. Until well into the twentieth century, sheepherders, including the creek's namesake, used the upper slopes extensively to graze their flocks, and they often set fire to these areas to improve grazing conditions.

No one claimed that this was an absolutely pristine environment, but for many it was a place of tremendous solitude, physical beauty, fine fishing, and convenient recreation. From the road along the McKenzie River the most popular trail ascended alongside French Pete Creek, where hikers were quickly engulfed in the dominating evergreen forest. Among the local hiking community, it was a very popular site for year-round recreation. In the decade since the Forest Service removed it from the wilderness area in 1957, backcountry recreation in Oregon and throughout the country had exploded. Whereas few people knew this valley and its neighboring hills in the mid-1950s, now this area had a large and growing constituency.

Much of the pressure that kept the French Pete Valley undeveloped came from the same individuals who unsuccessfully campaigned to protect it as wilderness in the 1950s. Even after the secretary of agriculture made his decision in 1957, Karl Onthank and others in the Friends of the Three Sisters sustained the pressure. They sponsored outings through the area, promoted surveys of the recreational and scientific resources there, organized photographic exhibits, and supported scientific study of the botanical and geological features unique to this section of the Old Cascades.[2] When the Forest Service finalized management plans for timber harvesting in the area in 1964, the Friends and others filed administrative appeals to delay the work. By the time of Karl Onthank's death in 1967, roads and timber sales had altered the landscape to the north of French Pete, but French Pete itself remained completely unroaded and unlogged.

Early in 1968, the Willamette National Forest announced its intent to sell timber in the valley of French Pete Creek and started building access roads southward from the existing road system east of the Cougar Reservoir and west of Horse Creek. Its proposal called for eleven cutting units to remove 18.5 million board feet, 2.5 percent of the valley's total timber volume.[3] Local conservationists learned of the planned sale and reacted to stop it.

Brock Evans, who took over the job of Northwest conservation representative for the Sierra Club and the Federation of Western Outdoor Clubs in 1967, immediately turned to a coalition of veterans who had fought the Forest Service to protect the lands west of Horse Creek since the mid-1950s. As regional representative, his job was to organize, assist, and coordinate the efforts of local activists. He gathered Richard and Winninette Noyes, Holway Jones, and others in Eugene early that year to form a new organization devoted to preventing logging in French Pete Valley. These veterans were exhausted from their years of seemingly fruitless efforts, Evans remembers, but he persuaded them to launch another campaign to challenge once again the decision of 1957.[4]

They formed the Save French Pete Committee, chaired by Dick Noyes, who was also chair of the chemistry department at the University of Oregon. Like the Alpine Lakes Protection Society, which Evans helped to form later that same year, the Save French Pete Committee focused attention on a single issue. Their first action was to offer an alternative management plan: the creation of an "intermediate recreation area" in the valley, which would allow neither logging nor road construction. Although it did not offer the firm protection of wilderness areas, this new designation seemed to the committee to be a more realistic option, given the very limited time before cutting might begin.

Forest Service district ranger Michael Kerrick submitted a new logging plan in June, and the Save French Pete Committee recruited the support of local congressman John Dellenback, who asked the agency to delay its decision until further public input could be heard. Pressured from both within and outside the agency, the forest supervisor postponed the timber sales until 1969 and embarked on developing new plans for logging and road building.[5]

The issue gathered significant public and media attention in western Oregon over the following years. The Forest Service received support for its logging plans from local chambers of commerce, the Oregon Sheep Growers Association, regional chapters of the Society of American

Foresters (SAF), as well as the timber industry.[6] In opposition, a similar coalition of groups and individuals that fought declassification of this area in the 1950s now joined with newer organizations, such as the Oregon Environmental Council. Generating public attention from across the country was the primary goal of the antilogging coalition. Douglas Scott, a forestry student at the University of Michigan and a native of Oregon, read a pamphlet sent by Brock Evans. He found the publication "very forceful" and proceeded to draft a letter to the supervisor of the Willamette National Forest asking for a "'go slow' approach to this decision."[7] "[Wilderness] conditions do still exist in the valley of French Pete Creek," he noted. "And they persist in a much different context than even as recently as the 1957 decision. The area has obtained a uniqueness and an enhanced value as a wilderness resource precisely because it has, to this point, remained undeveloped." In Scott's case the pamphlets sent out were unusually significant: Scott eventually replaced Evans as Northwest representative for the Sierra Club in 1973, in which position he coordinated the campaigns for both French Pete and the Alpine Lakes.[8]

The timber industry, for its part in this increasingly public debate, generated many thousands of letters and postcards from its workers over the next few years that urged the Forest Service to maintain its policy of maximum timber production for these lands. Although these comments in favor of Forest Service policy greatly outnumbered those opposed, the vast majority were postcards and form letters. Such mass mailings created a problem for public agencies and members of Congress, who deliberated over how much credence to give postcards as opposed to other forms of comment. The wilderness lobby later took up this strategy of producing overwhelming numbers by way of postcards, form letters, and petitions, and both sides to this day still employ the technique, though public agencies have come to view cards and form letters as less significant than personal letters. Senator Bob Packwood, writing to the secretary of agriculture in 1971, commented, "I can recall instances where I was advised 'in confidence' that one's job was in jeopardy if he did not write to Bob Packwood opposing the French Pete Intermediate Recreation Bill and supporting the Forest Service Management Plan for the area."[9]

Advocates of preserving French Pete Valley from logging tried to convince people of the unique and rare qualities of the area that would be lost if it was logged. This was the "hook" with which Evans tried to garner public support for preserving the valley.[10] French Pete was, they claimed, one of three remaining low-elevation valleys at least ten miles long in the Oregon Cascades that had not yet been developed. Representatives in the timber industry argued that the number was actually four, and the Forest Service counted five, but this did not diminish the fact of scarcity, because the original count was at least sixty-five.[11] Rhetorically, advocates sought to gain sympathy and support by focusing on saving one of the last remnants of undisturbed low-elevation forests. This argument gained increasing influence in the late-1960s, when concern over ecology and a coming "resource crisis" became widespread.[12]

The costs of not logging the valley would be minor, wilderness activists argued. The seven hundred million board feet contained in the 19,000-acre drainage represented merely 1 percent of the timber volume available on the Willamette National Forest. As a relatively young forest of just over one hundred years old, it also was not among the most valuable of timber stands in the region. "The commercial timber value within French Pete is miniscule when one considers the entire Willamette National Forest," Senator Packwood commented in 1971. "French Pete is little for the Forest Service to give up."[13]

The Forest Service, however, faced consistent pressure during these years to expand the timber supply, and any action that removed volume from the annual cut faced a storm of opposition from within the agency and from the industry.[14] As a symbol of the debate over competing values and bureaucratic authority, the valley of French Pete Creek became far more important than the sum of its timber. The Forest Service officials of the Willamette National Forest maintained their intent to develop timber sales in the valley, however, justifying their actions by reference to both the secretary of agriculture's 1957 decision and the broader Forest Service mandate to maximize timber production. The forest supervisor, David Gibney, represented the arm of the Forest Service which gave the timber program the highest priority in the decades after World War II. He once said, "We must keep every acre of land outside of wilderness fully productive. A decrepit old-growth stand depresses me."[15]

Gibney was an "old saw-and-axe" forester to his colleagues and "an extreme timber beast" to wilderness activists.[16] Evans recalled his first meeting with Gibney in July 1967: "He eyed me coldly, put his feet up on his desk, lit up a black cigar, blew smoke in my face, and said, 'I don't like your ethics,' and then proceeded to lecture me on the fact that all the forests would turn into a jackstraw of downed logs and rot away unless loggers came to clean them up and cut them down."[17] Evans soon afterward suggested that public comments be directed to the chief of the Forest Service and the regional forester rather than to Gibney; "The forest supervisor is hopeless," he told others.[18]

Gibney's approach certainly eliminated any room for compromise in this debate, but even when Zane Smith replaced him as forest supervisor in 1970 and brought a more conciliatory approach with greater opportunity for public input, there was no middle ground on the question of whether or not to allow logging in the French Pete Valley. Until 1977, every agency land use plan for the area included proposals for logging, and the environmental coalition would not accept a plan that did.[19] The Forest Service claimed that the 1957 decision did not allow it to consider this option. In that decision, the secretary of agriculture, Orville L. Freeman, wrote, "The 53,000 acres, more or less, west of Horse Creek which were formerly a part of the Three Sisters Primitive Area will be managed hereafter as a multiple-use area. . . . Timber harvest will proceed in an orderly manner."[20]

Richard Noyes spoke for most of his colleagues when he lashed out at the agency's definition of "multiple use," which did not include wilderness. From his temporary post at Oxford University in 1971, Noyes wrote to the assistant secretary of agriculture:

> At the turn of the century, the Central Oregon Cascades had hundreds of valleys containing millions of acres of low altitude Douglas fir forests. By your letter of September 10, you have conclusively demonstrated to me that the Forest Service does not intend to leave a single one of those valleys so that American citizens can stand on a ridge and look across a sweep of unbroken forest such as was once part of their heritage. A policy that leaves no such opportunity is a clear violation of the principle of Multiple Use. . . .
>
> If you disagree in any way with the way I have interpreted that policy in this letter, please tell me how my interpretation is in error. *If you do not do*

so, I shall be prepared to assume, in court if necessary, that the Forest Service policy is indeed as I have interpreted it. I very much wish you would enlighten me as to how such a policy is to be reconciled with the principle of Multiple Use.[21]

As we have seen in earlier case studies, the definition of "multiple use" had long been in contention. Conservationists had worked hard to ensure that wilderness was written into the legal definition that was agreed to in the Multiple Use and Sustained Yield Act of 1960, and letters like this demonstrate that they made a point of seeing that the 1960 definition was upheld. Support for their position came from studies such as the 1970 Bolle Report from the University of Montana School of Forestry, which criticized the Forest Service emphasis on timber production and found that "multiple use management, in fact, does not exist as the governing principle on the Bitterroot National Forest" in Montana.[22]

Members of the timber industry in Oregon supported the agency's insistence that the 1957 decision had settled the matter and that logging was the established policy for the area. They expressed frustration with what they saw as unnecessary delays. Wendell Barnes, of the Western Wood Products Association, wrote, "It seems to me every aspect of the French Pete situation has long ago been presented to, and considered by, the Department [of Agriculture]. I suspect, however, that these appeals may simply be a part of an overall strategy of the appellants not just to be heard, but to use these procedures and others as a means of creating in the French Pete drainage a 'de facto wilderness' in which timber sales would be forever precluded, Wilderness Act or no Wilderness Act."[23] Although French Pete already was, by its nature, a de facto wilderness, Barnes was correct that opponents sought any means to delay the agency's final decision. They received help in these efforts from a series of events distant from French Pete.

In the 1970s, a greater concern arose for designating wilderness near urban areas. The Alpine Lakes, Seattle's "backyard wilderness," gained support from this emphasis, as did French Pete. The SAF supported this concept in their official policy statement on forested wilderness, approved by the governing council in 1975: "Efforts should be made to acquire and restore lands which are readily accessible to large population centers for use and management as forest wilderness. While this will be difficult and costly, it will allow more people the opportunity to obtain a forest wilderness experience."[24] French Pete Creek, forty miles east of Eugene, fit this description very well. It was one of the most accessible undeveloped portions of the Willamette National Forest for residents of Eugene and Springfield, the second largest metropolis in the state.

As the stalemate over French Pete deepened in 1969, Congress became more directly involved. The coalition opposed to Forest Service plans appealed to Congress for support after Supervisor Gibney announced new logging plans in 1969. Agreeing that Gibney's schedule did not allow the public enough time to fully mount a legitimate administrative appeal to the plan, Senators Mark Hatfield and Bob Packwood and local Congressman John Dellenback requested Secretary of Agriculture Clifford Hardin to intervene so that more time could be provided for public discussion. Hardin relented, placing a sixty-day delay on the timber sales.[25]

Hatfield and Dellenback requested the delay based on procedural concerns of due process; otherwise, they openly supported Forest Service plans for logging in the area. But Packwood, who had won election to the Senate over legendary incumbent Wayne Morse the previous year, began to speak out against logging plans. He met with President Nixon to generate additional pressure on the Forest Service from above, for which he was attacked by the timber industry.[26] Packwood understood the political capital of growing environmental awareness, and he sought to take advantage of it. He publicly declared that "there has been a dramatic change in public opinion about environmental concern."[27] In December 1969, Packwood introduced a bill based on the Save French Pete Committee's proposal for an "intermediate recreation area." Although the Forest Service made plans to resubmit the timber sale in February 1970, they admitted to representatives of the timber industry that "nothing would be done with the French Pete timber sales until Congress acted upon Packwood's bill."[28]

Other national events worked to further delay logging plans for French Pete. In January 1970, President Nixon signed the National Environmental Policy Act (NEPA), which would become arguably the most far-reaching and influential piece of environmental law in American history. NEPA mandated thorough reviews of the potential environmental impact of actions taken by the federal government. The Forest Service realized that it must meet this new requirement for any timber sales in the French Pete Valley.

The agency completed a draft environmental impact statement (EIS) in the fall of 1970, then submitted a revised, final EIS in July 1971. Its new plan for logging in the valley promised to delay development in the lower third of the French Pete drainage, confining the timber sales to the middle and upper portions. In addition, it promised to close any logging roads to public use once the timber harvest ended. This would limit the environmental impact, the Forest Service claimed, by "emphasizing preservation of scenic values in designing cutting areas and locating roads."[29] Other government agencies criticized the Forest Service for assuming that scenic values were the sole concern. The president's Council on Environmental Quality found that the revised plan "poses a serious ecological problem."[30]

Political criticism was also strong. Senator Packwood wrote, "The modifications suggested in that environmental statement were so minor as to be almost insignificant."[31] Steve McCarthy commented to the annual meeting of the Federation of Western Outdoor Clubs in September, "The final statement is not a particularly good one. [The Forest Service] has dressed up the draft and made it look like they know a little bit about ecology." "Our strategy will be to go into the court" to challenge the agency decisions based on the inadequacy of their planning and the requirements of NEPA.[32] Although the EIS for French Pete was never challenged in court, as McCarthy and Noyes had threatened, the issue did get caught up in broader court battles and rulings on the inadequacy of Forest Service EIS documents.

The Roadless Area Review and Evaluation (RARE) added further delays to logging in French Pete. In early 1972, the Willamette National Forest finalized a survey of all its designated roadless lands as part of the national EIS on roadless lands. The draft statement did not identify a single area on the entire forest for further study or designation as wilderness. After public pressure mounted, the forest supervisor chose four areas for study as possible wilderness recommendations in the final EIS. All other roadless lands were to be opened to timber harvesting.

In addition, the agency's definition of "roadless" simply ignored much of its undeveloped land. Bill Worf, who helped to develop the RARE process from Forest Service headquarters in Washington, DC, said of the inventory to identify roadless areas for study, "It wasn't honestly done on all Forests. . . . Some supervisors saw this as a real threat and they didn't want to identify roadless country. They figured the next step was wilderness, you know. They didn't trust me, and they didn't trust the public. So they just flat out ignored some roadless country."[33] Out of three roadless areas identified in the French Pete region, not one was given further consideration for wilderness. To wilderness advocates, this reinforced their deepest fears that "the Forest Service had plans to cut essentially every old growth tree in the state."[34]

The RARE process provided wilderness activists with very little to cheer about. Most of the acreage it proposed for wilderness was in areas with very little conflict over resources. The recommendations for French Pete Valley exemplified a number of problems with the RARE process that opponents identified. They charged that the Forest Service arbitrarily divided the area up into three units. It also applied such strict interpretations of wilderness, reflecting the agency's purity doctrine, that few low-elevation sites would qualify for further protection. Holway Jones labeled the process, "at the very least, arbitrary and prejudiced."[35] Facing potential legal defeat in federal court, the Forest Service admitted the inadequacy of its first RARE process throughout the country and set to work assessing each roadless area individually under the guidelines of NEPA.

By 1970, the effort to protect French Pete Creek from commercial logging turned to Congress, where it joined other efforts to preserve de facto wilderness. Frustration with the agency's unwillingness to consider an alternative to logging in the valley and their combative relations with the Willamette National Forest pushed wilderness activists toward cultivating support in Congress. Holway Jones wrote to Senator Packwood in 1973, "Our sincere hope is that you, as our strongest champion for preservation of wilderness lands in Oregon, will help us overcome legislatively, if at all possible, what we apparently cannot accomplish administratively."[36]

By the 1980s, most Oregonians could not stretch their imaginations far enough to define Senator Packwood as a champion of wilderness preservation. "Bob Plywood" was a derogatory moniker used by environmentalists in later years, but in his first term, as environmental activist Andy Kerr later noted, "there wasn't an Oregon politician better on environmental issues than Senator Bob Packwood."[37] When French Pete activists turned to Congress to find a way to challenge Forest Service insistence on logging in the area, Packwood was their strongest supporter. His political courage at the time cannot be overestimated. Packwood stood alone within the state congressional delegation. Even Governor Tom McCall, the political maverick who exemplified Oregon's image in the early 1970s as a haven of environmental concern, would not take on the timber industry. He remained an opponent of wilderness designation in forested regions of the state.[38]

In 1972, Packwood reintroduced the Save French Pete Committee's measure to designate an intermediate recreation area, which would ban commercial timber sales and road construction in the valley. It did allow for salvage logging of dead or dying trees by use of helicopters, but dispersed backcountry recreation would receive priority status for the area. The Senate held committee hearings in May 1972, where Doug Scott, then with the Wilderness Society, noted, "This is the first time, in 20 years of continuing controversy, as Senator Packwood has noted, that this issue has been taken out of administrative channels to be heard at the Congressional level."[39]

It was also the first time since 1955 that any public hearing had been held on the issue. Although Senator Hatfield, who opposed Packwood's bill, did not allow his committee to hold field hearings in Eugene, students and citizens there organized their own hearings, complete with an empty chair for Senator Hatfield. Packwood later had the transcript printed in the *Congressional Record*.[40] Hatfield's status as the senior senator in the state delegation and his seat on the Interior Committee ensured that Packwood's bill would not pass, but it continued to cultivate awareness of French Pete as a major national issue in environmental politics.

Senator Packwood's bill was not a wilderness bill, and it raised strategic concerns among those who wanted to prevent logging in French Pete. Although their ultimate goal was to add this area to the Three Sisters Wilderness, many felt they did not have the time for a long-term campaign. This concern led the Save French Pete Committee to push for the intermediate recreation area status, but by 1973 this strategy clashed with a broader national debate over the purity doctrine.

In 1973, the Forest Service urged Congress to create such an alternative to wilderness as a designation for lands that it felt were not pristine wilderness but that were valuable for primitive, backcountry recreation. This was the agency's failed approach to Marion Lake during the debates over the Mount Jefferson Wilderness, but it did not want this intermediate designation applied to French Pete, which was at a lower elevation and held far more timber. The eastern United States, where all lands had clearly been transformed by human use since colonial times, was the main battleground for this debate. The Forest Service successfully persuaded the Senate to pass the National Forest Wild Areas Act in 1973, which would have set different criteria for wilderness in the eastern and western states, thus codifying the agency's purity doctrine.

One result of this effort, if not the main goal itself, would have been to limit potential wilderness designations on national forests in the West. (Another result would have been to move debate over such proposals to the Senate and House Committees on Agriculture, which were far more sympathetic to the Forest Service than the Interior Committees, which controlled wilderness bills.) A successful, national campaign ensued by environmental groups to stop that bill in the House of Representatives and to replace it with an Eastern Wilderness Areas Act, which became law in 1975. This was the major victory for conservationists in the long debate over the definition of what type of land did or did not qualify for protection under the Wilderness Act, and it strongly undermined the agency's purity doctrine. To push for an intermediate recreation area during this debate would have undermined the larger issue of whose definition of the Wilderness Act would win out; thus, the Save French Pete Committee decided to try for wilderness status for the French Pete region.[41] The next bill Packwood introduced in 1975, after his successful reelection, was a wilderness bill.

In addition, French Pete came to include far more than just the single drainage of 19,000 acres. Ironically, the Forest Service played a significant role identifying a larger area of roadless land than the French Pete Valley. This was a common, though unintended result of the RARE process. Forest Service documentation of roadless lands and citizen oversight of its studies greatly increased the general knowledge of these relatively unknown parts of the national forests.[42] RARE studies identified 8,600 acres in the Rebel Creek valley, south of French Pete, and 9,900 acres in Walker Creek valley, to the north, as undeveloped and roadless. The survey also found 3,500 acres in the "Mosquito Creek Triangle" between French Pete Valley and the western boundary of the Three Sisters Wilderness Area.

This was not breaking news to wilderness advocates who had monitored these areas for two decades as roads and timber sales altered the lower portions of each valley, but official identification and acknowledgment of their status by the Forest Service and the failure of the RARE provided the opportunity to ask why those lands not yet developed should not also be wilderness. In addition, agency studies provided the necessary evidence to argue that they should be wilderness. Evans noted that the RARE meetings and public hearings served "to identify and bring out in the open several other important areas in Oregon considered to be of vital importance for the necessary diversity of Oregon's wilderness." Among several sites he listed was "the French Pete area together with Rebel Creek and Walker Creek."[43] The longer Forest Service logging plans were delayed, the bigger French Pete became. By 1973, "French Pete" had more than doubled to 42,000 acres.[44]

By the mid-1970s, public attention from a growing grassroots environmental movement placed French Pete into a stalemate position, just as the broader pattern of social protest at the time was changing the nature of wilderness debates. Debates over French Pete provided great theater by a diverse cast. Although the land and the trees were the main characters, center stage was in Eugene, home of the University of Oregon. Student participation became a key element of the opposition to logging in French Pete. Student support had been common since the 1950s, but the culture of student activism had changed. Karl Onthank recruited Michael McCloskey when he was a law student at the University of Oregon in the 1950s to work as the first Northwest conservation representative of the Federation of Western Outdoor Clubs; McCloskey went on to become the executive director of the Sierra Club. The Save French Pete Committee also turned to the university student body for help. The University of Oregon was a more politically active campus than the average American college in the 1960s. Student protests against the war in Vietnam and the university administration and for civil rights had become common events on campus and in Eugene. The university was a rich source of ideas and people to join in a second campaign against logging in the lower valleys around Horse Creek.

On 15 November 1969, "Mobilization Day," Vietnam moratorium demonstrations brought out the largest antiwar crowds of the era. Some 300,000 in Washington, DC, and an estimated 700,000 across the nation, including groups in Eugene and Portland, marched that day.[45] Three days later, another set of moratorium marches occurred in Oregon's two major cities, Eugene and Portland. But this second call for moratorium was not aimed at the war; it was aimed at logging in the valley of French Pete Creek.[46] In Eugene, fifteen hundred students and community members marched to the headquarters of the Willamette National Forest. A new student organization, Nature's Conspiracy, organized the rally with support from the Save French Pete Committee. One observer described the crowd as "bearded, long-hair students, . . . girls with long stringy hair, and clean-cut persons as well." Among the signs they carried were "Make Love, Not Lumber" and "Keep Oregon Green—Save French Pete."[47] Although they had no formal connection with antiwar groups on campus, many participants undoubtedly joined both moratorium demonstrations. The same day, a much smaller group marched from Portland State University to the regional office of the Forest Service, where they met with regional forester Charles Connaughton.[48]

The growing counterculture movement at the time lent support and participants to this new era of wilderness protests. Historian Roderick Nash noted in 1973, "The environmental renaissance of the late 1960s and early 1970s paralleled a deep-rooted questioning of established American values and institutions on the part of what some labeled the 'counterculture.' Wilderness and the idea of wilderness played a key role in both social-intellectual movements."[49] Protests in Eugene to preserve French Pete from logging gave that community a national reputation for environmental activism. Bob Wazeka compared Eugene's role in the wilderness movement of the 1970s to the role of Paris as the center of the Western literary world of the 1920s.[50]

Regardless of hyperbole, the campaign to preserve French Pete garnered a lot of attention from a wide variety of interests. For many, especially those who were not part of the older hiking and climbing community in the region, it was their first introduction to wilderness issues. Andy Kerr, a high school student in the logging town of Creswell, Oregon, at the time of the Nature's Conspiracy rally in 1969, had little interest in the antiwar protests that week, but the French Pete debate made him take notice. "What a novel concept," he thought, "part of the national forest that you don't log."[51] Participation in the second Earth Day events in 1971 further helped Kerr to develop an awareness of environmental issues. He went on to Oregon State University in Corvallis in 1973, where he founded a student environmental center. In 1976 he joined the staff of the Oregon Wilderness Coalition (OWC) for fifty dollars per month, lobbying to pass a wilderness bill in Congress that included French Pete.[52]

Aesthetic appreciation and recreational opportunities were not what drove Andy Kerr and his colleagues at the OWC, and in this way they were quite different from the "old guard" of the Sierra Club and the Friends of the Three Sisters. The OWC began in 1972 to provide a local coordinating body for grassroots organizing. The Sierra Club had done this work in previous years, but it had become too much of a lightning rod by this point to go into rural communities recruiting support. Holway Jones, Bob Wazeka, and Joe Walicki founded the OWC to carry out this work. Several of the early staff members and organizers were biologists by training, and they brought a stronger ecological perspective to the wilderness campaign.

They also brought a new rhetoric, based more on reason, science, and economics than the former emotional appeals for preserving aesthetic beauty. The OWC produced a button that read "Wilderness, More than Recreation." The strong presence of scientists in the Friends of the Three Sisters in the 1950s demonstrates that this was not a new awareness, but it was a new emphasis that the OWC brought to the public campaign. Economist and forester Randall O'Toole opposed the dominance of clear-cutting on public lands, but he also disliked opposition to clear-cutting based solely on aesthetic and emotional values. When he joined the OWC in the mid-1970s, he challenged the Forest Service on its own grounds of forest economics. O'Toole recalled, "The wilderness movement in Oregon was changing from one based on emotion to one based on reason."[53] The OWC focused on watershed health, wildlife habitat, and salmon habitat as the intrinsic values of wilderness.

This created some conflict with the traditional strategy, which focused on human-centered values, and some feared that a divided movement would be weakened. Thomas Kimball, of the moderate National Wildlife Federation, warned, "In a democracy the people need to know the facts to make sound decisions about their environment. But whom do they hear the loudest? The militants—the emotionalists—the eco-freaks when they should be hearing the professionals." Kimball reflected many common prejudices against social activists at the time when he called outspoken activists like O'Toole and student demonstrators "emotionalists" and distinguished them from "professionals."[54] The Mazamas in Portland had long been inconsistent in their support for wilderness protection, and now they refused to join the protests against Forest Service plans for French Pete because they worried about losing their tax-exempt status as a nonprofit organization.[55]

Karl Onthank was once disturbed by the multitude of voices representing different interests in wilderness protection. He blamed some of the difficulties faced by the Friends of the Three Sisters in the mid-1950s on the mixed messages sent to the Forest Service by conservationists. By the mid-1970s, however, a relative cacophony of individuals and interest groups coalesced behind efforts to stop Forest Service plans to build roads and sell timber in the French Pete region. Kirkpatrick Sale wrote of the environmental movement in the 1970s that "the range of interests and causes (not to mention styles and strategies) was absolutely protean, diverse, and varied as no other movement to date. . . . The kind of movement that evolved in these years and the kind of public support that sustained it were both largely without precedent, at least in this century."[56]

Despite Onthank's earlier reservations, the growing diversity of the drive to preserve French Pete gave that movement greater strength. Boundary decisions for new wilderness areas were still concluded by well-dressed lobbyists and congressional staff members in Capitol Hill offices, but the broader social activism that arose out of Eugene provided wilderness advocates in Congress and national organizations with greater leverage to negotiate for their interests. By 1977, Doug Scott had become one of the leading lobbyists for the Sierra Club in Washington, DC. He followed an incremental approach, taking what gains were available at a given time and then working for more in the next round of debates. At times he decried the "bomb throwers" on both sides, who threatened to cripple negotiations for compromise, but many of those more radical supporters of expanded wilderness provided an essential base of support from which he and others could negotiate.[57] In addition, their principled stands and stated refusal to compromise made moderates like Scott seem quite reasonable in their demands, thus increasing their political leverage.

The public attention on French Pete placed Forest Service plans there in a stalemate, but a major step forward in breaking the impasse came in 1974 when Jim Weaver was elected to Congress, representing the district that included French Pete and Eugene. He joined Senator Packwood by sponsoring legislation in the House to add the expanded French Pete into the Three Sisters Wilderness Area. But even with Weaver's support, a French Pete wilderness faced too much opposition from the timber industry, which remained a dominant branch of Oregon's economy, and from Mark Hatfield in the Senate. Although some in the industry realized that French Pete was already a lost cause for them, most dug in their heels to prevent it from becoming part of the Three Sisters Wilderness.[58]

Industry opposition frustrated Weaver, who sought to both support the industry and declare French Pete as wilderness. When Dave Burwell, of the Rosboro Lumber Company in Springfield, objected to Weaver's support of French Pete and offered as a compromise the original 19,000-acre proposition of the Save French Pete Committee in 1968, the congressman scrawled a response: "Dammit, Dave—I'm back here *fighting* for forest mgmt. funds to *increase* the productivity of our forests and all I hear from you people is bitching about wilderness. Let's get to work and tackle the *real* job."[59]

Final approval of French Pete as a 42,000-acre addition to the Three Sisters Wilderness Area came as part of a national initiative able to overcome opposition within the state. Doug Scott conceived of an omnibus de facto wilderness bill in 1976, which would carefully select a variety of national-forest wilderness disputes from around the country. One of his goals was to overcome local opposition with a national bill, and another was to create a precedent for preserving de facto wilderness. Critical to his strategy was to select only those sites where "the local politics are either favorable or at least neutral."[60]

French Pete as wilderness had the support of the local congressman, and the attention from grassroots wilderness activists had long neutralized its potential timber supply. Three candidates for the Democratic nomination for president in 1976 jumped on Scott's bill as a popular endeavor. Senator Frank Church (Idaho), Congressman Morris Udall (Arizona), and Georgia governor Jimmy Carter all endorsed what became known as the Endangered American Wilderness Act. The bill passed both houses in 1977, but Senator Hatfield removed French Pete from the Senate version. It was returned in the House-Senate compromise, and President Carter signed it in February 1978.[61] In many ways, wilderness debates have always swung on the political cycles in Congress and the White House.[62] Yet years of work on the ground and in local communities had sorted out the options for what was possible when the debate reached its final stages. This combination was certainly true for French Pete.

Hiking into this new western portion of the Three Sisters Wilderness Area today, one can go back in time, if not to the mythical forest primeval, then at least to 1968. The lines that mark the boundaries between logging and wilderness in the French Pete region are basically where they were in 1968, when David Gibney announced his intent to push that boundary further up into the Cascades. The road from Cougar Reservoir along the South Fork of McKenzie River still passes over the mouth of French Pete Creek, and the same trail still leads hikers into the dense forests along the creek and up to the meadowed ridges more than ten miles away. With sufficient physical strength and food, one can continue on foot up and over the Cascade Crest to reach the eastern boundary of the Three Sisters Wilderness among dry forests of ponderosa pine a few days later. Or one can take a shorter hike north into the upper drainage of Walker Creek and rest at the shores of Karl and Ruth Onthank Lakes. While at these forested lakes, named in their honor in 1989, one can look back and consider that significant events and movements can originate with the actions of a small group of people committed to a particular place.

The Endangered American Wilderness Act was a major symbolic victory for wilderness advocates. Forest Service historian Gerald Williams has argued, "Basically, the back of the Oregon timber industry was broken—it would never have the same power and influence that it once felt and could no longer act with impunity in matters dealing with logging on the national forests."[63] But the fact that numerous French Petes' worth of public timberland in the Oregon Cascades fell to logging during the ten years of this dispute after 1968 (and far more since 1957) suggests that the industry remained very strong despite this loss.

In the big picture of logging on public lands, preserving French Pete as wilderness made little difference. The year 1978 also saw the highest level of timber production in Oregon since 1950: 8.2 billion board feet. Prices and demand were high, providing a boom time for the industry.[64] In this regard, it was not much of a victory for conservationists, but the wilderness movement in Oregon never sought to stop all logging on public lands. Nor was it an effort to preserve only areas of pristine and sublime representations of wild nature. It was an effort to prevent industrial development in particular areas. In many places, such as Horse Creek, that effort failed as roads and tree plantations replaced native forests. In the valley of French Pete Creek, it succeeded.

For the Forest Service, passage of the Endangered American Wilderness Act was an embarrassing rebuke of its policies, but in the case of French Pete it was also a relief. Increasingly, forest managers after the retirement of Supervisor Gibney in 1970 felt that their hands were tied in regard to French Pete. They claimed to sympathize with efforts to put recreation above logging, but they also argued that the secretary of agriculture's 1957 decision was a mandate for logging that they could not ignore. French Pete required a lot of energy from the agency for a relatively small amount of its land.

Regardless of its stated sympathy, the agency maintained a strong intransigence throughout the debate, which clashed strongly with the increasingly aggressive approach of many of the new participants in the wilderness movement. This conflict caused the agency to lose much of its vaunted respect and authority, and a combative tone dominated debates over wilderness and forest management in the following decade.

The logging boom of 1978–79 was followed by a bust in the regional timber industry, which also shaped later debates and fueled a backlash against the wilderness movement. In 1978 the Carter administration sought to weaken inflation and lower prices in the housing market by increasing the supply of building material.[65] When the demand for lumber and housing fell rapidly in 1980, Oregon lumber companies found themselves with expensive timber that they had purchased earlier in speculative contracts from federal land and now could not sell. The state's lumber industry tumbled precipitously into the 1980s.[66] In the search for a scapegoat, many pointed fingers at the wilderness movement for "locking up" timber, but the culprit was an erratic timber market and a national recession. In the following decade the industry and its workers organized a combative backlash against wilderness in the Northwest in an effort to regain political power and economic security. At the same time, wilderness preservation continued to gain in popularity, and the 1980s would see even greater numbers of acres and valuable forests added to the wilderness system in both Oregon and Washington. In Oregon, the organizations and leadership in the wilderness campaign that came of age during the French Pete battle would lead the debates in the 1980s and beyond.

6 PICKING UP THE PIECES, 1977–1984

B ald Eagle Ridge winds westward from Dishpan Gap on the Cascade Crest, just south of the Glacier Peak Wilderness Area. Looking out to the north on a clear day, few places offer a better view of the high, alpine country on the flanks of Glacier Peak than this grassy ridge, sweet with the blossom of wildflowers in midsummer and fluorescent red and orange with the turning of the mountain ash and huckleberry in the fall. Facing around to the south, one's gaze is drawn downward to the verdant canopy of evergreen forest carpeting the floor of the valley several thousand vertical feet below. The North Fork of the Skykomish River offers a stretch of impressive timber stands to rival those of the White Chuck and Suiattle Rivers to the north. To this day, however, this valley of the North Fork remains a relatively quiet backwater and has never endured the spotlight of land use debates, such as occurred over the Suiattle and White Chuck Valleys since the 1950s.

While those debates focused on the gateway valleys to Glacier Peak and in the 1970s skipped southward to the Alpine Lakes country, the managers of the Snoqualmie National Forest slowly, but surely, extended a road and sold timber in the lower stretches of the North Fork Skykomish River valley. Past the mouth of Goblin Creek, then Quartz Creek, this road reached within ten miles of the Cascade Crest

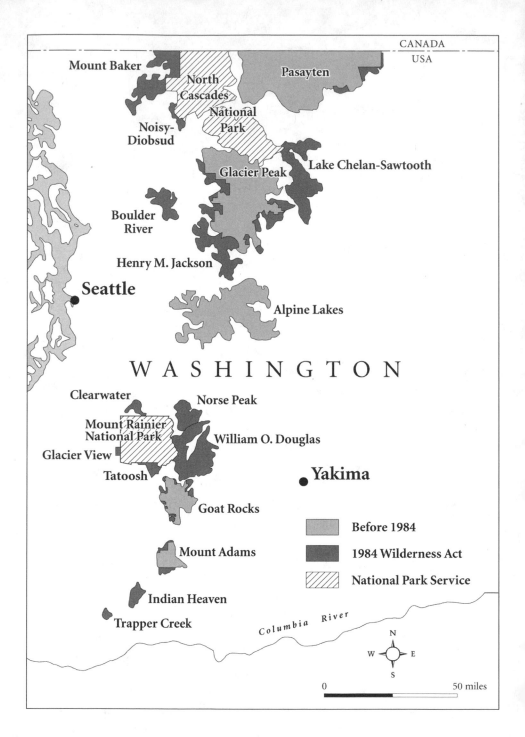

CANADA
USA

Mount Baker

North
Cascades
National
Park

Pasayten

Noisy-
Diobsud

Glacier Peak

Lake Chelan-Sawtooth

Boulder
River

Henry M. Jackson

Seattle

Alpine Lakes

W A S H I N G T O N

Clearwater

Norse Peak

Mount Rainier
National Park

William O. Douglas

Glacier View

Tatoosh

Yakima

Goat Rocks

Before 1984

Mount Adams

1984 Wilderness Act

National Park Service

Indian Heaven

Trapper Creek

Columbia River

N
W · E
S

0

50 miles

MAP 7. Washington Cascade Wilderness Areas Designated in 1984. Map by
Peter Morrison and Barry Levely.

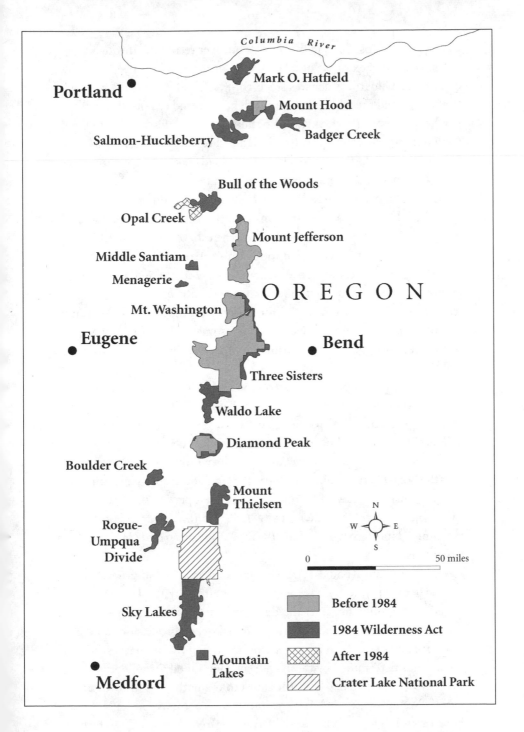

MAP 8. Oregon Cascade Wilderness Areas Designated in 1984. Map by Peter Morrison and Barry Levely.

by the early 1980s. Beyond the road's end, ever retreating through these years, was a fine example of de facto wilderness that has been the crux of Cascade wilderness debates since 1968. After the fights over French Pete Creek and the Alpine Lakes, the debate turned to countless valleys just like the North Fork Skykomish. Like the North Fork, most of these were not entirely roadless valleys, such as French Pete Creek was. The question, instead, was where should the roads end? Where should we draw the lines in the remaining old-growth forests?

More than ever before, the wilderness debates culminating in 1984 turned on how to manage the remaining unroaded and undeveloped low-elevation lands within the national forests of Oregon and Washington. The Forest Service tried to regain control over these decisions; Congress searched for a long-term compromise that would please competing interest groups; the timber industry sought to establish guaranteed, secure access to a reliable timber supply for the foreseeable future; and wilderness advocates tried to include some of the remaining pieces of forested terrain into the National Wilderness Preservation System.

In testimony to Congress in 1977 on the Endangered American Wilderness Act (which became law in 1978), Rupert Cutler, assistant secretary of agriculture and former assistant to Howard Zahniser at the Wilderness Society, shocked his former colleagues in the wilderness movement and representatives of the timber industry by announcing that the Forest Service, under his jurisdiction, would commence another comprehensive review of its roadless, undeveloped lands. The goal of this project, quickly dubbed "RARE II," was for the agency to make recommendations to Congress on the final disposition of de facto wilderness lands.

Like the initial Roadless Area Review and Evaluation process (now called "RARE I"), RARE II was clearly an effort by the Forest Service to regain lost influence over the decision-making process for its undeveloped lands.[1] The agency promised to make speedy decisions and then move forward with land management, including timber harvesting, on those lands determined by the agency as unqualified for wilderness status. Forest Service chief John McGuire told a gathering of foresters in 1979, "We initiated RARE II to promptly allocate most of the National Forest roadless areas either to wilderness or to other uses. . . . The goal was to bring a quick end to the slow, piecemeal allocation of these road-less areas."[2] The delays caused by citizen lawsuits and the study requirements of the National Environmental Policy Act (NEPA) process frustrated land use planners in the Forest Service, and they hoped that RARE II would help to break the stalemate.

RARE II was to be far more comprehensive than RARE I. It included national-forest lands in the eastern United States, a decision that dis-solved much of what remained of the purity doctrine. As Assistant Sec-retary Cutler explained, "A critical reading of the Wilderness Act of 1964 confirms that its framers intended that lands which bear some indica-tions of man may be wilderness." The immediate result was that the Forest Service studied significantly more land in RARE II than it had in RARE I, over sixty-two million acres nationwide.[3]

In the summer of 1977, the Forest Service held over two hundred workshops around the country to help identify certain areas that should or should not be included in the RARE II evaluation and to deter-mine criteria for assessing those roadless lands.[4] Reflecting the grow-ing participatory nature of wilderness debates in this era, RARE II eventually surpassed its predecessor by garnering the largest public input to any federal hearing in U.S. history to that point.

The responses to the work in this first stage were typically mixed. Wilderness advocates praised the expanded definition of roadless lands and extension of the hearings to the eastern United States, but they continued to challenge the way the agency applied its RARE II criteria in the Cascades. The Forest Service planned timber sales in many areas that wilderness advocates felt should be in the RARE II study.

One example of their dispute over defining roadless lands arose in the Bull of the Woods region, in the lower-elevation foothills north-west of Mount Jefferson in Oregon. Straddling both the Willamette and Mount Hood National Forests, the roadless area covered 49,000 acres of mostly forested terrain, with a core of higher, rocky ridges. Portland area conservationists had long promoted its value as wilderness, and Senator Mark Hatfield had included the entire area into his proposed Oregon omnibus wilderness bill in the early 1970s, but the legislation had never passed the House of Representatives. The Forest Service divided the area in its RARE II inventory, leaving out 22,000 acres along Opal Creek and Hot Springs Creek "primarily due to high mineral and timber values."[5] Statewide, the Oregon Wilderness Coalition (OWC) identified one million acres of roadless forests that were not in the RARE II inventory.[6]

The timber industry was initially very wary of RARE II as another potential bureaucratic delay to timber harvests in the lands under review. Gus Kuehne, of the Tacoma-based American Plywood Association, responded quickly and cynically to Cutler's initiative, saying that RARE II "has speeded the process right up to where we were in 1971."[7] As the Forest Service gathered public input on which areas to inventory and what set of criteria to use in classifying land, Kirk Ewart, of the Boise Cascade Corporation, claimed that RARE II "has severely reduced the available supply of timber to western mills and is creating crisis conditions for communities dependent on National Forest timber."[8]

By the end of 1977, the Forest Service had completed the preliminary stages of inventory and polling, and the timber industry reaction noticeably perked up. The input from 50,000 people during the public hearings that previous summer strongly favored development of roadless lands. The top-ranked priority was the need to make "significant" timber, energy, and mineral resources "available for extraction."[9] Satisfied with the outcome of this initial stage of the process, timber industry representatives urged that the process continue as rapidly as possible.

Rupert Cutler had promised a short timeline for completion of RARE II when he first introduced the proposal, and the Forest Service maintained that tight schedule, completing the entire review by the end of 1978. That year saw important decisions being made on one-third of the national forests as well as unprecedented public participation through comments on the Forest Service proposals. The agency identified an inventory of sixty-two million acres of roadless lands: 2,919 parcels of at least 5,000 acres each. Following NEPA guidelines for environmental assessments, the Forest Service released its draft environmental impact statement (EIS) in June 1978, which listed ten alternatives for the distribution of these lands between three categories: wilderness, future planning (a category that prohibited development while the agency considered options for its use), and nonwilderness. The agency did not choose a preferred alternative from among the ten it presented.

The public response that flowed in over the next few months was unprecedented in scale. Nearly 360,000 people commented on some aspect of the plan, some with detailed letters, some by signing petitions. No other proposed federal land use action had ever received such a volume of public input. In Oregon and Washington, 76,000 people sent in comments on the study proposals, which covered 5.5 million acres in both states.[10] It also, in the words of historian David Clary, "set off an incredible storm." The economic malaise of the 1970s and the post-Watergate distrust of the federal government combined with the inherent conflict between incompatible uses of the public forests to create angry public meetings and demonstrations. Police protection accompanied Forest Service representatives at some meetings.[11]

In January 1979, the Forest Service released its final EIS on RARE II. In it, the agency did establish a clear recommendation. Out of the 62 million acres studied, the Forest Service recommended 15 million acres for wilderness, 11 million acres for further study, and 36 million acres for nonwilderness. One-third of the area recommended for wilderness was in Alaska and had already been listed as future wilderness under an earlier land use study. Out of 2.5 million acres assessed in Washington State, the recommendations called for 269,000 acres for wilderness, 219,000 acres for further study, and slightly over 2 million acres for nonwilderness uses. In Oregon, out of 3 million acres studied, the agency recommended 368,000 acres for wilderness, 400,000 acres for further study, and 2.2 million acres for nonwilderness.[12]

Nationally, environmental organizations expressed "acute disappointment" that nearly 60 percent of the lands in the study would be opened to development, but in Oregon especially, where the percentage for nonwilderness was much higher, the response among environmentalists was angrier.[13] Holway Jones, who had helped organize the Save French Pete Committee in 1968, wrote to Rupert Cutler, "It's hard for me to believe, Rupe, that the RARE II recommendations are going to be allowed to stand the way they came out on January 4. There are a lot of unhappy people here in the Northwest, especially in Oregon. Most of them feel downright cheated—in fact, angry."[14]

Although the Forest Service and timber industry hoped the RARE II process would avoid the threat of lawsuits, local activists in Oregon immediately spoke of challenging the decision in court. The regional and national leadership of the Sierra Club opposed this confrontational approach, fearing that it would create a strong, widespread political backlash against wilderness. A split arose between the Sierra Club and the OWC, as well as within the OWC itself. These strategic and philosophical divisions had begun during the French Pete campaign, and they became stronger after RARE II.[15]

Members of the Sierra Club had founded the OWC in the early 1970s to promote wilderness advocacy in small towns throughout the state, and this had become both a source of strength and a source of conflict between the organizations. The RARE II procedures as established by the Forest Service gave preference to public comments on specific roadless lands, and the OWC's main achievement was to organize groups of citizens who would represent their local roadless tracts. Part of their work would be to study these areas in great detail. In congressional hearings on post–RARE II wilderness bills, the OWC was able to muster a lineup of local citizens who knew each specific area with deep personal knowledge and passion. They created a constituency that did not reflect the dominantly urban, middle-class membership of the Sierra Club in Oregon, and they expressed pride that they represented more than just "the wine and brie set," as OWC director James Montieth referred to the "old guard" environmentalists.[16] The OWC also pushed the focus of their arguments for wilderness toward purely ecological issues of habitat and biodiversity and away from the recreational and aesthetic concerns of traditional wilderness campaigns. Although protection of old-growth forests had been at the core of the conservationist agenda since the 1950s, the OWC made it their sole purpose in the 1980s.

In Washington State, environmental organizations also expressed immediate outrage at the RARE II decisions, which recommended for nonwilderness several areas in the Cascades that had been at the center of wilderness debates since the 1950s. Most glaring of all was Cougar Lakes, a rugged, forested region of roughly 280,000 acres east of Mount Rainier National Park with one road cutting through the middle at Chinook Pass. In 1961 a coalition of regional conservation organizations had proposed that the Cougar Lakes Limited Area, established in the 1940s, become part of a broader Cougar Lakes Wilderness. The North Cascades Study Team had proposed a wilderness area there in 1965, and Congress later considered several bills to add the area to the National Wilderness Preservation System.[17] In their final RARE II statement, the

Forest Service first divided the Cougar Lakes area into six separate units and then proposed for wilderness designation only 23,000 acres, 8 percent of the total roadless area, centered on the Cascade Crest. Cougar Lakes, however, was an obvious choice for wilderness and had a broad, visible supporting constituency on both sides of the Cascades. William O. Douglas had long been an outspoken advocate of preserving this part of the Cascades, where, as a young boy in Yakima, he had first explored wild country. If they lost there, conservationists felt, where could they win?[18]

Before the Forest Service's final EIS was released in 1979, wilderness advocates in Washington State had organized their own coalition to coordinate efforts to challenge RARE II. Citizens for Washington Wilderness was formed in the summer of 1978 to generate public response to RARE II and to develop an alternative plan. Citizens for Washington Wilderness also sought to expand upon the research conducted by the RARE II study teams. They distributed Roadless Area Summary Sheets to their local constituents and urged them to catalogue all unroaded areas, their history, attributes, and threatened land use actions. The summer of 1978 was an important time for field research, and the information gathered would be used to generate site-specific comments during the RARE II public-comment period.

Like the members of the OWC, Washington conservationists sought to become the experts on each roadless area and then focus public attention on specific, controversial ones.[19] They hoped to take advantage of the stated Forest Service policy that site-specific, personal comments would weigh more than others in the final assessment. Don Campbell, supervisor of the Mount Baker–Snoqualmie National Forest, wrote, "This is not a vote counting, so the value is in the letter's content rather than the number of signatures that support that decision."[20] After organizing their efforts to satisfy the agency's requests, wilderness advocates were deeply frustrated when, by the final RARE II decision in 1979, that work seemed to have been in vain. They turned, with all others in the debate, to Congress.

The timber industry in Oregon and Washington reacted with similar intensity to organize their response to RARE II and their lobbying efforts in Congress after the final RARE decision. William Hagenstein, of the Industrial Forestry Association (IFA), wrote to member corporations in 1978: "Because there is nothing more important this year to our Region's future timber supply than RARE II, the IFA staff has been heavily preoccupied in RARE II activity all this year."[21] Under the leadership of the IFA in Portland and the National Forest Products Association (NFPA) nationally, the regional timber industry organized coalitions, established teams to further study the roadless areas, and instituted lobbying strategies to take their message to the public and to political leaders.[22]

These timber industry groups organized on-the-ground studies of each roadless area to accumulate their own data on timber supply and other attributes to support their case in calling for opening most of those forests to timber harvesting. Foresters from IFA-member companies scoured the woods that summer collecting data not just on timber resources but also on the social and economic impacts of policy decisions for local communities. They next developed this information into individual responses "to the RARE II draft EIS in the manner prescribed by USFS which has indicated that greatest attention would be paid to 'narrative responses' which show knowledge of individual roadless areas."[23]

The industry coalition also set out on a public-relations campaign to generate broad awareness of and support for their position. This was not new; the industry had been sponsoring an aggressive public-relations effort since the late 1960s, but now it sought to present a unified, substantial message on the specific issues of RARE II. The IFA provided a "RARE II kit" to every media outlet in Oregon and Washington. Borrowing a tactic long-used by wilderness advocates, they developed a traveling slide program. And they created several television programs specifically on RARE II, free copies of which were widely distributed by the Oregon Managed Forest Council. The IFA provided the media with free helicopter tours of particular roadless areas, such as Waldo Lake in Oregon, just south of the Three Sisters Wilderness Area, in August 1978. Their goal was to generate "a groundswell of response" during the RARE II public-comment period.[24]

Nationally, their work paid off as the volume of signatures supporting the option of no additional wilderness exceeded the number supporting full wilderness protection by a margin of three to one.[25] The industry presented an impressive display of public-relations organizing. John Hall, of the NFPA, commented, "We played all of the subsets of RARE II and we played them well."[26]

The RARE II final EIS required presidential review, and in April 1979, the White House released its final approval of the RARE II findings with very few modifications. President Carter did expand the proposed Cougar Lakes Wilderness Area from the 23,000 acres suggested in RARE II to 129,000 acres in his final recommendations to Congress, but this was the only significant change in Oregon and Washington. All sides knew that Congress would be the final arbiter of the continuing dispute over these lands. Meanwhile, the Forest Service embarked on its plans to develop the roadless areas it released from wilderness consideration in RARE II. It began to plan timber sales in many valleys such as the Middle Fork Santiam and Opal Creek in Oregon.[27]

Although it had been critical of the RARE II process at times, fearing further delays in land management decisions, the timber industry immediately began a campaign to make sure that the RARE II decisions became law. Don-Lee Davidson, president of the NFPA in 1979, asserted, "The goals of the study can only be realized if the non-Wilderness lands are returned promptly to management as part of the working forest."[28] RARE II recommendations offered a solution that provided "certainty" in the timber supply market for those companies that relied on national-forest timber for their business. "To plan ahead," the NFPA concluded, "the forest industry needs certainty about the timber supply that will be available. Plant modernization and expansion are not possible in a climate of basic raw material insecurity." The NFPA urged a speedy and firm resolution: "All multiple-use users of the National Forests urge prompt, wise decisions—the sooner the better—because the long debate has created enormous uncertainty and insecurity that only Congress and the Administration can resolve."[29]

The judicial branch of the federal government only added to the uncertainty of the whole process when it ruled in 1980 that the RARE II documentation and opportunities for public input were both insufficient to satisfy the demands of NEPA, at least in the case of California. The federal district court rejected the RARE II findings in California and required the Forest Service to file site-specific environmental reviews for each roadless area. In 1982, the Ninth Circuit Court of Appeals upheld the lower court.

The ruling did not surprise many people involved with RARE II; the legal holes were clearly visible. The federal Environmental Protection Agency found the draft EIS to be "inadequate," and it predicted legal problems with a system in which the Forest Service chose its preferred alternative only after the opportunity for public comment had ended. Officials in the timber industry also understood the legal problems. The NFPA noted, "[The] Forest Service is proceeding with planning on RARE II non-Wilderness lands under a regulation which staff and attorneys view as extremely vulnerable to legal challenge." The Sierra Club's Doug Scott fought to restrain environmental lawyers who salivated at the ease of such a high-profile court victory because he feared that destroying RARE II in court would fuel antiwilderness legislation in Congress. The state of California went ahead with its own lawsuit anyway.[30] The associate editor of *Timber Harvesting* magazine stated the case dryly: "Ten years and two RAREs later, the Forest Service was beginning to understand the meaning of the National Environmental Policy Act."[31]

The timber industry's legislative priority focused on passage of a national law to codify the nonwilderness recommendations of RARE II, with certain modifications. The industry wanted "release bills" that made timber on public lands that did not become wilderness permanently available for logging. The administrative decisions of RARE II and other Forest Service land use reviews were never set in stone; they were susceptible to political trends, judicial review, and future wilderness debates. In an ironic twist, the industry sought in its release bills the same permanence and reliability that wilderness advocates had sought in their campaign to pass the Wilderness Act two decades earlier. The "uncertainty" of the administrative boundaries of the Three Sisters Primitive Area, and other similar sites, in the 1950s led to the conservationists' campaign to make Congress permanently "release" those areas from the timber sale program. By 1980, neither side was willing to trust the Forest Service to meet its needs.

Over the next several years, the roadless lands left out of the wilderness category by RARE II became the focus of political debate, and "release language" for those lands was the crux of each individual piece of wilderness legislation. The NFPA instructed its lobbyists, "Acceptable release language is essential, independent of boundary questions." The "bottom line" for negotiating was release language that would prevent the Forest Service from considering roadless lands for wilderness until at least the year 2000, which they hoped would allow the Forest Service to sell timber in these areas. NFPA policy was to "oppose even acceptable boundaries if release is not included."[32] Once again, the wilderness debates focused on the lands outside the potential wilderness boundaries.

The strategy behind release language was not necessarily unique to these debates after RARE II. Exchanging land for guaranteed supplies of timber was at the crux of the Alpine Lakes debate. The industry-led Alpine Lakes Coalition asked Congressman Lloyd Meeds to include language in the final bill that would expedite Forest Service roadless reviews elsewhere in Washington State, with the hope that completion of these reviews would accelerate logging in these areas. An earlier version of Meeds's Alpine Lakes bill did include such language, but wilderness lobbyists were successful in having that proposal rejected in House committee meetings in 1975 and in demanding a "clean bill" of their own.[33]

The Forest Service, which strongly supported permanent-release language in the 1980s, had pursued policies since the 1950s that had led to an unwritten tradition of releasing all nonwilderness lands to resource extraction. In its view, forestlands should be zoned as either wilderness or multiple use, and thus all lands not included within a wilderness area should be subject to timber management. It was either one or the other. This helps to explain why the agency consistently rejected wilderness for the French Pete region in the 1960s and 1970s as contradictory to the 1957 decision of the secretary of agriculture to "release" the lands west of Horse Creek to timber management.

There were two interconnected aspects to release language in the post–RARE II wilderness bills. First, the timber industry and the Forest Service, frustrated by seeing land use planning for roadless areas blocked in court, wanted RARE II decisions protected from lawsuits. The federal court decision against RARE II applied only to California, but industry representatives realized that it could quickly be transferred to other states if a lawsuit were filed. The California ruling said that site-specific EISs, which themselves could be challenged in court, were required by NEPA prior to developing roadless areas. Release language would free the agency from this restriction. This type of release was also called "sufficiency language," because Congress could simply declare the existing RARE II documentation and decisions legally sufficient.

The second purpose of release language was to open for nonwilderness use those lands that Congress did not declare wilderness or wilderness study areas. Congress would state that the Forest Service did not have to consider wilderness preservation in developing land use plans for these areas although, as wilderness advocates were quick to point out, the agency certainly could still choose to leave the "released" lands undeveloped.[34]

The industry's demand for "hard," or permanent-release, language and environmentalists' demand for significant acreage of new wilderness created a stalemate in Congress. Both sides could stop each other's bills, but nothing could be resolved. The main source of dispute in the debates over release language was the duration of the release period during which roadless lands could not be considered for wilderness designation. The first post–RARE II bill, introduced by Congressman Tom Foley (Washington State) in 1979, called for permanently releasing all RARE II lands recommended for nonwilderness from further consideration for wilderness. Even the fifteen million acres that RARE II recommended as wilderness would be permanently opened to logging under his proposal if Congress had not acted on those by 1984. Foley's bill would have sabotaged parts of the Wilderness Act and thus it angered conservationists.[35] NFPA lobbyists tried to use Foley's bill as a vehicle to generate support in Congress for more moderate release language. After facing stiff opposition, Foley offered an amended bill that kept the release language but would immediately designate as wilderness the fifteen million acres so recommended by RARE II. Yet this too faced widespread and bipartisan opposition.[36]

As both the timber industry and wilderness activists sought legislative solutions to the stalemate, they struggled with internal divisions. The court decision against RARE II in California pushed many timber companies there to seek a compromise in order to break the court injunction against timber sales in roadless areas. A California statewide bill was introduced in 1980, but seeing the political winds shifting in their favor toward the more conservative Reagan era, the leadership of NFPA worked to obstruct it. They felt that the "urgency" created by the federal court decision would lead "to adverse boundary trade-offs for industry." NFPA members were divided between the hard-liners, who would not compromise on release language, and those looking for a more immediate resolution.[37]

Unity was also a struggle for wilderness advocates in Washington and Oregon, and distinct differences emerged between environmental groups in these two states. Release language was a critical issue for environmentalists in Washington State. Doug Scott, who directed the Seattle-based Northwest office of the Sierra Club, led the national effort to minimize the impact of release language. He strongly campaigned against RARE II lawsuits, fearing that they might create a political backlash that would result in stronger release language. Washington activists felt confident in their ability to work within Congress instead of the courts to achieve more wilderness protection for lower-elevation lands.[38]

Leaders of the Oregon Wilderness Coalition, which changed its name to the Oregon Natural Resources Council (ONRC) in 1982, felt that they faced a far more desperate situation than their colleagues in Washington, and they cared little for the seemingly arcane battle over release language. The ONRC represented a coalition of local grassroots organizations, each of which desperately wanted to save some piece of its own backyard from logging. In Oregon, timber harvesting was occurring so fast that to these activists the difference between ten years or thirty years or forever in the competing release bills was meaningless. They did not believe that they had even ten years to work with. The time was now or never for these activists, and they did not want to give up their local forests for the national cause, nor were their leaders willing to ask them to do so. Others in Oregon expressed their frustrations with the slow pace of legislative action by joining the civil-disobedience efforts of the radical environmental group Earth First! which debuted in the state in the spring of 1983 by blocking road construction into a roadless area in the Klamath Mountains of southern Oregon.[39]

Beginning during the French Pete debate, the ONRC (then OWC) sought to distance itself from the traditional rhetoric of promoting wilderness protection for aesthetic and recreational reasons, and this increased after RARE II. The organization deliberately focused on areas that had relatively few of the traditional characteristics of high, alpine wilderness. The Forest Service itself had opened a window for this when it stated a preference for RARE II to give protection to underrepresented ecological features.[40] Low-elevation old-growth forests in Oregon certainly fit this description, but the end product of RARE II did not change the existing imbalance in wilderness protection. The ONRC emphasized that the next wilderness bill should protect significant examples of old-growth forests. French Pete was a mature forest, valuable to the timber industry, but at just over 100 years old, it was not an example of the classic old-growth stand of 500- to 1,000-year-old trees.[41]

The ONRC came to focus on a small, 24,000-acre roadless pocket surrounded by logging roads along the Middle Santiam River and the forests west of Waldo Lake, once part of the Waldo Lake Limited Area, which Karl Onthank and others had fought to preserve in the 1950s. Andy Kerr, of the ONRC, expressed some of the passion with which he and his colleagues in Oregon approached this issue: "By the time the fight came in the 1984 bill, it was God damn it, we want the Middle Santiam *because* it's old growth. Because it *has* the most volume per acre. And we wanted Waldo because it *had* the most volume of timber of any roadless area in the debate, in Oregon or anywhere else. With those areas we got some of the first wildernesses for old-growth forests, which was an emerging political concept at that time."[42]

The ONRC was not unique in expressing its concern for protecting old-growth forests with wilderness status; such forests had been at the center of every wilderness debate in the Cascades since the 1950s. Its arguments, however, shifted more toward scientific justifications than had any previous lobbying efforts. The distinction between the Sierra Club and the ONRC rested mainly in strategy and in their perceived timeline to achieve their goals. The ONRC dismissed the relatively slow, incremental approach favored by Sierra Club activists such as Doug Scott. You take what you can get and then come back for more, Scott explained.[43] The ONRC strongly felt that they could not compromise in the short run because there might be few forests left to come back for. These competing approaches engendered open conflict that lingers to this day throughout the environmental movement, but they hid the common concern for preserving forests that lay at the foundation of the wilderness movement in the Northwest.

While an Oregon wilderness bill was stuck in Congress in 1983 over release language and a dispute between Congressman James Weaver's proposal for 1.2 million acres of new wilderness and Senator Mark Hatfield's 600,000-acre proposal, Oregon activists decided to separate themselves from the national strategy of wilderness proponents and the "old guard" of Northwest wilderness advocates. Openly defying the strategy of the Sierra Club and the Wilderness Society, in 1983 the ONRC filed suit in federal court against the RARE II decision in Oregon. Modeled after the state of California's successful lawsuit, this seemed certain to shut down logging operations in all the lands studied under RARE II.[44] To many, this was like throwing gasoline on a fire that seemed on the verge of coming under control, and it exacerbated growing divisions between wilderness activists. For the ONRC, the intent was clearly to put more pressure on the timber industry and the legislative process, and it was successful. James Montieth, director of the ONRC, explained the rationale behind the use of this legal weapon: "A RARE II suit may provide the necessary incentive, since the 'locking up' of three million acres will be anathema to them [the timber industry], and the only way to 'unlock' those lands is to pass legislation. . . . The lawsuit is the best catalyst we can provide, short of total capitulation on the acreage. If it's not an adequate incentive for the industry, so be it."[45] In his public press conference, Montieth stated, "Conservationists have asked the court to halt road building and timber sales on slightly less than 3 million acres of roadless areas until an adequate wilderness review is completed, or preferably until Congress passes legislation to resolve this issue."[46]

Although Senator Hatfield intensely disliked being coerced in this way, he recognized the renewed urgency of passing an Oregon wilderness bill. He made it known that he was willing to negotiate with Weaver and include additional acreage in exchange for some form of temporary-release language, but Senator James McClure (Idaho) remained the main stumbling block for all pending RARE II wilderness bills in western states. As chair of the Senate Interior Committee, which oversaw legislation on wilderness, he exercised his powers to insist that all wilderness bills contain permanent-release language.[47] Hatfield responded to McClure,

"I think unlike any of the other western states at this moment, we are in a very unique situation in Oregon in that we have had suits filed that are now being litigated. . . . And considering the basic economics of Oregon is related to the timber industry, we are in a very urgent situation."[48]

Hatfield joined Dan Evans (Washington) and other western senators to use their political leverage to force McClure to agree to a compromise in which the Forest Service was not required to consider any areas for wilderness designation in its management options until the second round of forest planning required by the National Forest Management Act (NFMA) of 1976. The first round of NFMA planning was to be completed by 1985, and revisions were not required until ten to fifteen years later. Only in the second round of forest planning, the final, compromise, "soft" release language stated, could citizens insist that the Forest Service fully reconsider the issue of wilderness for roadless lands. Most important to Hatfield and the Oregon timber industry, the bill included sufficiency language that nullified the ONRC's lawsuit.[49]

After the dam broke on the release language debate in May, Congress passed wilderness acts for Oregon, Washington, and sixteen other states. Ironically, President Ronald Reagan, a strong opponent of wilderness, signed more acres of national-forest wilderness into law than any of his predecessors since 1964. One lobbyist for the timber industry quipped as Congress reached its compromise, "You realize, of course, that they just turned Ronald Reagan into Teddy Roosevelt."[50] The resulting statewide wilderness acts in Oregon and Washington in 1984 added more acreage and more forested areas to the wilderness system of the Cascades than did any other previous year of legislative action. These laws did more than just designate wilderness, however; they prescribed that the land outside the boundaries of newly designated wilderness areas be opened, or "released," to development for a period of at least ten to fifteen years (until the second round of NFMA planning). Never before had Congress protected so much land in the Northwest by wilderness designation in a single year; yet never before had Congress directly instructed that so much land be opened to resource extraction.

The 1984 laws are often called RARE II bills, because they were in direct response to the zoning proposals presented by the Forest Service in its RARE II analysis. But these laws in many ways signify the failure of

RARE II. The Forest Service began the roadless review process as an attempt to regain control over the wilderness issue from the judicial and legislative branches. The lawsuits in California and Oregon clearly demonstrated that the agency was not able to escape its legal dilemma. Congress added sufficiency (release) language to the 1984 wilderness bills to bail out the Forest Service, but the acreage that Congress added to the wilderness system in Oregon and Washington very clearly gives the opposite message: that RARE II was actually politically insufficient. The agency's RARE II recommendations meant very little to Congress as it hammered out a compromise between competing public interests, and its final decisions added to the wilderness system several times more acres than the Forest Service desired.[51]

The Forest Service decisions in the final RARE II proposal were embarrassingly unrealistic in the political realm. Whereas the agency called for 368,000 acres of new wilderness in Oregon, Congress, even with Mark Hatfield's strong distaste for adding old-growth forests to the wilderness system, passed a bill for over 853,000 acres. In Washington, the 1979 recommendation for 269,000 acres ballooned to well over one million. The Forest Service, having opposed those increases throughout, once again found itself on the outside of the process of designating the land use category of wilderness that it had invented many decades before.[52]

It is difficult to identify a clear winner in the struggle between the timber industry and wilderness advocates. Certainly the acreage eventually added to the wilderness system in both Oregon and Washington was much greater than many had thought possible, and much of that contained old-growth forests. In Oregon, the new wilderness areas on the Middle Santiam and Waldo Lake granted protected status to a tremendous volume of timber, but the acreage of both areas was well below that requested by the ONRC. Out of 24,000 acres of roadless land along the Middle Santiam River studied in RARE II, only 7,500 became wilderness in 1984.

The ONRC had fought hard for these places solely for their biological value, and they had won a number of small victories.[53] A map of Oregon wilderness shows several of these in the pocket wilderness areas along the lower, western slopes of the Cascades. The Bull of the Woods, Salmon-Huckleberry, Middle Santiam, and Grassy Knob Wilderness

Areas still see little recreational use, but their ecological value is very important to those who study old-growth forests. They are a visible symbol of how Oregon activists reshaped the wilderness campaigns after the 1960s.

The 1984 bills picked up pieces left over from wilderness campaigns going back to the 1950s. In Washington, conservationists successfully obtained two wilderness areas in the Cougar Lakes region—the Norse Peak and the William O. Douglas Wilderness Areas—which protected most of the area under dispute since the 1950s. For the third time since 1964, Congress changed the boundaries of the Glacier Peak Wilderness Area, adding acres along the ridges and in the forested valleys that were at the center of the struggle leading to the creation of the North Cascades National Park in 1968. A new wilderness area, named after Senator Henry M. Jackson, who died in office in 1983, was attached to the southern border of the Glacier Peak Wilderness Area, creating an almost solid block of protected alpine land in the Cascades from Canada to Snoqualmie Pass. In Oregon, Congress once again expanded the Three Sisters Wilderness Area and also created the Waldo Lake Wilderness Area out of what remained of the Waldo Lake Limited Area.

When the results of the 1984 bills are measured in terms of acres, the timber industry clearly came out on top, however. The acres released to development added up to more than double the additions to the wilderness system. Nationwide, Congress added 6.6 million acres to the wilderness system in 1984 while "releasing" 13.6 million. As Doug Scott has said, these were not wilderness bills; they were release bills.[54] The security of the timber supply to be achieved by release language motivated the industry to fight so hard for passage of these bills. Gene Bergoffen, vice president for resources of NFPA, praised the economic security offered by the final negotiated release language: "We view the compromise as a win-win solution. . . . The land isn't left in a state of limbo."[55] Senator Hatfield was also optimistic about the impact of his own legislation: "This bill resolves the wilderness issue on Oregon's national forests, bringing to a close that 20-year chapter of wilderness controversy in Oregon."[56]

Smaller timber companies were not as satisfied. They depended far more on public lands for timber supply than the large landholders represented by NFPA. Don Johnson, of the Johnson Lumber Company of Prairie City in eastern Oregon, reflected the fears of many small operators when he warned, "There will be some companies who'll have to quit. It's the survival of the fittest. I like some wilderness myself, but I don't like to see old growth timber or timber producing lands locked up. We went too far this time."[57] Large timber companies have always been more able and willing to trade more wilderness acres for greater economic stability.

The industry got the release language it wanted, but it was not enough to save it from economic decline. The 1984 bills were passed during one of the most severe recessions in the timber industry in the twentieth century. The secure access to timber supplies promised by the release language and the increased timber sales on national-forest lands under Reagan administration policies of the 1980s were insufficient to protect lumber mills from powerful market forces that had little to do with wilderness debates. Lumber companies in the Northwest bought high-priced contracts for national-forest timber during the 1970s, when lumber prices were high, but those prices collapsed in the 1980s. The price of Douglas fir lumber on national forests west of the Cascades dropped over 70 percent over the course of two years.[58] Release language would not provide noticeable security under such conditions.

The federal government pursued other means to assist the industry during these years. Beginning in 1981, the Forest Service allowed interest-free contract extensions for logging companies that faced deadlines for cutting timber they had agreed to purchase in earlier years. In 1984, after approving both the Washington and Oregon wilderness acts, Congress passed a timber contract buyout bill, which allowed companies to dissolve their contract obligations at an affordable cost.[59]

ONRC lobbyists joined their rivals in the timber industry to support legislation for timber contract relief because it also promised a reduction in logging on national forests in the Cascades. Andy Kerr, on his way to Washington, DC, to lobby for the bill, ran into Senator Hatfield in Chicago's O'Hare airport. The exchange that occurred was very telling with respect to Hatfield's emphasis on release language as the primary legacy of the 1984 bills. Kerr explained to the senator that he was going to support the timber contract buyout bill, which Hatfield himself had introduced, "because it would slow the development of roadless areas." According to Kerr, Hatfield responded, "There are no more roadless areas. We released them."

"Oh, well, Senator, but you know, they are still out there in fact, and they still don't have any roads."

"There are no more roadless areas," the senator repeated.[60]

If the history of the wilderness debates proves anything, it is that such confidence, on either side, is often not justified, as the forests below Bald Eagle Ridge can now attest. After twenty years, wilderness debates are returning to these forests along the North Fork Skykomish River. The upper stretches of the North Fork are part of the 100,000-acre Henry M. Jackson Wilderness Area, created by the 1984 Washington Wilderness Act, but the lower forests were left out of the final boundaries. In the summer of 2001, Washington's senior senator, Patty Murray, and Representative Rick Larsen promised to introduce legislation for a Wild Sky Wilderness Area that would extend the boundaries of the existing wilderness farther into lower-elevation forests and protect a large, rugged area of roadless lands studied in RARE II and "released" by the Washington Wilderness Act of 1984. Standing in a grove of second-growth trees at an elevation below one thousand feet, Senator Murray said, "In 1984 we protected the high ground. We now know what happens when we don't have any lowland protected." She referred primarily to the loss of habitat for salmon and other endangered species, an issue that has rapidly gained prominence since 1984.[61]

Their proposal, the first national-forest wilderness bill in Washington since 1984, reflects the consistently flexible nature of wilderness designation as a practical tool for land and resource protection. In Oregon, a broader initiative led by the ONRC seeks to identify new roadless areas and add up to five million acres of low-elevation forest to the wilderness system, much of which was not considered in the 1984 negotiations.[62] In the beginning of the twenty-first century, wilderness protection is once again becoming a dominant issue in the land use debates of both states.

EPILOGUE

The broken-down cabin along the banks of Camp Robber Creek in the Alpine Lakes Wilderness lies quietly today, disappearing into the growing forest vegetation. Its immediate surroundings have not visibly changed in the past half century. No fires or landslides have come to transform the species composition of the site, and the planned logging roads and clear-cuts never reached that far up the valley. When Congress defined the boundary of the Alpine Lakes Wilderness in 1976, it stopped Forest Service plans to extend its road and logging operations. To the loggers of the region, the Forest Service, the hundreds of hikers who walk up the trail to Dorothy Lake every summer weekend, and the local environment, that boundary matters. The lines of wilderness areas are significant to all these groups and more because they define places for distinct forms of human land use on both sides of the border. The cabin itself might serve to undermine a mythology of pure, pristine nature that is often attached to wilderness ideology, but the more important factor for land use and history over the past several decades is the boundary line within which that cabin site sits.

The central lesson of wilderness debates in the Oregon and Washington Cascades—one that applies nationwide—is that boundaries matter. Since World War II wilderness in the United States has been less an idealized abstraction than a set of very real, valued pockets of the American landscape. Within those wilderness areas Americans practice a very different form of land use than is allowed outside those boundaries, with particular restrictions on resource extraction and motorized recreation. From the 1950s to 1984, an increasing number of Americans became directly involved in the debates over where to draw those dividing lines.

In terms of number of bills passed and acreage of national forest preserved, the year 1984 could be considered the apex of the wilderness movement, when the last great flurry of congressional designation of protected forest lands under the Wilderness Act occurred. In the midst of the combative, polarized politics that have characterized American public discourse since then, the idea of Congress passing so many wilderness bills in one session now seems a far-fetched dream. The environmental movement became increasingly divided between the vision of wilderness areas as recreation sites and as ecological reserves; the fault lines emerged during the French Pete debate in Oregon in the 1970s. Wilderness itself, as a concept, came under fire from various directions in the 1990s. The environmental movement had diversified to encompass countless concerns—such as pollution, endangered species, and environmental justice—compared to which wilderness areas often seemed an idealized abstraction. In light of the more critical assessment of European-based ideological traditions, scholars and activists insisted that "the time has come to rethink wilderness." [1] Yet despite these developments and the reduced number of wilderness bills passed by Congress, wilderness designation has remained very relevant to environmental politics, not just in the Cascades but throughout the country.

Much of the explanation for the lasting power of wilderness designation comes from its history since World War II, which documents it as a very flexible and practical political tool for drawing boundaries—not a rigid ideology of pristine nature, as academic and prodevelopment critics of the 1990s often characterized it. Wilderness ideas and laws have responded to the perceived concerns of their day, and it is within the specific contexts of time and place that we should assess wilderness. Before World War II, as Paul Sutter has observed, the consumer ethos of providing motorized recreational opportunities was a prime motivation toward wilderness preservation. Yet, as Sutter further noted, each generation of activists has redefined wilderness in terms of the perceived environmental threats of its own times.[2] Beginning in the 1950s, rapid expansion of resource extraction from public lands, and the resulting scarcity of aesthetic and ecological resources such as old-growth forests, fueled the environmental movement to create and expand a legislated system of wilderness protection. By 2004, timber harvests from national forests in the Northwest occurred at a fraction of the rate seen in 1984, a decline in which wilderness legislation played little to no part. As logging receded from its dominant position in national forest management and the regional economy, wilderness boundaries began to represent more than merely the difference between clear-cuts and old-growth forests; nevertheless, drawing lines in the forest has remained an essential tool in debates over land use and zoning on public land.

In the early twenty-first century, two competing visions of the process of determining wilderness boundaries have emerged. On the one hand, the administration of President George W. Bush supported a return to the centralized decision making that characterized the years prior to the Wilderness Act. Citing complaints over the gridlock and "analysis paralysis" caused by countless public hearings and extensive public documentation of land use impacts, the administration sought to limit public involvement and streamline the decision-making process, particularly in regard to the management of roadless areas.[3] On the other hand, similar frustrations over divisive land use debates and their uncertain results have precipitated an extraordinary rise in the level of collaboration between competing interests groups. Throughout the West, ranchers, loggers, farmers, off-road vehicle clubs, and environmentalists have negotiated a series of proposed compromises on zoning wide swaths of public land. In these discussions, wilderness is an essential land use tool, but just one of many options on the table.

In the statewide wilderness bills of 1984, Congress established zoning guidelines for over two million acres of national forest in Oregon and Washington. But the fundamental conflict remained over how much of the Northwest's old-growth forests to protect from logging, and when Congress declared in release language that this issue could not be addressed by the Wilderness Act for a period of up to fifteen years, it was bound to find another outlet.

That outlet was the federal court system, where groups such as the

Oregon Natural Resources Council, the Sierra Club, and local chapters of the Audubon Society filed lawsuits to protect roadless lands because of their wildlife habitat and biological diversity. Environmental public-interest lawyers had cut their teeth on wilderness lawsuits, from the Parker Decision in 1970—which protected de facto wilderness lands contiguous to existing primitive and wilderness areas—to the RARE II challenges in California and Oregon. Tony Ruckel, the lead attorney who argued for the Parker Decision, correctly predicted in 1970, "The aroused citizen, frustrated by an uncomprehending branch of the executive department, confused and angered by the frequently sluggish pace of the legislature . . . will turn to the arbiter of disputes unsettled in these two branches of our government, a court of law."[4]

In the legal arena since 1984, the release language has had little impact.[5] Sufficiency language in the 1984 bills ruled that RARE II had provided for enough study of wilderness values, but there were other values that would be asserted and contested in the federal courts, such as wildlife habitat for the northern spotted owl. Environmental groups filed many lawsuits challenging Forest Service management of public forests after 1984, but none of the results were as momentous as the decisions handed down by District Judge William Dwyer in 1991 that ordered the Forest Service to halt all timber sales in remaining old-growth forests until the agency complied with National Forest Management Act requirements to protect the viability of the northern spotted owl. The Forest Service timber program never recovered from "the Dwyer Decision," which sped up the inevitable crash in the old-growth-based timber economy.[6]

The legal cases were not about preserving a pure and pristine wilderness, but then neither were the wilderness debates. Like wilderness legislation, lawsuits were a very effective tool for limiting logging on public land, but they lacked the longevity of wilderness boundaries. Rather than resolving the basic dispute in 1984, Congress inadvertently reduced its influence over forest politics and pushed these debates into the federal court system by the late 1980s. In 1994, President Bill Clinton conferred with leaders throughout the Northwest to negotiate the Northwest Forest Plan, an attempt to resolve the disputes through systematic, long-range planning and zoning of the region's forests.

The issues of de facto wilderness and roadless lands remain central throughout the ongoing debates. RARE I and RARE II failed in defining the final status of many of these areas, partially because federal courts rejected both processes for insufficient attention to National Environmental Policy Act (NEPA) requirements. At least 58 million acres of designated roadless lands remained undefined at the beginning of the twenty-first century, and in January 2001, President Bill Clinton signed an executive order representing another stage of the de facto wilderness debates. The "Roadless Intitiative" was a plan proposed by the Forest Service to prohibit road construction and most timber harvests within its inventoried roadless areas. Critics challenged the ruling as desperately rushed through by the departing Clinton administration, but it was clearly part of the ongoing debate over de facto wilderness lands that goes back before the Wilderness Act.

Part fiscal conservatism, part holistic ecology, the Roadless Initiative represented a significant cultural shift within the Forest Service since the 1980s. In response to public pressure, federal environmental laws, and diminishing timber supplies, the ranger districts throughout the country diversified their workforce to include many more employees trained in various fields of ecology. Frustrated by the diminishing influence and respect toward their organization in matters of land use, many of this younger generation rebelled against the "old guard" of the timber program. The Association of Forest Service Employees for Environmental Ethics emerged in Oregon in 1989 to lead internal discussions of reform away from the focus on timber sales. New, holistic policies of "ecosystem management" emphasized stewardship of interconnected ecosystems rather than of single commodities. In the light of an $8.4 billion backlog of maintenance costs on its 386,000 miles of existing roads, the Forest Service moved to place its roadless areas off-limits to development.[7]

Although the agency's preferred outcome was materially different from that of the RARE processes, which sought to support the timber sale program, the Roadless Initiative continued in the tradition of increasing public involvement. Over the course of four months in 2000, the Forest Service collected well over one million written responses to its proposal. Added to the testimonies from over 600 public meetings, this exceeded the record participation of RARE II. Environmental organizations used techniques employed by the industry during RARE II to flood the agency with postcards, and the majority of comments supported the road-building ban. Those in the minority—this time, industry supporters—again asked that the postcards be devalued in the final analysis. Cynthia Lummis of the Wyoming Board of Land Commissioners complained, "NEPA is not a process for voting. NEPA is a process for public ideas and concerns to be aired and reviewed."[8]

While wilderness advocates ironically found themselves reunited with the Forest Service to support one of its conservation proposals, resource industries, antipreservation groups, and western states turned to the federal courts for relief. In July 2003, federal judge Clarence Brimmer ruled against the new roadless plan in a case brought by the state of Wyoming. Although the decision went against the prowilderness stand, it was quite similar to earlier court rebukes of administrative hubris. The judge rejected what he called a "thinly veiled attempt to designate 'wilderness areas.'"[9]

Appeal of this case and other legal challenges continued, while the administration of George W. Bush openly pushed to eliminate the roadless plan and to reduce public participation in land use decisions. In May 2005, the Bush administration finalized a new rule for the development of roadless national forest lands. With the new guidelines, the Department of Agriculture eliminated the Roadless Initiative and returned to the existing Forest Service protocols for land management, with the added measure of inviting state governors to petition the agency with specific requests. By the end of 2005, several western states had challenged the new ruling because of its limited public involvement and added burden on state officials.[10]

In the meantime, renewed public activism led Congress to reassert its role in defining wilderness lands in the Northwest. By 2006 the effort to pass a "Wild Sky Wilderness" bill in Washington State was the most advanced, while a proposal by Oregon Senator Ron Wyden for a new wilderness area near Mount Hood had also been introduced. Although Congress was deeply polarized, wilderness bills demonstrated the ability to progress in this political environment if they were built on collaboration between competing interest groups.[11]

The proposal for Wild Sky reflected many of the patterns of earlier wilderness debates, yet with a somewhat different cast. Many of the issues were familiar, and the debate focused once again on the boundaries. The emphasis was on 16,000 acres of low-elevation forests within the 106,000-acre proposed wilderness area. Its proponents, including the state's bipartisan congressional delegation, argued that this inclusion of lands along the valley bottoms was critical to the whole proposal.[12] It was near the urban centers of Puget Sound, and it provided critical habitat for salmon.

In attempts to exclude land from within the proposed wilderness area, opponents revived a pure definition of wilderness, arguing that the former logging and mining sites within the boundaries disqualified the area from wilderness consideration. As evidence, they pointed to the over 10,000 acres within the proposed area that had been logged up to eighty years previously and the thirty miles of logging roads there, but the history of the Wilderness Act does not support their case for excluding these lands. Roads and old logging sites have been consciously included by Congress into wilderness areas since 1964.[13]

Although unanimously approved by the Senate, the Wild Sky bill had not received either a floor or a committee vote in the House, mainly because the leader of this latest incarnation of the purity doctrine tended a powerful seat as chair of the House Resources Committee. Congressman Richard Pombo of California was the main obstacle to passing the bill in 2004.[14]

Although timber companies voiced opposition because they felt the Northwest Forest Plan promised timber harvesting in areas proposed for wilderness, much of the concern came from off-road vehicle groups. The proposed boundary lines of the wilderness were drawn between motorized and nonmotorized recreation groups, a major shift from the previous division between logging and preservation. This tension has now become a dominant issue in wilderness debates, and will likely shape the future even more as timber harvests continue to decline in the region. In the case of Wild Sky, advocates of the wilderness sat down well ahead of time with other user groups to negotiate acceptable boundaries before the bill was introduced in Congress. The Washington State Snowmobile Association agreed not to lobby against the bill if 4,000 acres of popular snowmobiling routes were removed from the original draft. The lines were also redrawn so that Barclay Lake, popular among large church groups and Boy Scouts, was left outside of the wilderness area, where group size limits are common. And floatplane operators would retain the right to land on isolated Lake Isabel, even though they agreed for the lake to be within the new wilderness area.[15]

Praise for the bill focused more on the participatory and collaborative process than on the actual proposal. "You did it the way it ought to be done. It was an inclusive process," Idaho Senator Larry Craig told the Washington delegation before the Senate overwhelmingly approved the measure in 2002. The *Seattle Post-Intelligencer* observed, "The Wild Sky proposal unites people rather than divides them."[16] The strategy of negotiating the lines ahead of time won broad support and undermined opposition, which made this bill far less combative on the local level than previous campaigns.

Collaborative compromises on small wilderness areas scratched out before congressional debate were the operative system for a series of wilderness proposals in the early twenty-first century, some of which have become law. One writer recently suggested, "It's a sign of the times for the wilderness movement, which can either move forward incrementally, or risk grinding to a complete standstill."[17]

An example of such compromise legislation came in 2003 in Nevada, a state traditionally far less supportive of wilderness designation than Washington. To gain support, the Nevada Wilderness Coalition cut its proposal from 4.1 million acres to 425,000 acres of new wilderness centered near Las Vegas and agreed to attach its bill to a land exchange that would provide a new airport for the city. Tying wilderness to urban growth seemed deeply contrary to wilderness ideals, but wilderness bills in the Northwest were often tied, at least indirectly, to logging. Nevada activist Bart Koehler saw the process as an opening for democratic participation: "The Wilderness Act is a real example of democracy at work. It is a citizens' law."[18]

In Idaho, two proposals emerged in 2004 from negotiations that epitomized the new collaborative approach. A coalition of ranchers, off-road vehicle groups, and the Idaho Conservation League developed joint proposals for broad land use plans for the Boulder and White Cloud Mountains of central Idaho and for the Owyhee Canyonlands in the southwest corner of the state. Much of the state congressional delegation had long been openly opposed to new wilderness areas, yet they were directly involved in both processes. At 300,000 acres, the Boulder–White Clouds

Wilderness would be fairly large, but, in a state with nearly 11 million acres of de facto wilderness, it was merely an example of the piecemeal approach. Both plans created a zoning system that would provide for economic development in local communities, ranching, off-road vehicle routes, and statutory wilderness.[19]

While critics arose on all sides of each of these proposed deals, the process exemplified many aspects of the debates in the previous decades. A political give-and-take had always been part of the story, as had growing citizen involvement. Although the compromises may not have seemed balanced to all sides in each case, the players in the process matured to the point where they—not Congress or the land management agencies—divided access to public lands among incompatible uses. Perhaps such diversity of interest groups was a culmination of changes that had occurred since passage of the Wilderness Act. As Congress and the executive branch declined in political civility and effectiveness, these citizen committees were especially impressive and welcome.

The focus of wilderness debates on specific areas of land and resources cultivated an increasingly participatory process after World War II that attracted more direct public input than any other political issue in American history. Passage of the Wilderness Act of 1964 opened the door for all citizens to get involved on all sides of the debates over where to draw the lines, and the process of defining perimeters of wilderness areas played a major role in expanding the participatory nature of American politics in the post-war era.

Into this new public arena emerged not only the advocates of wilderness preservation but their opponents as well. Leaders of the timber industry in Oregon and Washington were deeply involved in these debates, on a national level, and they played an essential role in the final determination of where to draw the lines. Since passage of the Wilderness Act, there have been few cases in which representatives from resource extraction industries in the Northwest have refused to participate in defining wilderness boundaries due to blanket philosophical opposition to wilderness preservation, because many did not share this philosophy and because they could gain more benefits by participating. Drawing wilderness boundaries often opened up more acreage for potential logging than it placed into wilderness areas. The debate over

French Pete Creek in Oregon from 1968 to 1978 stands out as an an example of the local timber industry's digging in its heels on principle, yet it represents the industry's arguably biggest defeat during those years.

Wilderness status is not permanent; economic or cultural changes can readily lead Congress to reconsider the boundaries. Previously criticized as being a burden to economic growth, wilderness areas have now been touted for their benefits to the economy.[20] Congress and later generations have the right to change these boundaries, but, as the debates of the past forty years clearly show, it is a very difficult process. Making reductions in wilderness difficult is exactly what the Wilderness Act of 1964 was meant to do in the wake of the Forest Service's eager willingness to reduce wilderness protection in the Three Sisters region in 1957.

To acknowledge wilderness as a form of land use—one with its own consumer ethos of outdoor recreation—does not diminish from the aesthetic beauty and biodiversity of many of these lands but reinforces the importance of the lines drawn around them. Hike down from Jefferson Park into the Whitewater Creek valley, crossing the boundary of the Mount Jefferson Wilderness. The trail terminates in the clear-cuts at the end of the Whitewater Creek road, which sparked such animosity from wilderness advocates in the 1960s. The transition between forest and clear-cut, between the wilderness area and developed land, is stunning. On a hot summer day, the cool temperatures in the shade of the forest canopy give way to the much hotter, drier conditions of the cut-over land around the parking lot. Songs of the varied thrush in the forest yield to the chirping of grasshoppers. The transformation from one landscape to another is aesthetically and physically significant. All of us to some degree value aspects of both. The line is not a simple demarcation between good and evil or human and natural, and was never meant to be. Basically, it is a division between two broad patterns of land use. The significance of wilderness preservation in modern U.S. history rests in the boundaries of wilderness areas, where they lie, and who placed them there.

NOTES

INTRODUCTION

1. Gilligan, "Forest Service Primitive and Wilderness Areas"; Keyser, *Preservation of Wilderness Areas*, 23–26.

2. Cronon, "The Trouble with Wilderness," 69–78; Nash, *Wilderness and the American Mind*, 1–7.

3. Thomas R. Vale finds "no appreciable difference between 'wilderness' and 'wild' and between the various meanings (statutory and cultural) of 'wilderness'" (*American Wilderness*, 7). I believe the recent debates over wilderness are inadequate partially due to the lack of precise definitions.

4. The romantic idea of wilderness as a place apart from humanity, which has deep cultural roots, has been thoroughly discounted, yet such a strict and unrealistic definition continues to arise in wilderness debates. Labeled "the purity doctrine," such a definition is used by opponents to wilderness to argue that the lands in question do not qualify. Chapter 4 focuses on the use of this strategy in Oregon in the 1960s.

5. Some of the most effective criticism of the idea of a pure wilderness has come in recent years from non-Western and postmodernist critiques. See particularly Guha, "Radical American Environmentalism and Wilderness Preservation," Cronon, "The Trouble with Wilderness," and other essays republished in Calicott and Nelson, *Great New Wilderness Debate*.

In the recent criticisms and traditional celebrations of the wilderness idea,

I object mainly to the habit of applying the nineteenth-century ideology of pristine and sublime landscapes to late-twentieth-century debates and negotiations over land use boundaries. Although ideological traditions were employed as tools by all sides of the debates, they were among the least effective in shaping the final decisions on wilderness boundaries. Critics of wilderness have also too often equated postwar deliberations in the United States over wildlands with wilderness as an imperial tool for displacing native peoples in both the early American West and colonized regions such as British Africa. In the following case studies, wilderness designation did not displace people. That process had already occurred in the Cascades through treaties, wars, and industrial development. Looking at specific case studies helps to clear away some of the problems caused by universalizing assumptions about the concept of wilderness.

6. This description is not meant to be a thorough catalogue of the range but rather is given as an aid in locating the areas discussed in the case studies in the following chapters. Especially (and regretfully) neglected in these descriptions is the drier, east side of the mountains. For sources on the Cascade Range see Mathews, *Cascade Olympic Natural History*; Beckey, *Cascade Alpine Guide*, 3–12; Schwartz, *Cascade Companion*; McKee, *Cascadia*.

7. Catton, *Wonderland*, 45–47, 63–69. Neither the Forest Service nor the National Park Service existed at this time, but transferring forest reserves to the national park still upset many foresters.

8. George Draffan, Ken Favrholdt, Mitch Friedman, and Bob Mierendorf, "History of the Greater North Cascades Ecosystem," in Friedman and Lindholdt, *Cascadia Wild*, 30; see also Beckey, *Range of Glaciers*, 27, 41–45.

9. Wilkeson, *Wilkeson's Notes on Puget Sound*, 10, 18.

10. Robbins, *Landscapes of Promise*, 229; J. Granville Jensen, "Commercial Timberland Resources," in Jackson and Kimerling, *Atlas of the Pacific Northwest*, 103–7.

11. Hays, *Beauty, Health, and Permanence*. Paul S. Sutter also notes a shift in the broader debate itself in *Driven Wild*, 248.

12. Hirt, *Conspiracy of Optimism*, xx–xxiv; Steen, *U.S. Forest Service*, 280–85.

13. Hays, *Beauty, Health, and Permanence*, 13–39; Hirt, *Conspiracy of Optimism*, xxv–xxvi.

14. Brock Evans, interview by author, 28 July 2001. Evans was responding directly to the historiographical emphasis on the intellectual history of wilder-

ness ideology when he discounted the ideology of wilderness as the underlying conflict in wilderness debates.

15. A. W. Greeley to M. Brock Evans, 3 June 1969, BEP, box 15, folder: Oregon–Mt. Jefferson Wilderness, 1961–69, Incoming Letters U.S.

16. Sutter, *Driven Wild*, 248; Beierle and Cayford, *Democracy in Practice*, 2–6.

17. Langston, *Where Land and Water Meet*, 9. Striking parallels emerge in the same era in the history of nuclear power, as documented in Balogh, *Chain Reaction*, 16–20, 221–301. Also see Caldwell, Hayes, and MacWhirter, *Citizens and the Environment*, xi–xxx.

18. For the intellectual development of wilderness ideology, see Nash, *Wilderness and the American Mind*; Oelschlaeger, *Idea of Wilderness*. For the development of the political movement, see Allin, *Politics of Wilderness Preservation*; Roth, *Wilderness Movement and the National Forests, 1980–1984*; Doug Scott, *Enduring Wilderness*; Sutter, *Driven Wild*; Harvey, *Wilderness Forever*. One of the most impressive and helpful contributions is Jay (James Morton) Turner's 2004 dissertation, "Promise of Wilderness," which examines the history of the Wilderness Society and the wilderness movement since 1964.

19. Hays, "Structure of Environmental Politics since World War II," 721; Hays, *Explorations in Environmental History*, 88–89.

20. Doug Scott, *Enduring Wilderness*, 15.

21. Robert Frost, "Mending Wall," in *Collected Poems, Prose, and Plays*, 39–40.

22. National Wilderness Preservation System, *U.S. Code* 16 (1964), sec. 1131.

23. Cronon, *Changes in the Land*, 12.

24. Eric T. Freyfogle, "Bounded People, Boundless Land," in Knight and Landres, *Stewardship across Boundaries*, 15–21.

25. Allin, *Politics of Wilderness Preservation*; Nash, *Wilderness and the American Mind*, 200–237.

26. Limerick, *Legacy of Conquest*, 55.

27. Fisher, "1932 Handshake Agreement," 187–217; Haeberlin and Gunther, *Indians of Puget Sound*, 12; Allan Smith, *Ethnography of the North Cascades* (1987).

28. Schwantes, *Pacific Northwest*, 142, 173–74, 121.

29. U.S. Congress, Public Land Law Review Commission (Paul W. Gates), *History of Public Land Law Development*, 566.

30. Waldo, *Letters and Journals from the High Cascades of Oregon,* vii; Rakestraw, *History of Forest Conservation,* 45–53. The Willamette National Forest and part of the Deschutes National Forest were both created out of the Cascade Forest Reserve.

31. Rakestraw, *History of Forest Conservation,* 44, 64–66; Steen, *U.S. Forest Service,* 74–75.

32. For a more thorough discussion of the value invested in public land, see James C. Foster, preface to Robbins and Foster, *Land in the American West,* vii.

33. Nash, *Wilderness and the American Mind,* 189; Stegner, "Coda: Wilderness Letter," 153. Stegner's letter, written in 1960 to the Outdoor Recreation Resources Review Commission, is a prominent example of the rhetorical focus on an idealized wilderness in support of preservation. However, in his eloquent and poetic plea for the "idea of wilderness," he grounds his argument in specific places.

34. For a summary of antiwilderness attitudes, see Nash, *Wilderness and the American Mind,* 239–43.

35. Limerick, *Legacy of Conquest,* 55.

1 THE THREE SISTERS, 1950–1964

1. Merriam, *Saving Wilderness,* 2; Olaus J. Murie, "To the Council of the Wilderness Society," 25 July 1951, and Olaus J. Murie to Wm. N. Parke, forester, 26 July 1951, DSP; John Scott, "Three Sisters Primitive Area," 53–54. See also Rakestraw and Rakestraw, *History of the Willamette National Forest,* 111–12.

2. John Scott, "Three Sisters Primitive Area," 53–54; Murie, "To the Council of the Wilderness Society," 2.

3. Murie, "To the Council of the Wilderness Society," 2. See also Merriam, *Saving Wilderness,* 2–4.

4. This feeling is reflected in handwritten notes from a Forest Service meeting of 26 April 1955. See "Notes—Three Sisters Analysis," 26 April 1955, and Information and Education, L. G. Jolley to Supervisor Mt. Baker et al., 10 May 1955, NA-PNW, box 25219, FRC #73A898, folder: Three Sisters Wilderness Area, 1954–66. *Crow's Lumber Digest* called the opposition a "dramatic surprise"; see "People's Forests . . . for Wilderness—How Much," *Crow's Lumber Digest,* 14 February 1957, 28.

5. Steen, *U.S. Forest Service,* 153–56; Pyne, *Fire in America,* 278–79. On

Leopold, see Meine, *Aldo Leopold*; on Carhart, see Baldwin, *Quiet Revolution*; and on Koch, see Koch, *Forty Years a Forester*, 189–92.

6. Gilligan, "Forest Service Primitive and Wilderness Areas"; Doug Scott, *Enduring Wilderness*, 29.

7. Steen, *U.S. Forest Service*, 210–13; Nash, *Wilderness and the American Mind*, 203–6, 220; Glover, *Wilderness Original*, 230–33; Sutter, *Driven Wild*, 252–55.

8. Glover, *Wilderness Original*, 145; see also Sutter, *Driven Wild*.

9. For an extended discussion of the L-20 Regulations and the U Regulations, see Gilligan, "Forest Service Primitive and Wilderness Areas"; Keyser, *Preservation of Wilderness Areas*, 24–26.

10. Merriam, *Saving Wilderness*, 1; Doug Scott, *Enduring Wilderness*, 32–34; Steen, *U.S. Forest Service*, 209–13.

11. U.S. Department of Agriculture, Forest Service, "Fact Sheet for the Proposed Three Sisters Wilderness Area," n.d., NA-PNW, box 25219, FRC #73A898, folder: Three Sisters Wilderness Area, 1954–66.

12. True D. Morse, "Decision of the Secretary of Agriculture Establishing the Three Sisters Wilderness Area," 6 February 1957, 1, NA-PNW, box 25219, FRC #73A898, folder: Three Sisters Wilderness Area, 1954–66.

13. Glover, *Wilderness Original*, 233.

14. J. Granville Jensen, "Commercial Timberland Resources," in Jackson and Kimerling, *Atlas of the Pacific Northwest*, 103–7.

15. For further geological description of the western Oregon Cascades, see McKee, *Cascadia*, 174–90. Also see Orr and Orr, *Geology of Oregon*, which was originally published in 1959 by University of Oregon geologist Ewart Baldwin, who was active with the Friends of the Three Sisters beginning in the early 1960s.

16. For a thorough discussion of the role of the Dinosaur National Monument controversy in the national movement for wilderness legislation, see Harvey, *Symbol of Wilderness*. This debate over a dam at Echo Park dealt as much with questions of National Park Service policy as with wilderness policy, however. See Harvey, *Symbol of Wilderness*, 54–66. In Oregon, as in the final, 1964 version of the Wilderness Act, wilderness was mainly a question of national-forest policy. See Cox et al., *This Well-Wooded Land*, 243; Thomas R. Cox, "Changing Forests, Changing Needs: Using the Pacific Northwest's Westside Forests, Past and Present," in Goble and Hirt, *Northwest Lands*, 468–69.

17. Merriam, *Saving Wilderness*, 3; Rakestraw and Rakestraw, *History of the Willamette National Forest*, 202–3.

18. In *Conspiracy of Optimism*, Hirt provides the most comprehensive discussion of how, throughout these years, estimations of timber yields escalated beyond actual timber supplies.

19. The preliminary proposal in 1951 included a wild area at Waldo Lake. That was removed from the proposal, presumably due to the high volume of timber there. See J. Michael McCloskey, "The Waldo Lake Battle," *Western Outdoor Quarterly* 29, no. 1 (Winter 1962): 3–6.

20. Merriam, *Saving Wilderness*, 2; Morse, "Decision of the Secretary of Agriculture"; E. L. Peterson to Doug McKay, 10 September 1956, KOCP, box 1, folder: Three Sisters, Incoming Correspondence, U.S. Secretary of Agriculture.

21. At this time, many foresters distinguished between wilderness and multiple-use areas, arguing that wilderness was a "departure from [the latter] principle." See "People's Forests," 27; Bultena and Hendee, "Foresters' Views of Interest Group Positions on Forest Policy," 337–42; Hirt, *Conspiracy of Optimism*, 38–39; Steen, *U.S. Forest Service*, 302–7.

22. "Notes—Three Sisters Analysis"; Information and Education, L. G. Jolley to Supervisor Mt. Baker et al.

23. The Industrial Forestry Association (IFA), headquartered in Portland, played a central role in coordinating industry response to wilderness debates up through the Oregon Wilderness Act of 1984. For many years William Hagenstein was director of the IFA. See Hagenstein, "Forestry's Advocate."

24. Merriam, *Saving Wilderness*, 4–5.

25. Karl Onthank to Hubert G. Schenck, 7 October 1955, KOCP, box 1, folder: Three Sisters, Outgoing Correspondence. Other letters in this folder demonstrate Onthank's attempts to bring a national voice to the debate by recruiting efforts outside the local region.

26. Hays, *Beauty, Health, and Permanence*, 120. Also see Hays, "Structure of Environmental Politics since World War Two," 719–20.

27. Karl W. Onthank to Dr. Olaus Murie et al., 9 February 1957, 2, DSP.

28. Leslie Tooze, "Opponents to Reductions of Primitive Area Heard," *Portland Oregonian*, 17 February 1955, 5; "Panel Scores Logging Plan for Three Sisters," *Portland Oregonian*, 12 February 1955, 7.

29. A. F. Hartung, international president, to Dave Charlton, 12 January 1955, 1, NA-PNW, box 25219, FRC #73A898, folder: Three Sisters Wilderness Area, 1954–66. Union leaders were strong allies in the efforts to maintain

protection for Horse Creek. Al Kaufman, secretary of the Machinists Union in Eugene, was a founding member of the Friends of the Three Sisters.

30. Ibid., 1–2.

31. Karl W. Onthank to Janet Calkins, 28 February 1955, 1, KOCP, box 1, folder: Three Sisters, Outgoing Correspondence.

32. Howard Zahniser, "Statement on the Three Sisters Wilderness Area," 17 February 1955, 5, DSP.

33. Mrs. Karl W. [Ruth] Onthank, "Further Remarks," 1, KOCP, box 10, folder: Sierra Club Projects, Three Sisters.

34. On the role of these scientists in the Friends of the Three Sisters, see Merriam, *Saving Wilderness*, 35–46.

35. Bonita J. Miller, "'Overmature Timber' and Rotting Logs," n.d., KOCP, box 1, folder: Three Sisters Associated Documents.

36. Karl W. Onthank to Dave Brower, 31 May 1956, 1, KOCP, box 10, folder: Sierra Club Correspondence, Brower, David R.

37. Douglas W. Scott, *Wilderness-Forever Future*, 10–13.

38. Howard Zahniser, "Statement on the Three Sisters," 6.

39. Karl W. Onthank to Mrs. G. P. Schumacher, 17 January 1955, KOCP, box 1, folder: Three Sisters, Outgoing Correspondence.

40. Karl W. Onthank to Janet Calkins, 2.

41. Gilligan, "Forest Service Primitive and Wilderness Areas," 2; Wengert, "Ideological Basis of Conservation and Natural Resources Policies and Programs," 71.

42. David Brower to Ezra Benson, secretary of agriculture, 26 January 1956, and Sigurd Olson to Fred Packard, 4 February 1956, DSP.

43. McCloskey, "Wilderness Movement at the Crossroads," 347–48.

44. Brock Evans, memo from Brock Evans to Oregon Cascades—Campaign File, 15 January 1973, 1, DSP.

45. Karl W. Onthank to Dave Brower, 1.

46. Manning, "You Don't Have to Be Old to Be an Elder," 59.

47. U.S. Department of Agriculture, "Three Sisters Action Adds 32,000 Acres to Oregon Wilderness," 8 February 1957, NA-PNW, box 25219, FRC #73A898, folder: Three Sisters Wilderness Area, 1954–66.

48. Charlotte E. Mauk, "Now if Ever," statement presented for the Sierra Club at the annual convention of the Federation of Western Outdoor Clubs, Nesika Lodge, OR, 4 September 1954, 1, KOCP, box 10, folder: Sierra Club, Projects, Three Sisters.

49. Zahniser, "Statement on the Three Sisters," 6. Also see further elaboration on wilderness and zoning in Hirt, *Conspiracy of Optimism*, 129, 162–66.

50. Karl W. Onthank to Dr. Olaus Murie et al., 2. Forest Service Region 6, headquartered in Portland, encompasses all the national forests in Oregon and Washington.

51. Merriam, *Saving Wilderness*, 6.

52. Richard L. Neuberger, press release, 8 February 1957, and Wayne Morse, "Morse Warns against Wilderness Decision," 18 January 1957, KOCP, box 1, folder: Three Sisters Editorials.

53. Thomas Cox makes this point in "Changing Forests, Changing Needs," 468. Also see Hays, *Beauty, Health, and Permanence*, 118–19.

54. Howard Zahniser to Frank Church, 11 April 1961, 4, KOCP, box 1, folder: Three Sisters, Associated Documents.

55. "Primitive Heritage at Stake," *Redmond (OR) Spokesman*, 14 February 1955, 2; "The Three Sisters Wilderness Decision—the Last Word or Just the Beginning?" *Eugene (OR) Register-Guard*, 10 February 1957, 10A.

56. Much has been written on conservation and the Progressive Movement. The standard work remains Hays, *Conservation and the Gospel of Efficiency*. For a discussion of a similar situation in the realm of nuclear science, where policy decision making excluded public participation, see Balogh, *Chain Reaction*, 1–20.

57. The leading interpretations of this shift in postwar environmental politics are Hays, *Beauty, Health, and Permanence*, see especially 13–39; and Hirt, *Conspiracy of Optimism*.

58. Karl W. Onthank to Dr. Olaus Murie et al., 2.

2 THE NORTH CASCADES, 1956–1968

1. Karl Onthank to Dr. Olaus Murie et al., 9 February 1957, 1, DSP. The announcement that Onthank refers to is *Glacier Peak Land Management Study*, a copy of which is available in NFPAR, box 192a, folder: Glacier Wilderness.

2. Karl W. Onthank to David Brower, 9 September 1956, KOCP, box 10, folder: Sierra Club Correspondence, Brower, David R.

3. Frome, *Battle for the Wilderness*, 135.

4. George C. Wall to A. Z. Nelson, 3 July 1957, NFPAR, box 192A, folder: Glacier Wilderness.

5. *Glacier Peak Land Management Study*, 5.

6. Allan Smith, *Ethnography of the North Cascades*; Beckey, *Range of Glaciers*, 21–23.

7. Manning, "You Don't Have to Be Old to Be an Elder," 58.

8. David R. Simons to J. Herbert Stone, regional forester, 6 April 1957, 1, KOCP, box 10, folder: Sierra Club Correspondence, Simons, David R.; *Glacier Peak Land Management Study*, 1; North Cascades Study Team, *North Cascades*, 30; Frome, *Battle for the Wilderness*, 135–36.

9. North Cascades Study Team, *North Cascades*, 30; Frome, *Battle for the Wilderness*, 136; Frank B. Folsom, assistant regional forester, to Karl W. Onthank, 7 January 1957, 1, KOCP, box 1, folder: Three Sisters, Incoming Correspondence, U.S. Forest Service, Pacific Northwest Region.

10. Frome, *Battle for the Wilderness*, 136.

11. Quoted in Manning, "You Don't Have to Be Old to Be an Elder," 59.

12. Polly Dyer, interview by author, 14 September 2001.

13. "Will We Discover the Northern Cascades in Time?" 13.

14. Sommarstrom, "Wild Land Preservation Crisis," 48–49. Philip Zalesky was the first president of the NCCC, but Goldsworthy was president through most of the North Cascades debate. See Goldsworthy, "Protecting the North Cascades."

15. Brower's "missing million" did not include the 801,000-acre North Cascades Primitive Area along the U.S.-Canada border, established in 1931 and expanded in 1935 (Brower, "The Missing Million," 10, 12).

16. *Glacier Peak Land Management Study*; J. Herbert Stone, "Proposed Establishment of Glacier Peak Wilderness Area," 16 February 1959, NFPAR, box 192A, folder: Glacier Wilderness.

17. Frome, *Battle for the Wilderness*, 136.

18. Brock Evans to editor, *Journal of Forestry*, 15 July 1968, 2, SAFR, box 401, folder: Responses on Receiving Copies of "Decision in the North Cascades."

19. McConnell, "Wilderness World," 14.

20. George C. Wall to A. Z. Nelson, 1; Dyer, interview by author.

21. George Wall to J. Herbert Stone, 25 March 1957, 1, NFPAR, box 192A, folder: Glacier Wilderness.

22. Clepper, "A Calm View of a Heated Subject," 2.

23. Hirt, *Conspiracy of Optimism*, 36–39; Frome, *Battle for the Wilderness*, 137–38. Wilderness advocates would turn the rhetorical tables on foresters,

calling logging a "single-use" operation because it destroyed, or at least delayed for many years, several other recreational and ecological values of the land and streams. John Hammond, of Portland, wrote to Senator Hatfield in 1969: "It is not 'multiple use' when any area outside dedicated wilderness and park lands is fair game for fulfilling the allowable cut. That is to make a *single-use* paramount, to give it the highest priority" (John L. Hammond to Honorable Mark O. Hatfield, 4 April 1969, BEP, box 15, folder: Oregon–Mt. Jefferson Wilderness, 1963–69, Incoming Letters, A–K).

24. Hirt, *Conspiracy of Optimism*, 39.

25. On Mount Rainier National Park, see Catton, *Wonderland*. On Olympic National Park, see Lien, *Olympic Battleground*.

26. Hirt, *Conspiracy of Optimism*, 37–39. An early example of interagency rivalry is clearly expressed in H. H. Chapman, "A Policy to Coordinate National Parks and National Forests," 1 June 1917, reprint with a new foreword from 28 July 1937 found in SAFR, box 68, folder: Referendum on National Parks, Forests, and Wilderness Areas; Herman Haupt Chapman was president of the Society of American Foresters. Also see Steen, *U.S. Forest Service*, 113–22.

27. Ralph D. Hodges Jr. to E. L. Kolbe, Western Pine Association, 9 October 1959, NFPAR, box 192A, folder: Glacier Wilderness.

28. Industrial Forestry Association, "Recommended Boundary for Glacier Peak Wilderness Area," 27 October 1959, 2, NFPAR, box 192A, folder: Glacier Wilderness.

29. J. D. Bronson, Statement of J. D. Bronson, President Western Pine Association, Glacier Peak Wilderness Area Hearing, Wenatchee, WA, 16 October 1959, 1, 3, NFPAR, box 192A, folder: Glacier Wilderness.

30. Good examples of this internal, policy debate are collected in SAFR, box 401, folder: Forest Policies.

31. *Journal of Forestry*, 64, no. 8 (August 1966): 525.

32. Ibid., 525–26.

33. Jay Gruenfeld, Personal Statement, Glacier Peak Wilderness Area Hearing, Wenatchee, WA, 16 October 1959, 2–3, NFPAR, box 192A, folder: Glacier Wilderness.

34. Warren G. Magnuson and Henry M. Jackson, press release, 18 March 1957, and Ernest L. Kolbe, Western Pine Association, to A. Z. Nelson, National Lumber Manufacturers Assn., 15 March 1957, NFPAR, box 192A, folder: Glacier Wilderness.

35. Douglas, *My Wilderness*, 124.

36. Ruth [Onthank] to Gerry [Sharpe], 9 August 1961, 2, 5, KOCP, box 10, folder: Sierra Club, Outgoing Correspondence.

37. Manning, "You Don't Have to Be Old to Be an Elder," 57–59. For more on Simons, see David Brower's 27 December 1960 obituary of him in KOCP, box 10, folder: Sierra Club Correspondence, Simons, David R.

38. David Simons to Dr. Karl W. Onthank, 13 April 1957, 1, KOCP, box 10, folder: Sierra Club Correspondence, Simons, David R. Emphasis retained from the original.

39. Wayburn, "Join the Glacier Peak Task Force"; outings schedule in *Sierra Club Bulletin* 41, no. 3 (March 1956): 18–19, 24–25.

40. McConnell, "Wilderness World," 14.

41. H. R. Glascock to subscribing members [Western Forestry and Conservation Association], 31 July 1959, 1–2, NFPAR, box 192A, folder: Glacier Wilderness; *Wilderness Alps of Stehekin*, 16mm film, written and narrated by David Brower; Goldsworthy, "Protecting the North Cascades," 79. Polly Dyer, interview by author, also emphasized the importance of Brower's film in the publicity campaign.

42. Stegner, *This Is Dinosaur*; Harvey, *Symbol of Wilderness*, 257–59; Karl W. Onthank to David Brower, 1.

43. Manning, *North Cascades*; Manning, *Wild Cascades*, 14.

44. Sommarstrom, "Wild Land Preservation Crisis," 68–69; Rothman, "A Regular Ding-Dong Fight," 141–61.

45. Gilligan, "Forest Service Primitive and Wilderness Areas," 2.

46. David R. Simons to editor, *Eugene Register-Guard*, 2 January 1960, 2, KOCP, box 10, folder: Sierra Club Correspondence, Simons, David R.; "North Cascades Park," *Living Wilderness*, no. 85 (Winter–Spring 1964): 36.

47. Quoted in Runte, *National Parks*, 210.

48. North Cascades Study Team, *North Cascades*, 21.

49. Runte, *National Parks*, 209–12.

50. Brooks, *Pursuit of Wilderness*, 47–56. In the 1960s Kennecott Copper Corporation proposed construction of a large mine on its claims at Miner's Ridge, just north of Glacier Peak itself, in the heart of the Glacier Peak Wilderness Area. The possibility of a strip mine at this location created a storm of controversy and pushed many to support a national park, where mining would not be allowed, instead of a wilderness area, where mining could continue. A fine essay on this controversy, which pits David Brower against geologist Charles Park, is McPhee's *Encounters with the Archdruid*, 1–75.

51. See Glover, *Wilderness Original*, 233; Washington State Planning Council, *Cascade Mountains Study*. Lauren Danner, of Olympia, Washington, is currently working on a book that will document this history.

52. Quoted in H. R. Glascock to subscribing members, 2. Emphasis retained from the original. Ruth Onthank expressed concern that the focus on a national park for the Oregon Cascades, modeled after the North Cascades campaign, would undermine all the previous work toward wilderness protection and would only serve to accelerate Forest Service timber sales in disputed areas. See Ruth Onthank to Recter Johnson, 7 February 1961, 2, KOCP, box 10, folder: Sierra Club, Outgoing Correspondence.

53. Robert Marshall to Irving M. Clar, 12 November 1938, NA-PNW, box 75835, FRC #70B0825, folder: 2320 Wilderness and Primitive Areas, North Cascade Primitive Area, 1934–1962.

54. Zalesky quoted in Sommarstrom, "Wild Land Preservation Crisis," 49. Also see more on Zalesky's position in Goldsworthy, "Protecting the North Cascades," 43–47.

55. David R. Brower to Karl Onthank, 25 November 1955, 2, KOCP, box 10, folder: Sierra Club Correspondence, Brower, David R.

56. Simons, *Need for Scenic Resource Conservation*.

57. Quoted in Manning, "You Don't Have to Be Old to Be an Elder," 87.

58. Dyer, interview by author.

59. E. L. Peterson, "Decision of the Secretary of Agriculture Establishing the Glacier Peak Wilderness Area, Mt. Baker and Wenatchee National Forests, Washington," 6 September 1960, 2, NA-PNW, Dec. files 2100–2310 Special Planning Areas, 1927–73, box 6, folder: Moratorium Areas [1 of 2].

60. Sommarstrom, "Wild Land Preservation Crisis," 46, suggests that the national-park campaign played a significant role in frightening the Department of Agriculture into expanding the wilderness proposal against the wishes of the Forest Service.

61. John A. Baker to Honorable Thomas M. Pelly, 13 September 1962, 2, NA-PNW, Dec. files 2100–2310 Special Planning Areas, 1927–73, box 6, folder: Moratorium Areas [1 of 2]. The High Mountain Policy was developed in response to concerns expressed by senators from both Oregon and Washington, who urged the Forest Service to delay and reevaluate development plans for Waldo Lake and the Minam River in Oregon and the Cougar Lakes and North Cascades areas of Washington. Most of each of these areas was eventually protected as wilderness or national park. For the origins of the policy,

see "Freeman Issues North Cascades Stop Order," *Living Wilderness*, no. 77 (Summer–Fall 1961): 28.

62. Quoted from Orville Freeman and Stewart Udall to President John F. Kennedy, 28 January 1963, reprinted in North Cascades Study Team, *North Cascades*, 153–54; McCloskey, *Prospectus;* McCloskey, *In the Thick of It,* 42–43.

63. McConnell, "Northern Cascades," 22.

64. David Simons to Dr. Karl W. Onthank.

65. North Cascades Study Team, *North Cascades*, 18–20.

66. Ibid., 85–119. See Goldsworthy, "Protecting the North Cascades," 74; Evans, interview by author, 28 July 2001.

67. *U.S. Code 16*, sec. 90e-1.

68. Sommarstrom, "Wild Land Preservation Crisis," 94–95, 141–55. Mark Harvey emphasizes the importance of interagency rivalry in *Symbol of Wilderness*, 74–106.

69. Brock Evans to editor, *Journal of Forestry*, 1.

70. North Cascades Study Team, *North Cascades*, 21.

71. Sommarstrom, "Wild Land Preservation Crisis," 144.

72. McCloskey, "A Conservation Agenda for 1969."

73. Sommarstrom, "Wild Land Preservation Crisis," 78.

74. Evans, interview by author. Brower had apparently used this metaphor earlier in other contexts and reportedly borrowed it from Senator Richard Neuberger; McCloskey, interview by author, 7 November 2003; McCloskey, *In the Thick of It,* 44.

3 MOUNT JEFFERSON, 1961–1968

1. McCloskey, "Wilderness Movement at the Crossroads," 346–61.

2. Holway R. Jones, Statement of Holway R. Jones, 26 October 1966, 4–5, BEP, box 29, folder: Mt. Jefferson 1966 Hearings.

3. J. Michael McCloskey et al. to J. Herbert Stone, regional forester, 30 December 1963, BEP, box 29, folder: Mt. Jefferson 1964 Hearings; Stewart Brandborg, "A Call for Participation in Mt. Jefferson Wilderness Area Hearing, 26 October 1966," n.d., 4, BEP, box 29, folder: Mt. Jefferson 1966 Hearings.

4. Outdoor Recreation Resources Review Committee, *ORRRC Study Report 3*, 120, 335.

5. A. Robert Smith, "Oregon Wilderness Area Arguments Heard by Lands Subcommittee in Nation's Capital," *Portland Oregonian*, 20 February 1968, 7.

6. Rodger Pegues to D. R. Gibney, forest supervisor, 2 December 1966, and "National Forest Timber for Sale, Willamette National Forest, South Whitewater #3 Sale," November 1966, BEP, box 15, folder: Oregon–Mt. Jefferson Wilderness, 1961–69, Incoming Letters.

7. Rodger W. Pegues, "Mt. Jefferson Wilderness Proposal: A Report and Recommendation on the Proposal to Establish a Mt. Jefferson Wilderness Area in Oregon," 7 October 1966, 3, BEP, box 29, folder: Mt. Jefferson 1966 Hearings.

8. Jones, Statement of Holway R. Jones, 6–7; Polly Dyer, interview by author, 14 September 2001.

9. J. Michael McCloskey, "Draft of Proposed Federal Legislation to Restrict Cutting near Dedicated Areas," 14 January 1962, BEP, box 29, folder: Administrative Procedures.

10. See National Wilderness Preservation System, *U.S. Code* 16 (1964), sec. 1132(b). On the primitive area reviews, see Roth, *Wilderness Movement and the National Forests: 1964–1980*, 11–22; Douglas W. Scott, *Wilderness-Forever Future*, 16–20. In 1967 the San Rafael Primitive Area in California was the first primitive area that Congress declared as wilderness. The level and intensity of citizen activism in favor of an expanded wilderness area there surprised many in Congress and the Forest Service and set the tone for debates to follow. The Pasayten Wilderness Area, along with the northern section of North Cascades National Park, was created out of the North Cascades Primitive Area, but it never went through the Forest Service's primitive area review process. The passage of the North Cascades National Park Act in Congress overruled this agency review.

11. Orville L. Freeman, introduction to Baldwin, *Quiet Revolution*, x.

12. See *A Proposal: Mt. Jefferson Wilderness* (1966), copy in BEP, box 29, folder: Mt. Jefferson 1966 Hearings.

13. U.S. Department of Agriculture, Forest Service, *In the Matter of: Mount Jefferson Wilderness Proposal*, 8.

14. Ibid.

15. See USDA Forest Service, *In the Matter of: Mount Jefferson Wilderness Proposal*.

16. Evans, "Proposed Mount Jefferson Wilderness," 30.

17. J. Michael McCloskey et al. to J. Herbert Stone.

18. Concern over the impact of nearby roads on the wilderness character of protected areas was widespread by the early 1960s. A very clear statement of the problem can be found in Outdoor Recreation Resources Review Commission, *ORRRC Study Report 3*, 4.

19. U.S. Department of Agriculture, Forest Service, *In the Matter of: Mount Jefferson Wilderness Proposal*, 66, 68.

20. Lloyd Tupling to Albert J. McClure, 25 June 1968, SAFR, box 401, folder: Public Affairs—Miscellaneous—c. 1963–70.

21. Karl Onthank, "U.S. Forest Service Hearing on Reclassification of Mt. Jefferson Primitive Area," 2 June 1964, 2, BEP, box 29, folder: Mt. Jefferson 1964 Hearings. Conservationists split over which tactics to pursue in limiting logging in the area: a broader wilderness, a buffer zone, or a national park. Although the Oregon Cascades Conservation Council was formed in 1960 to promote a park, the idea never gained unified support and remained in the shadow of the North Cascades park campaign. See Simons, "These Are the Shining Mountains," 1–13; Evans, "Proposed Mount Jefferson Wilderness." Three Oregon senators, Wayne Morse, Bob Packwood, and Mark Hatfield, all introduced bills in the Senate between 1966 and 1972 to study the central Oregon Cascades for a possible national park.

22. Larry Williams to Kenneth K. Baldwin [1968], and Prince Helfrich to M. Brock Evans, 21 February 1968, BEP, box 15, folder: Oregon–Mt. Jefferson Wilderness, 1961–69, Incoming Letters A–K. Also see Statement of Senator Mark O. Hatfield on S. 2751, 19 February 1968, 1–2, BEP, box 15, folder: Oregon–Mt. Jefferson Wilderness, 1961–69, Speeches and Writings.

23. Outdoor Recreation Resources Review Commission, *ORRRC Study Report 3*, 327, 329.

24. Statement of Senator Mark O. Hatfield on S. 2751, 3, and Statement of Senator Wayne Morse on S. 2751, 20 February 1968, 2, BEP, box 15, folder: Oregon–Mt. Jefferson Wilderness, 1961–69, Speeches and Writings; A. Robert Smith, "Oregon Wilderness Area Arguments Heard," 7.

25. "Lumber Experts Begin Log Export Sessions," *Oregonian*, 21 February 1968, 19.

26. Testimony of David F. Berger, in U.S. Department of Agriculture, Forest Service, *In the Matter of: Mount Jefferson Wilderness Proposal*, 55. For a discussion of wilderness and Indian sovereignty, see Krahe, "Sovereign Prescription for Preservation."

27. Confederated Tribes of the Warm Springs Reservation, *People of Warm Springs*, 34–35.

28. "Minam and McQuinn," *Oregonian*, 26 May 1972, 40.

29. Frome, *Battle for the Wilderness*, 153.

30. Pyles, "Multiple Use of the National Forests," 120.

31. Orville L. Freeman, Address to the 10th Biennial Wilderness Conference, 7 April 1967, 4, USFSHQ, folder: Wilderness: General—Speeches. A good example of how the Forest Service proudly publicized its own heritage of preserving wilderness is the self-congratulatory pamphlet U.S. Department of Agriculture, Forest Service, *Wilderness*. It is clearly intended to divert criticism of Forest Service management of primitive areas and suggest that the Wilderness Act, then being debated in Congress, was not necessary. On the purity doctrine, see James Turner, "Wilderness East," 19–27.

32. U.S. Department of Agriculture, Forest Service, *In the Matter of: Mount Jefferson Wilderness Proposal*, 8.

33. Ibid., 38.

34. Stewart Brandborg, "A Special Memorandum to Members and Cooperators," 26 October 1966, 4, BEP, box 29, folder: Mt. Jefferson 1966 Hearings.

35. Ibid.; Statement of the Sierra Club on S. 2751, 19 February 1968, 3, BEP, box 15, folder: Oregon–Mt. Jefferson Wilderness, 1961–69, Speeches and Writings.

36. Douglas W. Scott, interview by author, 29 April 2001. Church quoted in Douglas W. Scott, "Congress's Practical Criteria for Designating Wilderness," 31.

37. RWP [Rodger Pegues] to Brandy [Stewart Brandborg], n.d., 3, BEP, box 29, folder: Mt. Jefferson 1966 Hearings.

38. J. Michael McCloskey et al. to J. Herbert Stone, 30 December 1963, 2. The Wilderness Act clearly allows preexisting use of motorized boats to continue in a wilderness area. See Special Provisions, sec. 4(d)(1), of the Wilderness Act. See also Roth, *Wilderness Movement and the National Forests: 1964–1980*, 14–15.

39. "Salem Man Leading Lake Change Drive," *Capital Journal*, 18 February 1969, 6; "Wilderness to Return," *Oregonian* 8 April 1969, 13; "Bills and Joint Resolutions Introduced," *Congressional Record* 125, pt. 9 (8 May 1969): 11798.

40. Senate Interior Committee, *Report on the Endangered American Wilderness Act*, 95th Cong., 1st sess., 11 October 1977, S. Rep. 95-490, 8; Douglas W. Scott, interview by author.

41. In 2004, from his seat as chair of the House Resources Committee, Congressman Richard Pombo, of California, used purity arguments to block wilderness proposals. See Alex Fryer, "Wilderness Backers Look to Nethercutt for Congressional Boost," *Seattle Times*, 22 March 2004.

1. The Seattle Mountaineers had proposed a similar road earlier in the century to promote preservation of the region and improve access to backcountry recreation, but in the postwar recreation and logging boom, the club switched its position and opposed road construction. Paul Sutter (*Driven Wild*) suggests that this shift to oppose road construction occurred among the leadership of the Wilderness Society during the interwar period and that limiting roads for recreation was their primary motivation for organizing the modern wilderness movement. In the Northwest, this shift does not seem to have occurred until after World War II.

2. As a limited area, one could argue that the Alpine Lakes was not entirely de facto wilderness. The Wilderness Act, however, did not recognize limited areas as it did primitive areas, where it mandated the Forest Service to conduct wilderness reviews before altering their status.

3. A large collection of correspondence on Cooper Lake can be found in NA-PNW, box 934902, FRC #76B2307, folder: Alpine Lakes Limited Area Out-Service Correspondence, 1957–1963. Also see the folder Wilderness and Primitives [sic] Area. Much of the land in the Cooper Lake area was privately owned by the Northern Pacific Railroad Company, and some of the roads were built to access private timber. Public and private land alternated in square-mile patches resembling a checkerboard, a direct legacy of the Northern Pacific Railroad Land Grant of 1864. The Northern Pacific had lost ownership of much of the central Alpine Lakes region by the 1930s due to congressional and judicial action, allowing the Forest Service to manage the alpine core as a single unit. Some of the land grant became part of the Alpine Lakes Wilderness Area through federal purchase and exchange in the late 1970s. Other parts remain under private ownership of a variety of timber companies. See Cotroneo, "United States v. Northern Pacific Railway Company," 110–11.

4. A. W. Greeley, deputy chief, to Dave James, Simpson Timber Company, 17 February 1964, NA-PNW, box 934902, FRC #76B2307, folder: Alpine Lakes Limited Area In-Service Correspondence, 1955–1964.

5. Herbert Stone approved a road along Mineral Creek to access potential mining sites being explored by the Phelps Dodge Corporation just northwest of Cooper Lake and a short spur road to access railroad land just west of Deception Falls, where he authorized a timber sale. He also approved construction

of the Smith Brook Road to access a timber sale at Rainy Pass, north of Stevens Pass. Although today the area this far north is not commonly considered in the Alpine Lakes, the road entered the limited area, which extended north to the Glacier Peak Wilderness Area, and thus Stone's approval was required before building the road. J. Herbert Stone to forest supervisor, Wenatchee N.F., 1 May 1963, and J. Herbert Stone, regional forester, to forest supervisor, Snoqualmie N.F., 14 March 1963, NA-PNW, box 934902, FRC #76B2307, folder: Alpine Lakes Limited Area In-Service Correspondence, 1955–1964; J. K. Blair, forest supervisor, to regional forester, 6 August 1965, NA-PNW, box 934902, FRC #76B2307, folder: Wilderness and Primitives Area.

6. In 1957 Polly Dyer suggested that all limited areas be automatically included in the wilderness system, then being proposed to Congress. See "Wilderness Bill Hearings," *Living Wilderness* 61 (Summer–Fall 1957): 29.

7. John R. Hazle, president, the Mountaineers, to J. Herbert Stone, regional forester, 30 May 1959, NA-PNW, box 934902, FRC #76B2307, folder: Alpine Lakes Limited Area Out-Service Correspondence, 1957–1963.

8. This point was made as an argument for including the lower valleys west of Glacier Peak into the wilderness or national park. See McConnell, "Wilderness World," 14.

9. Warth, "Wilderness Is for Families, Too!" 7. Though insufficient as a study of environmental politics in the Northwest, May's *Voice in the Wilderness* provides a very good example of the argument that preservation was elitist.

10. John Warth, board of directors, North Cascades Conservation Council, to Orville Freeman, secretary of agriculture, 20 June 1961, NA-PNW, box 934902, FRC #76B2307, folder: Alpine Lakes Limited Area In-Service Correspondence, 1955–1964. See also "You Hike From Lake to Lake," *Sunset: The Magazine of Western Living* 127, no. 1 (July 1961): 22–24; "Most Beautiful Lake?" *Seattle Times Sunday Pictorial*, 18 October 1959, 36.

11. North Cascades Conservation Council, the Mountaineers, the Mazamas, and Sierra Club, Pacific Northwest Chapter, "A Proposal for an Alpine Lakes Wilderness Area, Washington," December 1963, 1–2, copy in NA-PNW, box 934902, FRC #76B2307, folder: 2320 Alpine Lakes Wilderness; Evans, "Alpine Lakes: Stepchild of the North Cascades," 24. Many letters from individuals and organizations appealing to the Forest Service to delay timber sales are stored in the Alpine Lakes and Wilderness folders in NA-PNW, box 934902, FRC #76B2307.

12. Orville L. Freeman to John F. Warth, 28 August 1961, NA-PNW, box

934902, FRC #76B2307, folder: Alpine Lakes Limited Area In-Service Correspondence, 1955–1964.

13. Evans, "Alpine Lakes: Stepchild of the North Cascades." For a good expression of the growing frustration, see Brower, "Environmental Activist," 64–65. One exception to the neglect of conservationist pleas is the secretary of agriculture's 1960 decision to overrule the Forest Service and protect parts of the Suiattle and White Chuck Valleys in the Glacier Peak Wilderness Area, although too much of these forested valleys were still left unprotected to fully appease wilderness advocates at the time.

14. See John R. Hazle to J. Herbert Stone, 10 January 1959, and Stone's response of 22 January 1959, in NA-PNW, box 934902, FRC #76B2307, folder: Alpine Lakes Limited Area In-Service Correspondence, 1955–1964.

15. John R. Hazle to J. Herbert Stone, 30 May 1959, 1; and S. B. Olson, forester-Snoqualmie, to forest supervisor, 21 May 1959, 2, NA-PNW, box 934902, FRC #76B2307, folder: Alpine Lakes Limited Area In-Service Correspondence, 1955–1964.

16. John F. Warth to Orville Freeman, 20 June 1961, NA-PNW, box 934902, FRC #76B2307, folder: Alpine Lakes Limited Area In-Service Correspondence, 1955–1964.

17. S. B. Olson to forest supervisor, 21 May 1959, 2. Olson's use of the term "single use" is loaded with irony and is deeply entrenched in the rhetorical battle over "multiple use." Wilderness advocates labeled Forest Service timber policies as single-use activities because clear-cuts had very few other uses. Both sides tried to gain the upper hand by claiming that only their own policies represented multiple use.

18. J. Herbert Stone to John R. Hazle, 1 July 1959, NA-PNW, box 934902, FRC #76B2307, folder: Alpine Lakes Limited Area In-Service Correspondence, 1955–1964; J. Herbert Stone to John R. Hazle, 3 December 1959, NA-PNW, box 934902, FRC #76B2307, folder: Alpine Lakes Limited Area Out-Service Correspondence, 1957–1963.

19. Pauline Dyer, president, Federation of Western Outdoor Clubs, to Kenneth Blair, supervisor, Wenatchee National Forest, 10 February 1959, NA-PNW, box 934902, FRC #76B2307, folder: Alpine Lakes Limited Area Out-Service Correspondence, 1957–1963.

20. J. K. Blair, forest supervisor, to Pauline Dyer, president, Federation of Western Outdoor Clubs, 17 February 1959, NA-PNW, box 934902, FRC #76B2307, folder Alpine Lakes Limited Area Out-Service Correspondence, 1957–1963.

21. Kaufman, *Forest Ranger*. After World War II, this attitude became further ingrained; Hirt, *Conspiracy of Optimism*, xix–xxii.

22. John R. Hazle to J. Herbert Stone, 3 October 1959, and J. Herbert Stone to John R. Hazle, 3 December 1959, NA-PNW, box 934902, FRC #76B2307, folder: Alpine Lakes Limited Area Out-Service Correspondence, 1957–1963. It is interesting to compare Stone's language—public opinion is "cumbersome"—to complaints in 2002 by Dale Bosworth, Forest Service chief, that public scrutiny and appeals lead to "analysis paralysis." U.S. Congress, House, Committee on Resources, Subcommittee on Forests and Forest Health, *Oversight Hearing on Process Gridlock on the National Forests*, 107th Cong., 2nd sess., 12 June 2002, 2.

23. Snoqualmie and Wenatchee National Forests, "Administratively Confidential: A Management Proposal for Alpine Lakes Wilderness Area, Lake Dorothy Scenic Area, Enchantment Wild Area," [1964], 1, NA-PNW, box 934902, FRC #76B2307, folder: 2320 Alpine Lakes Wilderness.

24. Carl A. Newport, Written Testimony of Carl A. Newport to the Committee on Interior and Insular Affairs Subcommittee on National Parks and Recreation, 28 June 1975, 4, copy in LMP, box 212.

25. Evans, "Alpine Lakes: Stepchild of the North Cascades."

26. North Cascades Conservation Council et al., "Proposal for an Alpine Lakes Wilderness Area," 4–5; J. Michael McCloskey, interview by author, 7 November 2003. For example, there was little opposition at that time to Forest Service plans to build roads over Cady Pass and Curry Gap in what since 1984 is the Henry M. Jackson Wilderness Area.

27. Snoqualmie and Wenatchee National Forests, "Administratively Confidential."

28. Brock Evans, interview by author, 28 July 2001; Brock Evans, NW Rep., to Alpine Lakes–General File et al., 27 November 1972, 1, BEP, box 19, folder: Incoming Letters: Alpine Lakes–Eight Mile Creek.

29. Douglas W. Scott, *Wilderness-Forever Future*, 16–19; Douglas W. Scott, interview by author, 29 April 2001; Harvey, *Wilderness Forever*, 237–38.

30. Quoted in Douglas W. Scott, *Wilderness-Forever Future*, 18.

31. Quoted in ibid.

32. Ibid., 21; Douglas W. Scott, interview by author; Tom Price, "From Hardware to Software," 20; Roth, *Wilderness Movement and the National Forests: 1964–1980*, 24–34.

33. Roth, *Wilderness Movement and the National Forests: 1964–1980*, 33;

Douglas W. Scott, interview by author. Aspinall might have said the same about Henry M. Jackson, who leveraged the North Cascades bill past Aspinall's opposition in 1968.

34. Quoted in Roth, *Wilderness Movement and the National Forests: 1964–1980*, 32.

35. Some suggest that the Alpine Lakes was the first of the truly de facto wilderness bills because the Lincoln-Scapegoat bill concerned lands contiguous to the Bob Marshall Wilderness Area. The difference is too obscure to be of great importance here, though federal courts made such a distinction when they gave special status to contiguous lands in the Parker Case in 1970. See ibid., 19–22.

36. Patterson, *Grand Expectations*, 624; Douglas W. Scott, *Wilderness-Forever Future*, 16.

37. David Knibb, of the Alpine Lakes Protection Society (ALPS), and Brock Evans were both lawyers who used lawsuits as a tool to challenge Forest Service decisions. Knibb and ALPS filed lawsuits to stop construction of a road up the Middle Fork Snoqualmie River to access mining claims at Dutch Miller Gap in the heart of the Alpine Lakes. They also filed a lawsuit against the Forest Service for assisting the Pack River Lumber Company in constructing a road across public land to access its timber on private land in the Coulter Creek drainage, part of the area proposed for wilderness by ALPS. They argued unsuccessfully in court that such action illegally undermined the right of Congress to make decisions on wilderness boundaries. "Legislation by chain saw," they called it. See folders on both suits in ALPSP.

38. Evans, interview by author; Knibb, *Backyard Wilderness*, 22–26. Evans seems to remember the meeting precisely, though Knibb's account says that Evans was not there. Knibb was not at Hyas Lake that day.

39. Knibb, *Backyard Wilderness*, 22–31; "Alpine Lakes Proposals: Status Report, August 1973," 2, LMP, box 212.

40. Lloyd Meeds to David G. Knibb, 7 April 1970, LMP, box 212, folder: Subject Series—Alpine Lakes.

41. Knox Marshall, vice president, Forestry, to Owen Sawyer, Pack River Lumber Company et al., 13 January 1971, 1, NFPAR, box 191, folder: Alpine Lakes (II). The sheer volume of files collected by NFPA on the Alpine Lakes, in comparison to any other wilderness proposal, demonstrates the importance they attached to this issue.

42. Benneth to Burns, "Coalition on Alpine Lakes," 25 April 1973, and Albert

Stanley, president, Washington State Sportsmen's Council et al., to Representative Lloyd Meeds, 20 April 1973, NFPAR, box 191, folder: Alpine Lakes (II).

43. John Hall to Sonja Lehmer, "Private Meeting Room and Luncheon for Alpine Lakes Group," 10 June 1975, NFPAR, box 191, folder: Alpine Lakes (II). An especially clear and detailed example of the industry's effort to maintain a local image is R. S. Claunch to A. V. Smyth and K. R. Hundley, 19 January 1976, NFPAR, box 191, folder: Alpine Lakes (I).

44. Douglas W. Scott, interview by author; Polly Dyer, interview by author, 15 September 2001; McCloskey, interview by author. The Sierra Club assisted organization in the Pacific Coast states, and the Wilderness Society took the lead in the Rocky Mountain states. See Roth, *Wilderness Movement and the National Forests: 1964–1980*, 13.

45. Ray E. Johnson, vice president, Industrial Forestry Association, to Washington members, 9 June 1975, NFPAR, box 191, folder: Alpine Lakes (II).

46. Numerous examples can be found in the NFPAR. See Alpine Lakes Coalition, "10,000 Letters Urgently Needed!" 24 October 1973, NFPAR, box 191, folder: Alpine Lakes (II). See also Central Washington Cascades Study Team, *Central Washington Cascades Study;* Business Economics Advisory and Research, Inc., *Central Washington Cascades Study.*

47. "Legislative Plan," [1975], NFPA, box 191, folder: Alpine Lakes (II).

48. Evans, *Alpine Lakes;* Evans, interview by author.

49. Sommarstrom, "Wild Land Preservation Crisis," 112–13.

50. "Legislative Plan," 1.

51. Knibb, *Backyard Wilderness.*

52. Roth, *Wilderness Movement and the National Forests, 1964–1980,* 36–38. For a description of RARE from one of its leaders, see Bill Worf, interview by Gerald Williams, 1 May 1990, 27–29; copy of transcript obtained from the files of Gerald Williams, chief historian, U.S. Forest Service.

53. Ray E. Johnson, vice president, Industrial Forestry Association, to members, "House Interior Committee Action on Alpine Lakes HR 7792," 20 February 1976, NFPAR, box 191, folder: Alpine Lakes (I).

54. See the handwritten list of priorities 1–5 in "Amendments to Meeds Bill," 29 January 1976, NFPAR, box 191, folder: Alpine Lakes (I).

55. H. A. Chevara to James A. Haley, chairman, House Committee on Interior and Insular Affairs, 27 January 1976, NFPAR, box 191, folder: Alpine Lakes (I).

56. Congress, House, Congressman Meeds speaking for the Alpine Lakes Management Act, HR 7792, 94th Cong., 2nd sess., *Congressional Record* 122,

pt. 14 (8 June 1976): 16864–65. Also see the very clear review of events in Popovich, "Ah, Wilderness—an Admiring Look at the Alpine Lakes," 763–66.

57. Lloyd Meeds, Testimony before the Senate Interior Committee, 22 June 1976, copy in NFPAR, box 191, folder Alpine Lakes (I). Also see draft in LMP, box 214.

58. [H. A.] Buzz Chevara, Statement before the Senate Committee on Interior and Insular Affairs, 22 June 1976, copy in NFPAR, box 191, folder: Alpine Lakes (I).

59. Ralph D. Hodges Jr., executive vice president, NFPA, to James T. Lynn, director, Office of Management and Budget, 9 July 1976, 1–2, NFPAR, box 191, folder: Alpine Lakes (I).

60. Paul A. VanderMyde, Testimony before the Committee on Interior and Insular Affairs, United States Senate, copy in NFPAR, box 191, folder: Alpine Lakes (I).

61. Knibb, *Backyard Wilderness*, 223–24; "Alpine Lakes Bill," *Seattle Post-Intelligencer*, 9 July 1976, A10.

62. H. P. Newson, NFPA, to B. L. Orell, Weyerhaeuser Company, 13 July 1976, NFPAR, box 191, folder: Alpine Lakes (I).

63. Douglas W. Scott, interview by author. Knibb (*Backyard Wilderness*, 222) does not mention Ford's direct response, only that he was impressed. Joel Connelly, "Ford Approves Alpine Lakes Wilderness," *Seattle Post-Intelligencer*, 12 July 1976, A1; Daniel J. Evans, "Bipartisanship Protects Washington's Wilderness," *Seattle Times*, 8 September 2003.

64. Ralph D. Hodges Jr. to the president, 22 July 1976, NFPAR, box 191, folder: Alpine Lakes (I).

65. Knibb, *Backyard Wilderness*, 155.

66. Meeds, Testimony before the Senate Interior Committee.

67. See Hirt, *Conspiracy of Optimism*, 241–42.

5 RETURNING FRENCH PETE TO THE THREE SISTERS WILDERNESS AREA, 1968–1978

1. Brock Evans to Gerald Williams, 2 September 1992, 3, quoted in Williams, "French Pete Wilderness Controversy," 12.

2. Karl W. Onthank to David Brower, 21 February 1955, 1, KOCP, box 10, folder: Sierra Club Correspondence, Brower, David R. Also see David R. Brower to Ervin L. Peterson, assistant secretary of agriculture, 12 April 1957,

KOCP, box 10, folder: Sierra Club Projects, Three Sisters; Robert M. Storm, "Proposal for Grant from the National Science Foundation," 1, KOCP, box 1, folder: Three Sisters, Associated Documents; Ruth [Onthank] to Gerry [Sharpe], 9 August 1961, KOCP, box 10, folder: Sierra Club, Outgoing Correspondence; Karl Onthank, "Problems of Oregon's Central Cascades," 4.

3. USDA Forest Service, Willamette National Forest, "Background: Management of the French Pete Drainage," March 1971, copy included in Willamette National Forest, "French Pete Creek."

4. Brock Evans, interview by author, 28 July 2001; Polly Dyer, interview by author, 15 September 2001.

5. Williams, "French Pete Wilderness Controversy," 4–5; Noyes, "French Pete," 28.

6. Williams, "French Pete Wilderness Controversy," 5–6.

7. M. Brock Evans to Douglas W. Scott, 29 March 1968, Douglas W. Scott to M. Brock Evans, 15 April 1968, and Douglas W. Scott to supervisor, Willamette National Forest, draft, 10 April 1968, DSP.

8. Douglas W. Scott to supervisor, Willamette National Forest, draft, 2–3. The position of Northwest conservation representative had shifted by this time to be mainly under the Sierra Club rather than the Federation of Western Outdoor Clubs.

9. Bob Packwood to Clifford Hardin, secretary of agriculture, 26 July 1971, NA-PNW, box 36824, FRC #74B63, folder: French Pete Creek 2150. For one count of the public input to Willamette National Forest officials during a sixty-day comment period from December 1969 to February 1970, see Willamette National Forest, "Report of Ad-Hoc Task Force," [6 February 1970], 7–9, NA-PNW, box 36824, FRC #74B63, folder: French Pete Creek 2150. Of all comments received, 92 percent were postcards supporting the industry's perspective. The President's Council on Environmental Quality later scolded the Forest Service for a biased and "misleading" interpretation of these public comments by not taking into account the number and content of letters (not postcards) that had arrived prior to that particular sixty-day comment period. See Timothy Atkeson, general counsel, Council on Environmental Quality, to T. C. Byerly, U.S. Department of Agriculture, 4 January 1971, 2, copy attached to U.S. Department of Agriculture, "Environmental Statement: Management of French Pete Creek, Willamette National Forest," 14 July 1971, 5, NA-PNW, box 36824, FRC #74B63, folder: French Pete Creek 2150.

10. Quoted in Durbin, *Tree Huggers*, 28.

11. Andy Kerr, interview by author, 28 April 2001; Williams, "French Pete Wilderness Controversy," 5; Oregon Wilderness Coalition, "Three Sisters Wilderness Additions," [1973], DSP. Win Noyes wrote that it was "one of the last seven of the 273 valleys at least five miles long in the Oregon Cascades" ("French Pete," 28).

12. Sale, *Green Revolution*, 29–31; Mrs. Donald E. [Ruth] Clusen, "Broadening Conservation's Constituency," North American Wildlife and Natural Resources Conference, 5 March 1969, SAFR, box 244, folder: League of Women Voters.

13. Noyes, "French Pete," 26; Kerr, interview by author; Bob Packwood to Clifford Hardin.

14. Hirt, *Conspiracy of Optimism*, 249–51. Hirt demonstrates that the dominant trend in national-forest management after World War II was to increase production of timber to unsustainable levels; he refers to specific reports during the Nixon administration—and the French Pete debate—that continued that pressure.

15. Netboy, "French Pete for the People," 59.

16. Irving Brant and Brock Evans, both quoted in Williams, "French Pete Wilderness Controversy," 11.

17. Brock Evans to Gerald Williams, 2 September 1992, 2, quoted in Gerald Williams, "French Pete Wilderness Controversy," 11. Evans also tells the story in Evans, "Environmental Campaigner," 105.

18. Brock Evans to Mr. Scott, [n.d.], handwritten remark in margin of Douglas W. Scott to supervisor, Willamette National Forest, draft.

19. Williams, "French Pete Wilderness Controversy," 8. The final environmental impact statement for the Willamette National Forest Plan in 1977 listed the French Pete Valley as "undeveloped roadless recreation area," but by that point environmentalists had lost all faith in the agency and would not accept anything less than wilderness designation.

20. Morse, "Decision of the Secretary of Agriculture," 6 February 1957, 3, NA-PNW, box 25219, FRC #73A898, folder: Three Sisters Wilderness Area, 1954–66.

21. Richard M. Noyes to Thomas K. Cowden, Department of Agriculture, 7 October 1971, 2, NA-PNW, box 36824, FRC #74B63, folder: French Pete Creek 2150. Emphasis retained from the original.

22. Hirt, *Conspiracy of Optimism*, 248, 188–89. For how wilderness advocates defined multiple use, see, e.g., Brower, "Environmental Activist," 66–69.

23. Wendell B. Barnes, executive vice president, Western Wood Products Association, to Clifford Hardin, secretary of agriculture, 18 November 1969, 1–2, SAFR, box 256, folder: Sierra Club.

24. Society of American Foresters, "Forest Wilderness: A Position of the Society of American Foresters," 3, SAFR, box 276, folder: Statement of SAF on "Endangered Wilderness."

25. Netboy, "French Pete for the People," 18; Willamette National Forest, "Background: Management of the French Pete Drainage," March 1971, 2–3; "French Pete Delay Hailed," *Portland Oregonian*, 19 November 1969, 28; Roth, *Wilderness Movement and the National Forests: 1964–1980*, 49–50.

26. Rumors circulated at a logging conference that month that Packwood sought to gain Nixon's support for preserving French Pete by offering to vote for the president's controversial nomination of Clement Haynsworth to the Supreme Court. Packwood, who later voted against Haynsworth, shot back, "It's a damned lie . . . from men without conscience" ("Lumberman Shocked by Packwood Charge," *Portland Oregonian*, 20 November 1969, 36; "Packwood Denies Making Deal in Trade for Haynsworth Vote," *Portland Oregonian*, 18 November 1969, sec. 2, p. 8).

27. A. Robert Smith, "Conservation Splits Oregon's Senators," *Portland Oregonian*, 23 November 1969, 49; Kerr, "Browning of Bob Packwood," 2 (page number is from manuscript obtained from Andy Kerr, in author's possession).

28. "French Pete Again," *Western Forester* 15, no. 5 (February 1970): 1.

29. U.S. Department of Agriculture, "Environmental Statement," 5.

30. Timothy Atkeson to T. C. Byerly, 1, copy attached to U.S. Department of Agriculture, "Environmental Statement." Also see other responses from state and federal agencies attached to "Environmental Statement."

31. Bob Packwood to Clifford Hardin.

32. McCarthy's statement is given in George W. Williams to Philip L. Heaton, assistant regional forester, 4 October 1971, 3, NA-PNW, box 36824, FRC #74B63, folder: French Pete Creek 2150. This is Williams's report on the Federation of Western Outdoor Clubs annual convention held at Crystal Mountain, Washington, 4–6 September 1971.

33. Bill Worf, interview by Gerald Williams, 1 May 1990, 28. On the ongoing conflict over defining roadless areas, also see Roth, *Wilderness Movement and the National Forests: 1980–1984*, 27; Kerr, interview by author.

34. Kerr, "Browning of Bob Packwood," 2.

35. Holway R. Jones to Senator Robert Packwood, 4 February 1973, 1, DSP. Underline emphasis removed from the original.

36. Ibid., 2.

37. Kerr, "Browning of Bob Packwood," 2.

38. Walth, *Fire at Eden's Gate*, 331–32.

39. Douglas Scott, "Statement on S. 866," 25 May 1972, 3, DSP.

40. Phil Cogswell, "French Pete Argument Heard," *Portland Oregonian*, 26 May 1972, 1; Kerr, "Browning of Bob Packwood," 2; Williams, "French Pete Wilderness Controversy," 14–15.

41. Roth, *Wilderness Movement and the National Forests: 1964–1980*, 38–46; Douglas W. Scott, *Wilderness-Forever Future*, 24–25; Douglas W. Scott, interview by author. Also see articles on the theme, "Wild, Wild East" by Douglas Scott and James Morton Turner in the Spring 2001 issue of *Wild Earth*.

42. Roth (*Wilderness Movement and the National Forests: 1964–1980*, 38) makes this point, as does Kerr (interview by author).

43. Brock [Evans] to Senator Mark Hatfield, 13 October 1972, 3, DSP.

44. See Holway R. Jones, Oregon Wilderness Coalition, to Mark Hatfield, 20 March 1973, 11–13, DSP; Sierra Club, "Environmental Alert," 15 May 1972, 3, NA-PNW, folder: French Pete Creek 2150. The Sierra Club bulletin called for public support for Packwood's recreation area bill, but it also suggested that wilderness would be a more appropriate designation and would forestall strict interpretations of the Wilderness Act. Douglas Scott, "Statement on S. 866," 9–10.

45. Patterson, *Grand Expectations*, 753; "Trouble Flares at Conclusion of Capital Moratorium March," *Portland Oregonian*, 16 November 1969, 1. Marches in Eugene and Portland occurred on Friday, 14 November 1969.

46. Williams, "French Pete Wilderness Controversy," 6. Senator Frank Church, from Idaho, took advantage of the rhetorical connection between antiwar and environmental concerns. Speaking at an Earth Day rally in Pocatello in 1970, "he urged citizens to form a 'moratorium movement' to save the environment." See Ashby and Gramer, *Fighting the Odds*, 346.

47. Netboy, "French Pete for the People," 18, 56.

48. Roth, *Wilderness Movement and the National Forests: 1964–1980*, 50; Williams, "French Pete Wilderness Controversy," 12–13; Sierra Club Columbia Group, "French Pete Creek," 12 November 1969, SAFR, box 256, folder: Sierra Club; Netboy, "French Pete for the People," 18, 56.

49. Roderick Nash, abstract of "Wilderness and the Counterculture," a paper presented at the Organization of American Historians Convention, Chicago, 13 April 1973, USFSHQ, folder: Wilderness: General—Speeches. Also see Nash, *Wilderness and the American Mind*, 251–54, where he argues more simply that the counterculture embraced the wilderness movement but not that it reshaped the movement.

50. Wazeka, "Organizing for Wilderness," 52.

51. Kerr, interview by author. A very similar quote from Kerr is found in Durbin, *Tree Huggers*, 36.

52. Kerr, interview by author.

53. Durbin, *Tree Huggers*, 39–40.

54. Quoted in H. [Hardin] R. Glascock, "A Forester Views His Profession," address to the Fifteenth Annual Washington State Forestry Conference, Seattle, 5 November 1971, SAFR, box 244, folder: Washington State Forestry Conference, 1971.

55. Brock Evans to Robert Platt, Mazamas conservation chairman, December 1970, BEP, box 15, folder: Mazamas, 1967–71. Polly Dyer accuses the Mazamas of often having antiwilderness policies, depending on their leadership at the time (Dyer, interview by author).

56. Sale, *Green Revolution*, 31–32.

57. Scott quoted in Knibb, *Backyard Wilderness*, 202. Knibb claims that public feuding by "extremists on both sides" created an urgency to push through a final compromise over the Alpine Lakes in 1976.

58. Kerr, interview by author. Kerr comments that Arnie Ewing, of the Northwest Timber Association, understood the deadlock and suggested that French Pete be used as trading stock and that the industry drop its opposition to wilderness designation in exchange for guaranteed access to other lands.

59. Jim Weaver to Dave Burwell, 10 March 1977 (quotation), Dave Burwell to Jim Weaver, 16 March 1977, and Jim Weaver to Dave Burwell, 21 March 1977, SAFR, box 276, folder: Regional Policy Issues: Oregon and Maine, 1977. Emphasis and abbreviations retained from the original.

60. Doug Scott to Executive Committee of the National Wilderness Committee, Memorandum-Confidential, 3 March 1976, DSP; Douglas Scott, interview by author.

61. Frank Church's interest in the bill was genuine and was not feigned in order to promote his presidential aspirations. He had been an original supporter of the Wilderness Act, and he was the leading critic in the Senate of the Forest

Service's purity doctrine. On his efforts to pass the Endangered American Wilderness Act, including the 220,000-acre Gospel Hump Wilderness in central Idaho, see Ashby and Gramer, *Fighting the Odds*, 586–88.

62. Gerald Williams, national historian for the U.S. Forest Service, expressed this point in a discussion with the author at his office in Washington, 22 March 2001.

63. Williams, "French Pete Wilderness Controversy," 14.

64. Walth, *Fire at Eden's Gate*, 435.

65. Ibid., 435–38; Hirt, *Conspiracy of Optimism*, 265.

66. Walth, *Fire at Eden's Gate*, 436–41.

6 PICKING UP THE PIECES, 1977–1984

1. Roth, *Wilderness Movement and the National Forests: 1964–1980*, 54–55; Douglas W. Scott, interview by author, 29 April 2001; Andy Kerr, interview by author, 28 April 2001.

2. John R. McGuire, "RARE II: Where From?" Transcript of remarks presented to the Washington Section, Society of American Foresters, Washington, DC, 27 February 1979, 1, SAFR, box 364, folder: RARE II Legislation.

3. M. Rupert Cutler to chief, Forest Service, 2 November 1977, 1, USFSHQ, folder: Wilderness: Laws and Legislation—Dr. M. Rupert Cutler on Wilderness. RARE I studied fifty-six million acres. Not all the roadless areas from RARE I were simply reassessed in RARE II. The latter process used new criteria to define roadless areas and drew new boundaries. Much of the land within RARE I had been designated as wilderness by Congress, such as the Alpine Lakes and French Pete, or, more commonly, the Forest Service had built roads and sold timber in those areas since 1973.

4. U.S. Department of Agriculture, Forest Service, Pacific Northwest Region, "RARE II," 1, NA-PNW, box 36824, FRC #74B63, folder: North Cascades Plan, 11/71; *Wilderness Withdrawals and Timber Supply: How Wilderness Withdrawals Impact Timber Supply, Homebuilding, Employment, Recreation, and Community Stability*, 20 July 1978, 14, NFPAR, box 205, folder: Miscellaneous Materials; U.S. Department of Agriculture, Forest Service, Pacific Northwest Region, *State of Washington Supplement to the USDA Forest Service Draft Environmental Statement, Roadless Area Review and Evaluation II (RARE II)* (June 1978), 68.

5. John R. McGuire, chief, U.S. Forest Service, to Mark O. Hatfield, 28 September 1977, 1, DSP.

6. Roth, *Wilderness Movement and the National Forests: 1980–1984*, 27. Andy Kerr, of the OWC, has mentioned to me that this dispute continues. "To this day, you still see it," he said. "We're still fighting over the same god-damned boundaries. The criteria versus how they're applied" (Kerr, interview by author).

7. M. J. Kuehne, "Statement on S.1180 and H.R. 3454," 20 September 1977, 4, FKP, box 6, folder: Subject Series—RARE II.

8. Quoted in National Forest Products Association, "News: Forest Industry Leaders Urge Speed Up in National Forest Roadless Area Review," 22 September 1977, 1, SAFR, box 364, folder: RARE II Legislation.

9. *Wilderness Withdrawals and Timber Supply*, 14; McGuire, "RARE II: Where From?" 2.

10. U.S. Department of Agriculture, Forest Service, *RARE II*, iii–iv; Williams, "Creation of Wilderness in the Pacific Northwest," 5; R. E. Worthington, regional forester, to RARE II contributor, 20 February 1979, PDF.

11. Clary, *Timber and the Forest Service*, 176.

12. For figures, see U.S. Department of Agriculture, Forest Service, *RARE II*, iv, O-1, S-1.

13. Wilderness Society, Friends of the Earth, Sierra Club, and National Audubon Society, "Forest Service Abandons Wilderness to Developers," 4 January 1979, 1, SAFR, box 364, folder: RARE II Legislation.

14. Quoted in Roth, *Wilderness Movement and the National Forests: 1964–1980*, 58.

15. Roth, *Wilderness Movement and the National Forests: 1980–1984*, 23–27; Durbin, *Tree Huggers*, 57–58.

16. Roth, *Wilderness Movement and the National Forests: 1980–1984*, 26; Kerr, interview by author.

17. Sierra Club, Pacific Northwest Chapter, comp., *Critique and Analysis of the USDA Draft Environmental Statement on Selection of Proposed New Study Areas from Roadless and Undeveloped Areas and Sierra Club Recommendations on Roadless and Undeveloped Areas in Region Six, U.S. Forest Service*, 256–57; the Mountaineers, "Recommendations for Roadless and Undeveloped Areas within the National Forests, State of Washington and Alaska," 17 April 1973, II-1, NA-PNW, MBS Dec. Files 2100–2130, box 4, folder: Coordination, Identification, and Study of Undeveloped Areas [1 of 2].

18. U.S. Department of Agriculture, Forest Service, *RARE II*, S-3–S-8; "Cougar Lakes Wilderness Act (H.R. 4528)," [1979], FKP, box 6, folder: Miscellaneous 1978–79. See also Douglas, *Of Men and Mountains*.

19. Dave Pavelchek and Margie Gibson to assorted conservation and wilderness leaders, 14 July 1978, FKP, box 6, folder: RARE II—General Correspondence—Misc. 1978–79; Citizens for Washington Wilderness, "RARE II: Action Update," [1978], FKP, box 6, folder: RARE II—Organizational Features.

20. Quoted in Mount Baker–Snoqualmie National Forest, press release, 15 June 1978, FKP, box 6, folder: Subject Series—RARE II.

21. W. D. Hagenstein, executive vice president, IFA, to members, Industrial Forestry Association, 26 July 1978, 1, FKP, box 6, folder: RARE II—General Correspondence—Misc. 1978–79.

22. Ibid.

23. Ibid., 3.

24. Ibid., 2–3.

25. McGuire, "RARE II: Where From?" 2.

26. Quoted in Roth, *Wilderness Movement and the National Forests: 1964–1980*, 56.

27. Margot Hornblower, "Carter Will Open 36 Million Acres of U.S. Forests," *Washington Post*, 16 April 1979, A1; "Cougar Lakes Wilderness Act (H.R. 4528)."

28. National Forest Products Association, "News: Forest Industry Applauds Completion of Wilderness Study; Cautions against Delays in Returning Lands to Management," 4 January 1979, 1, SAFR, box 364, folder: RARE II Legislation.

29. National Forest Products Association, "Forest Industry Position, RARE II: A Process for Decision on National Forest Resource Lands," January 1979, 1, 6, SAFR, box 364, folder: RARE II Legislation.

30. National Forest Products Association, "Review of RARE II Objectives: 97th Congress," 6 November 1980, 7, NFPAR, box 206, folder: RARE II Reference Book, November 1980; William D. Dickerson, acting director, Environmental Protection Agency, to John McGuire, chief, Forest Service, 29 September 1978, 3–4, reprinted in U.S. Department of Agriculture, Forest Service, *RARE II*, V-6–V-8; Douglas W. Scott, interview by author; Roth, *Wilderness Movement and the National Forests: 1964–1980*, 59–60; U.S. Department of Agriculture, Office of the Secretary, "Our Response to the RARE II Court Decision," (1979), USFSHQ, folder: Wilderness: General.

31. Donnell, "Why RARE Failed," 39.

32. National Forest Products Association, "Review of RARE II Objectives," 1, 6. Comprehensive discussions of the history of release language can be found in Roth, *Wilderness Movement and the National Forests: 1980–1984*,

1–32. Donnell's "Release and Relief" provides detailed coverage from the perspective of the timber industry. Also see Douglas W. Scott, *Wilderness-Forever Future*, 22–23.

33. H. A. Chevarra, Ray E. Johnson, and George Casseday to Lloyd Meeds, 19 March 1976, NFPAR, box 191, folder: Alpine Lakes (I); Brock Evans to Doug Scott, 31 October 1975, SCP, acc. 2678-2, box 4.

34. For a brief review of the legislative history of release language, see Gorte and Baldwin, *Wilderness Legislation*, 5–8.

35. Roth, *Wilderness Movement and the National Forests: 1980–1984*, 1–3; "Rep. Foley Pushes Timber Industry's Nationwide Anti-wilderness Bill," *Sierra Club National News Report*, 18 December 1979, 1; "Club Finds Opposition to Foley Bills in Congress," *Sierra Club National News Report* 12, no. 14 (9 May 1980): 4.

36. National Forest Products Association, "Review of RARE II Objectives," 2, 6; "Foley Introduces New Bill," *Wilderness Report*, 29 February 1980, 1.

37. National Forest Products Association, "Review of RARE II Objectives," 2, 5; Roth, *Wilderness Movement and the National Forests: 1980–1984*, 3–5.

38. Douglas W. Scott, interview by author; Brock Evans, interview by author, 28 July 2001; Kerr, interview by author.

39. Roth, *Wilderness Movement and the National Forests: 1980–1984*, 24–33; Durbin, *Tree Huggers*, 56–59.

40. U.S. Department of Agriculture, Forest Service, *RARE II*, iii–iv.

41. This point about French Pete was made throughout the debate over that area. See Jones, "French Pete," 8.

42. Kerr, interview by author, emphasis retained from the original transcript; Roth, *Wilderness Movement and the National Forests: 1980–1984*, 26, 32–33.

43. Douglas W. Scott, interview by author.

44. Roth, *Wilderness Movement and the National Forests: 1980–1984*, 33–36; Durbin, *Tree Huggers*, 59; Donnell, "Release and Relief," 38.

45. Jim Montieth to Tim Wapato et al., 2 December 1983, quoted in Roth, *Wilderness Movement and the National Forests: 1980–1984*, 35.

46. Quoted in Durbin, *Tree Huggers*, 59.

47. Ross Anderson, "Wilderness Bill Held Hostage in Forests of D.C.," *Seattle Times*, 15 April 1984, A25; "Logrolling on Wilderness," *Seattle Post-Intelligencer*, 15 April 1984, A30; Donnell, "Release and Relief," 37–38.

48. U.S. Senate Energy Committee Business Meeting, 11 April 1984, quoted in Roth, *Wilderness Movement and the National Forests: 1980–1984*, 18.

49. Roth, *Wilderness Movement and the National Forests: 1980–1984*, 18–20; Donnell, "Release and Relief," 38.

50. Dale Russakoff, "Wilderness Compromise Is Reached," *Washington Post*, 3 May 1984, A1.

51. The Forest Service and the Department of Agriculture complained bitterly about this aspect of the Oregon wilderness bill. See John R. Block, secretary of agriculture, to Morris K. Udall, 15 March 1983, USFSHQ, folder: Wilderness—General.

52. Forest Service historian Dennis Roth argues that the Forest Service "played a significant role" in the compromise over release language, but the actual wilderness boundaries set in 1984 bear little of the agency's influence. See Roth, *Wilderness Movement and the National Forests: 1980–1984*, 20.

53. As an important victory in 1984, Kerr (interview by author) cites Cummins Creek Wilderness in the Oregon Coast Range, which he claims became the first wilderness area in the country that did not have any recreational trails. See also Roth, *Wilderness Movement and the National Forests: 1980–1984*, 33.

54. Roth, *Wilderness Movement and the National Forests: 1980–1984*, 19–20; Douglas W. Scott, interview by author.

55. Quoted in Donnell, "Release and Relief," 38.

56. Ibid., 40.

57. Ibid.

58. Mattey, *Timber Bubble*, 3–5.

59. Ibid., 5–9; *Federal Timber Contract Payment Modifications Act*, Public Law 98-478, *U.S. Code* 16, sec. 618.

60. Quoted in Durbin, *Tree Huggers*, 63.

61. Jim Haley, "Voices in the Proposed Wilderness," *Everett Herald*, 3 July 2001. Also see Joel Connelly, "Mission Possible—Bring Bush into the Wilderness," *Seattle Post-Intelligencer*, 4 July 2001; "Wilderness Close to Home," *Seattle Times*, 4 July 2001.

62. *Oregon Wild*.

EPILOGUE

1. Cronon, "The Trouble With Wilderness," 69. The clearest summary of the wilderness movement and its critics during these years comes from James Morton Turner, "Promise of Wilderness," 278–331.

2. Sutter, *Driven Wild*, 262–63.

3. U.S. Congress, House, Committee on Resources, Subcommittee on Forests and Forest Health, *Oversight Hearing on Process Gridlock on the National Forests*, 107th Cong., 2nd sess., 12 June 2002, 1–2.

4. H. Anthony Ruckel, "The Legal Dilemma of the Forest Service," in *The Case for a Blue Ribbon Commission on Timber Management in the National Forests*, 46. On the Parker Decision, see Roth, *Wilderness Movement and the National Forests: 1964-1980*, 20–22.

5. Klein-Robbehaar, "Judicial Review of Forest Service Timber Sales," 201–2; author's notes from Todd True's remarks made to the Oregon Wilderness Conference, Eugene, Oregon, 28 April 2001.

6. *Seattle Audubon Society v. John L. Evans*, Memorandum Decision and Injunction, C89-160WD (Western District of Washington 1991); Hirt, *Conspiracy of Optimism*, xlii–xliii.

7. U.S. Department of Agriculture, Forest Service, *Roadless Area Conservation Final Environmental Impact Statement Summary*, S-1–S-2; Hirt, *Conspiracy of Optimism*, xli.

8. U.S. Department of Agriculture, Forest Service, *Roadless Area Conservation Final Environmental Impact Statement*, vol. 3, *Agency Responses to Public Comments*, 1–2; Cynthia Lummis, "Public Ignored in Roadless Initiative," *Idaho State Journal*, 17 August 2003.

9. Jennifer Lee, "Administration to Exempt Forest from Road Act," *New York Times*, 16 July 2003, A14.

10. U.S. Department of Agriculture, Forest Service, Department of the Secretary, "Special Areas; State Petitions for Inventoried Roadless Area Management, Final Rule and Decision Memo," *Federal Register* 70, no. 92 (13 May 2005): 25654–57. In September 2006, U.S. District Court Judge Elizabeth Laporte reinstated the Roadless Initiative.

11. Matt Jenkins, "The Wild Card," *High Country News* 35, no. 4 (3 March 2003): 1.

12. Katherine Pfleger, "Wild Sky Isn't All Wild, Plan's Opponents Insist," *Seattle Times*, 16 September 2002

13. Ibid.;" Doug Scott, "All of the 'Wild Skykomish Wilderness' Qualifies under the Wilderness Act," 11–18.

14. Alex Fryer, "Wilderness Backers Look to Nethercutt for Congressional Boost," *Seattle Times*, 22 March 2004.

15. "Still Wild About Wild Sky," *Seattle Times*, 1 March 2003.

16. Ibid.; "Finish Wild Sky," *Seattle Post-Intelligencer*, 11 March 2003.

17. Jenkins, "Wild Card," 10.

18. Ibid., 8–10.

19. "Simpson Offers New Plan for Saving White Clouds Wilderness," *Idaho Statesman*, 18 June 2004; Jim Fisher, "A Middle Road Found Through Idaho's Owyhee's," *Lewiston Morning Tribune*, 18 April 2004, 1F.

20. Robert McClure, "Economists Urge Protection of Old-Growth Forests," *Seattle Post-Intelligencer*, 1 March 2002.

BIBLIOGRAPHY

MANUSCRIPT COLLECTIONS

ALPSP   Alpine Lakes Protection Society Papers. Manuscripts, Special Collections, University Archives. University of Washington Libraries, Seattle.

BEP   Brock Evans Papers. Manuscripts, Special Collections, University Archives. University of Washington Libraries, Seattle.

DSP   Papers obtained from the files of Douglas Scott. Copies in author's possession.

FCP   Frank Church Papers. Special Collections Department. Albertsons Library, Boise State University, Boise, Idaho.

FKP   Fayette Florent Krause Papers. Manuscripts, Special Collections, University Archives. University of Washington Libraries, Seattle.

KOCP   Karl Onthank Conservation Papers. Manuscripts and Special Collections. University of Oregon, Eugene.

LMP   Lloyd Meeds Papers. Manuscripts, Special Collections, University Archives. University of Washington Libraries, Seattle.

NA-PNW   U.S. Department of Agriculture. Forest Service. Record Group 95. National Archives, Pacific Northwest Region, Seattle.

NFPAR   National Forest Products Association Records. Forest History Society, Durham, NC.

PDF   Papers obtained from the files of Polly Dyer. Copies in author's possession.

PDP   Polly Dyer Papers. Manuscripts, Special Collections, University Archives. University of Washington Libraries. Seattle, Washington.

SAF-IER   Society of American Foresters, Inland Empire Section. Records, 1938–84. Manuscript Group 90. University of Idaho Special Collections, Moscow.

SAFR   Society of American Foresters Records. Forest History Society, Durham, NC.

SCP   Sierra Club Northwest Office Records. Manuscripts, Special Collections, University Archives. University of Washington Libraries. Seattle.

USFSHQ   U.S. Forest Service Headquarters History Collection. Forest History Society, Durham, NC.

OTHER SOURCES

Allin, Craig W. *The Politics of Wilderness Preservation*. Westport, CT: Greenwood Press, 1982.

Ashby, LeRoy, and Rod Gramer. *Fighting the Odds: The Life of Senator Frank Church*. Pullman: Washington State University Press, 1994.

Baldwin, Donald N. *The Quiet Revolution: Grass Roots of Today's Wilderness Preservation Movement*. Boulder, CO: Pruett Publishing Co., 1972.

Balogh, Brian. *Chain Reaction: Expert Debate and Public Participation in American Commercial Nuclear Power, 1945–1975*. Cambridge: Cambridge University Press, 1991.

Beckey, Fred. *Cascade Alpine Guide*. Vol. 1. Seattle: The Mountaineers, 1973.

———. *Range of Glaciers: The Exploration and Survey of the Northern Cascade Range*. Portland: Oregon Historical Society Press, 2003.

Beierle, Thomas C., and Jerry Cayford. *Democracy in Practice: Public Participation in Environmental Decisions*. Washington, DC: Resources for the Future, 2002.

Booth, Douglas E. *Valuing Nature: The Decline and Preservation of Old-Growth Forests*. Lanham, MD: Rowman and Littlefield Publishers, 1994.

Brooks, Paul. "A Copper Company vs. the North Cascades." *Harper's* 235, no. 1408 (September 1967): 48–50.

———. *The Pursuit of Wilderness*. Boston: Houghton Mifflin Co., 1971.

Brower, David R. "Environmental Activist, Publicist, and Prophet." Interviews conducted by Susan Schrepfer, 1974–78. Berkeley: Regional Oral History Office, Bancroft Library, University of California, 1980.

———. "The Missing Million: Crisis in the North Cascades." *Sierra Club Bulletin* 44, no. 2 (February 1959): 10–15.

Buckman, Robert E., and Richard L. Quintus. *Natural Areas of the Society of American Foresters*. Washington, DC: Society of American Foresters, 1972.

Bultena, Gordon L., and John C. Hendee. "Foresters' Views of Interest Group Positions on Forest Policy." *Journal of Forestry* 70, no. 6 (June 1972): 337–42.

Business Economics Advisory and Research, Inc. *Central Washington Cascades Study: An Economic-Ecological Evaluation, Summary Report*. Seattle: Central Washington Cascades Study Team, 1972.

Cafaro, Philip. "For a Grounded Conception of Wilderness and More Wilderness on the Ground." *Ethics and the Environment* 6, no. 1 (Spring 2001): 1–17.

Caldwell, Lynton K., Lynton R. Hayes, and Isabel M. MacWhirter. *Citizens and the Environment: Case Studies in Popular Action*. Bloomington: Indiana University Press, 1976.

Callicott, J. Baird, and Michael P. Nelson, eds. *The Great New Wilderness Debate*. Athens: University of Georgia Press, 1998.

Case, Robert Ormond, and Victoria Case. *Last Mountains: The Story of the Cascades*. Portland, OR: Binfords and Mort, 1945.

The Case for a Blue Ribbon Commission on Timber Management in the National Forests. Denver: Rocky Mountain Chapter of the Sierra Club and Western Regional Office of the Wilderness Society, 1970.

Catton, Theodore. *Inhabited Wilderness: Indians, Eskimos, and National Parks in Alaska*. Albuquerque: University of New Mexico Press, 1997.

———. *Wonderland: An Administrative History of Mount Rainier National Park*. Seattle: National Park Service Cultural Resources Program, 1996.

Central Washington Cascades Study Team. *Central Washington Cascades Study*. Seattle: Central Washington Cascades Study Team, 1972.

Clary, David A. *Timber and the Forest Service*. Lawrence: University Press of Kansas, 1986.

Clawson, Marion. *The Federal Lands: Their Use and Management*. Baltimore: John Hopkins Press, 1957.

————. *The Federal Lands since 1956: Recent Trends in Use and Management*. Washington, DC: Resources for the Future, 1967.

Clepper, Henry. "A Calm View of a Heated Subject." *Journal of Forestry* 60, no. 5 (May 1962): 297–300.

Confederated Tribes of the Warm Springs Reservation. *The People of Warm Springs*. Warm Springs, OR: Confederated Tribes of the Warm Springs Reservation, 1984.

Cooley, Richard A., and Geoffrey Wandesforde-Smith, eds. *Congress and the Environment*. Seattle: University of Washington Press, 1970.

Cotroneo, Ross R. "United States v. Northern Pacific Railway Company: The Final Settlement of the Land Grant Case, 1924–1941." *Pacific Northwest Quarterly* 71, no. 3 (July 1980): 107–11.

Cox, Thomas R., Robert S. Maxwell, Phillip Drennon Thomas, and Joseph J. Malone. *This Well-Wooded Land: Americans and Their Forests from Colonial Times to the Present*. Lincoln: University of Nebraska Press, 1985.

Cronon, William. *Changes in the Land: Indians, Colonists, and the Ecology of New England*. New York: Hill and Wang, 1983.

————. "The Trouble with Wilderness; or, Getting Back to the Wrong Nature." In *Uncommon Ground: Rethinking the Human Place in Nature*, ed. William Cronon, 69–90. New York: W. W. Norton, 1996.

Cutler, M. Rupert. "Land Trusts and Wildlands Protection." *Wild Earth* 8 (Summer 1998): 43–48.

Dana, Samuel Trask, and Sally K. Fairfax. *Forest and Range Policy: Its Development in the United States*. 2nd ed. New York: McGraw-Hill, 1980.

Danner, Lauren. "Cultural Values and Communication Content: The Environment and Washington State in the 1960s." Ph.D. diss., University of Oregon, 1999.

deBuys, William. *Enchantment and Exploitation: The Life and Hard Times of a New Mexico Mountain Range*. Albuquerque: University of New Mexico Press, 1985.

Devall, Bill. "The Deep, Long-Range Ecology Movement, 1960–2000: A Review." *Ethics and the Environment* 6, no. 1 (2001): 18–41.

Dilworth, J. R. *Land Use Planning and Zoning*. Proceedings of a Short Course for Foresters, Corvallis, OR, 6–7 February 1969. Corvallis: School of Forestry, Oregon State University, 1971.

Dirks-Edmunds, Jane Claire. *Not Just Trees: The Legacy of a Douglas-Fir Forest*. Pullman: Washington State University Press, 1999.

Donnell, Rich. "Wilderness: Cooler Heads Prevailed when the Wilderness System Became Law." *Timber Harvesting* 32, no. 5 (May 1984): 33–35.

———. "Purity: Lost in Wilderness, Part II." *Timber Harvesting* 32, no. 6 (June 1984): 32–34.

———. "Why RARE Failed: Lost in Wilderness, Part III." *Timber Harvesting* 32, no. 7 (July 1984): 34–39.

———. "Release and Relief: Lost in Wilderness, Part Four." *Timber Harvesting* 32, no. 8 (August 1984): 36–41.

Douglas, William O. *My Wilderness: The Pacific West*. New York: Pyramid Books, 1960.

———. *Of Men and Mountains*. New York: Harper, 1950.

———. "A Wilderness Bill of Rights." *Mazama* 43, no. 13 (December 1961): 12–13.

Dow, Edson. *Passes to the North: History of the Wenatchee Mountains*. Wenatchee, WA: Outdoor Publishing Co., 1963.

Durbin, Kathie. *Tree Huggers: Victory, Defeat, and Renewal in the Northwest Ancient Forest Campaign*. Seattle: The Mountaineers, 1996.

Dyer, Polly. Interview by author, 14 September 2001, Seattle, WA. Tape recording in author's possession.

———. "Preserving Parklands and Wilderness." Interview conducted by Susan Schrepfer, 1983. In *Pacific Northwest Conservationists*. Berkeley: Regional Oral History Office, Bancroft Library, University of California, 1986.

Eaton, Walter Prichard. *Skyline Camps: A Note Book of a Wanderer in Our Northwestern Mountains*. Boston: W. A. Wilde Co., 1922.

Egan, Timothy. *The Good Rain: Across Time and Terrain in the Pacific Northwest*. New York: Alfred A. Knopf, 1990.

Encyclopedia of American Forest and Conservation History. New York: Macmillan Publishing Co., 1983.

Evans, Brock. *Alpine Lakes*. With a foreword by David Brower. Seattle: The Mountaineers, 1971.

———. "The Alpine Lakes: Stepchild of the North Cascades." *Living Wilderness* 32, no. 101 (Spring 1968): 21–31.

———. "Environmental Campaigner: From the Northwest Forests to the Halls of Congress." Interview conducted by Ann Lage, 1982. In *Building* the Sierra Club's National Lobbying Program, 1967–1981, comp. Ann Lage. Berkeley: Regional Oral History Office, Bancroft Library, University of California, 1985.

———. "In Celebration of Wilderness: The Progress and the Promise." Wilderness Resource Distinguished Lectureship, no. 7. University of Idaho Wilderness Research Center, 14 November 1984.

———. Interview by author, 28 July 2001, Clarkston, WA. Tape recording in author's collection.

———. "New Effort to Save Oregon Wilderness." Western Outdoor Quarterly 35, no. 1 (Winter 1968): 1–9.

———. "Proposed Mount Jefferson Wilderness." Living Wilderness 31, no. 99 (Winter 1967–68): 30–34.

———. "Wilderness Myths and Misconceptions." In Voices for the Earth: A Treasury of The Sierra Club Bulletin, ed. Ann Gilliam, 411–14. San Francisco: Sierra Club Books, 1979.

Ficken, Robert E. The Forested Land: A History of Lumbering in Western Washington. Durham, NC: Forest History Society; Seattle: University of Washington Press, 1987.

Fisher, Andrew H. "The 1932 Handshake Agreement: Yakama Indian Treaty Rights and Forest Service Policy in the Pacific Northwest." Western Historical Quarterly 28 (Summer 1997): 187–217.

Flader, Susan L., and J. Baird Calicott. The River of the Mother of God and Other Essays by Aldo Leopold. Madison: University of Wisconsin Press, 1991.

Flores, Dan. Horizontal Yellow: Nature and History in the Near Southwest. Albuquerque: University of New Mexico Press, 1999.

Foreman, Dave. Confessions of an Eco-warrior. New York: Harmony Books, 1991.

———. "The Real Wilderness Idea." In Changing Perspectives and Future Directions: Proceedings of the "Wilderness Science in a Time of Change Conference" Held in Missoula, Montana, 23–27 May 1999, compiled by David N. Cole et al., vol. 1, 32–38. RMRS-P-15-VOL-1. Ogden, UT: USDA Forest Service, Rocky Mountain Research Station, 2000.

Foster, John Bellamy. Marx's Ecology: Materialism and Nature. New York: Monthly Review Press, 2000.

Fox, Stephen. The American Conservation Movement: John Muir and His Legacy. Madison: University of Wisconsin Press, 1981.

Franklin, Jerry F., and C. T. Dyrness. *Natural Vegetation of Oregon and Washington*. Pacific Northwest Forest and Range Experiment Station, General Technical Report PNW-8. Portland, OR: USDA Forest Service, 1973.

Friedman, Mitch, and Paul Lindholdt, eds. *Cascadia Wild: Protecting an International Ecosystem*. Bellingham, WA: Greater Ecosystem Alliance, 1993.

Frome, Michael. *Battle for the Wilderness*. Rev. ed. Salt Lake City: University of Utah Press, 1997.

———. *The Forest Service*. 2nd ed. Boulder, CO: Westview Press, 1984.

———, ed. *Issues in Wilderness Management*. Boulder, CO: Westview Press, 1985.

———. *Promised Land: Adventures and Encounters in Wild America*. New York: William Morrow and Co., 1985.

Frost, Robert. *Collected Poems, Prose, and Plays*. New York: Library of America, 1995.

George, Anthony J. *The Santiam Mining District of the Oregon Cascades: A Cultural Property Inventory and Historical Survey*. Salem, OR: Shiny Rock Mining Corp., 1985.

Giddens, Anthony. *The Consequences of Modernity*. Stanford, CA: Stanford University Press, 1990.

Gillette, Elizabeth R., ed. *Action for Wilderness*. San Francisco: Sierra Club, 1972.

Gilliam, Harold. "Shattering the Wilderness Myths." *The Mountaineer* 58, no. 12 (November 1965): 1–2.

Gilligan, James P. "The Development of Policy and Administration of Forest Service Primitive and Wilderness Areas in the Western United States." Ph.D. diss., University of Michigan, 1953.

Glacier Peak Land Management Study: Mt. Baker and Wenatchee National Forests, Washington. Portland, OR: USDA Forest Service, Pacific Northwest Region, 1957.

Glover, James M. *A Wilderness Original: The Life of Bob Marshall*. Seattle: The Mountaineers, 1986.

Goble, Dale D., and Paul W. Hirt. *Northwest Lands, Northwest Peoples: Readings in Environmental History*. Seattle: University of Washington Press, 1999.

Goldsworthy, Patrick D. "Protecting the North Cascades, 1954–1983."

Interview by Ann Lage, 1983. In *Pacific Northwest Conservationists*. Berkeley: Regional Oral History Office, Bancroft Library, University of California, 1986.

Gonzalez, George A. *Corporate Power and the Environment: The Political Economy of U.S. Environmental Policy*. Lanham, MD: Rowman and Littlefield Publishers, 2001.

Goodman, Doug, and Daniel McCool. *Contested Landscape: The Politics of Wilderness in Utah and the West*. Salt Lake City: University of Utah Press, 1999.

Gorte, Ross W., and Pamela Baldwin. *Wilderness Legislation: History of Release Language, 1979–1992*. Washington, DC: Congressional Research Service, Library of Congress, 1993.

Gottlieb, Robert. *Forcing the Spring: The Transformation of the American Environmental Movement*. Washington, DC: Island Press, 1993.

Graber, Linda H. *Wilderness as Sacred Space*. Monograph Series of the Association of American Geographers. Washington, DC: Association of American Geographers, 1976.

Graf, William L. *Wilderness Preservation and the Sagebrush Rebellions*. Savage, MD: Rowman and Littlefield Publishers, 1990.

Guha, Ramachandra. "Radical American Environmentalism and Wilderness Preservation: A Third World Critique." *Environmental Ethics* 11, no. 1 (Spring 1989): 71–83.

Gunther, Erna. *Ethnobotany of Western Washington*. Rev. ed. Seattle: University of Washington Press, 1973.

Haar, Charles S., and Jerold S. Kayden, eds. *Zoning and the American Dream: Promises Still to Keep*. Chicago: American Planning Association, 1989.

Haeberlin, Hermann, and Erna Gunther. *The Indians of Puget Sound*. University of Washington Publications in Anthropology, vol. 4, no. 1. Seattle: University of Washington Press, 1930.

Hagenstein, William David. "Forestry's Advocate." Interviews by Elwood R. Maunder and George T. Morgan, 1960, and by Harold K. Steen, 1992. Durham, NC: Forest History Society, 1995.

Harvey, Mark W. T. "Howard Zahniser: A Legacy of Wilderness." *Wild Earth* 8 (Summer 1998): 62–66.

———. *A Symbol of Wilderness: Echo Park and the American Conservation Movement*. Seattle: University of Washington Press, 2000.

————. *Wilderness Forever: Howard Zahniser and the Path to the Wilderness Act.* Seattle: University of Washington Press, 2005.

Hays, Samuel P. *Beauty, Health, and Permanence: Environmental Politics in the United States, 1955–1985.* Cambridge: Cambridge University Press, 1987.

————. *Conservation and the Gospel of Efficiency: The Progressive Conservation Movement, 1890–1920.* Cambridge, MA: Harvard University Press, 1959.

————. *Explorations in Environmental History.* Pittsburgh: University of Pittsburgh Press, 1998.

————. "The Structure of Environmental Politics since World War II." *Journal of Social History* 14, no. 4 (Summer 1981): 719–38.

Hendee, John C., George H. Stankey, and Robert C. Lucas. *Wilderness Management.* Miscellaneous Publication no. 1365. Washington, DC: USDA Forest Service, 1978.

Hirt, Paul W. *A Conspiracy of Optimism: Management of the National Forests since World War Two.* Lincoln: University of Nebraska Press, 1994.

————. "Institutional Failure in the U.S. Forest Service: A Historical Perspective." *Research in Social Problems and Public Policy* 7 (1999): 217–39.

Hollenbeck, Jan L. *A Cultural Resource Overview: Prehistory, Ethnography, and History, Mt. Baker–Snoqualmie National Forest.* Portland, OR: USDA Forest Service, Pacific Northwest Region, 1987.

Jackson, Philip I., and A. Jon Kimerling. *Atlas of the Pacific Northwest.* 8th ed. Corvallis: Oregon State University Press, 1993.

Jones, Holway R. "French Pete—Why We Must Save It." *Northwest Conifer* 9, no. 2 (March 1968): 7–9.

————. "The RARE Opportunity." *Sierra Club Bulletin* 61, no. 9 (October 1976): 10–15.

Kaufman, Herbert. *The Forest Ranger: A Study in Administrative Behavior.* Washington, DC: Johns Hopkins University Press, 1960.

Keane, John T. "The Wilderness Act as Congress Intended." *American Forests* 77, no. 2 (February 1971): 40–43, 61–63.

Kerouac, Jack. *The Dharma Bums.* New York: Viking Press, 1958.

Kerr, Andy. "The Browning of Bob Packwood." *Cascadia Times* 1, no. 6 (1995).

————. "The Browning of Bob Packwood." Unpublished paper in author's possession. N.d.

———. Interview by author, 28 April 2001, Eugene, OR. Tape recording in author's collection.

Keyser, C. Frank. *The Preservation of Wilderness Areas: An Analysis of Opinion on the Problem*. Washington, DC: Legislative Reference Service, Library of Congress, 1949.

Kimmins, Hamish. *Balancing Act: Environmental Issues in Forestry*. Vancouver, BC: UBC Press, 1992.

Klein-Robbehaar, John. "Judicial Review of Forest Service Timber Sales: Environmental Plaintiffs Gain New Options under the Oregon Wilderness Act." *Natural Resources Journal* 35, no. 1 (Winter 1995): 201–20.

Knibb, David. *Backyard Wilderness: The Alpine Lakes Story*. Seattle: The Mountaineers, 1982.

Knight, Richard L., and Peter B. Landres, eds. *Stewardship across Boundaries*. Washington, DC: Island Press, 1998.

Koch, Elers. *Forty Years a Forester, 1903–1943*. Missoula: Mountain Press, 1998.

Krahe, Diane L. "A Sovereign Prescription for Preservation: The Mission Mountains Tribal Wilderness." In *Trusteeship in Change: Toward Tribal Autonomy in Resource Management*, ed. Richmond L. Clow and Imre Sutton, 195–221. Boulder: University Press of Colorado, 2001.

Kruckeberg, Arthur R. *The Natural History of Puget Sound Country*. Seattle: University of Washington Press, 1991.

Landres, Peter, and Shannon Meyer. *National Wilderness Preservation System Database: Key Attributes and Trends, 1964 through 1998*. General Technical Report RMRS-GTR-18. Ogden, UT: USDA Forest Service, Rocky Mountain Research Station, October 1998.

Langston, Nancy. *Where Land and Water Meet: A Western Landscape Transformed*. Seattle: University of Washington Press, 2003.

Lien, Carsten. *Olympic Battleground: The Power Politics of Timber Preservation*. 2nd ed. Seattle: Mountaineers Books, 2000.

Limerick, Patricia Nelson. "Forestry and Modern Environmentalism: Ending the Cold War." *Journal of Forestry* 100 (December 2002): 46–50.

———. *Legacy of Conquest: The Unbroken Past of the American West*. New York: W. W. Norton, 1987.

Louter, David. *Contested Terrain: North Cascades National Park Service Complex, an Administrative History*. Seattle: National Park Service, 1998.

Luxenberg, Gretchen A. *Historic Resource Study, North Cascades National Park Service Complex, Washington*. Seattle: Cultural Resources Division, Pacific Northwest Region, National Park Service, 1986.

Manning, Harvey. *The North Cascades*. Seattle: The Mountaineers, 1964.

———. *Washington Wilderness: The Unfinished Work*. Seattle: The Mountaineers, 1984.

———. *The Wild Cascades: Forgotten Parkland*. With a foreword by William O. Douglas. The Exhibit-Format Series, ed. David Brower. San Francisco: Sierra Club, 1965.

———. "You Don't Have to Be Old to Be an Elder." *Backpacker* 3, no. 1 (Spring 1975): 56–59, 84–89.

Marsh, Kevin R. "'This Is Just the First Round': Designating Wilderness in the Central Oregon Cascades, 1950–1964." *Oregon Historical Quarterly* 103, no. 2 (Summer 2002): 210–33.

Mathews, Daniel. *Cascade-Olympic Natural History: A Trailside Reference*. Portland, OR: Raven Editions, 1988.

Mattey, Joe P. *The Timber Bubble That Burst: Government Policy and the Bailout of 1984*. New York: Oxford University Press, 1990.

May, Allan. *Voice in the Wilderness*. Chicago: Nelson-Hall, 1978.

McCloskey, J. Michael. "A Conservation Agenda for 1969." *Sierra Club Bulletin* 53, no. 12 (December 1968): 5.

———. *In the Thick of It: My Life in the Sierra Club*. Washington, D.C.: Island Press, 2005.

———. Interview by author, 7 November 2003, Portland, OR. Tape recording in author's collection.

———. "My Career Begins." 3 October 2002. Chapter 3 of unpublished memoir in author's possession.

———, ed. *Prospectus for a North Cascades National Park*. Seattle: North Cascades Conservation Council, 1963.

———. "The Waldo Lake Battle." *Western Outdoor Quarterly* 29, no. 1 (Winter 1962): 3–6.

———. "The Wilderness Act of 1964: Its Background and Meaning." *Oregon Law Review* 45 (June 1966): 288–314.

———. "Wilderness Movement at the Crossroads: 1945–1970." *Pacific Historical Review* 41, no. 3 (August 1972): 346–61.

McConnell, Grant. "The Cascades Wilderness." *Sierra Club Bulletin* 41, no. 10 (December 1956): 24–31.

————. "The Multiple-Use Concept in Forest Service Policy." *Sierra Club Bulletin* 44, no. 7 (October 1959): 14–28.

————. "Northern Cascades." *Sierra Club Bulletin* 42, no. 1 (January 1957): 20–23.

————. *Stehekin: A Valley in Time.* Seattle: The Mountaineers, 1988.

————. "Wilderness World." *The Mountaineer* 51, no. 4 (1958): 7–15.

McKee, Bates. *Cascadia: The Geologic Evolution of the Pacific Northwest.* New York: McGraw-Hill, 1972.

McPhee, John. *Encounters with the Archdruid.* New York: Farrar, Straus, and Giroux, 1971.

Meine, Curt. *Aldo Leopold: His Life and Work.* Madison: University of Wisconsin Press, 1988.

Meinig, D. W. *The Great Columbia Plain: A Historical Geography, 1805–1910.* With a foreword by William Cronon. Weyerhaeuser Environmental Classics. Seattle: University of Washington Press, 1995.

Merriam, Lawrence C. *Saving Wilderness in the Oregon Cascades: The Story of the Friends of the Three Sisters.* Eugene, OR: Friends of the Three Sisters Wilderness, 1999.

Milner, Clyde A., Carol A. O'Connor, and Martha A. Sandweiss, eds. *The Oxford History of the American West.* New York: Oxford University Press, 1994.

Nash, Roderick. *The Rights of Nature: A History of Environmental Ethics.* Madison: University of Wisconsin Press, 1989.

————. *Wilderness and the American Mind.* 4th ed. New Haven: Yale University Press, 2001.

National Parks and Conservation Association. *Nature Has No Borders: A Collection of Papers Presented at a Conference on the Protection and Management of the Northern Cascades Ecosystem, Held in Seattle, Washington, 15–17 March 1994.* Seattle: Peanut Butter Publishing Co., n.d.

Netboy, Anthony. "French Pete for the People." *American Forests* 76, no. 5 (May 1970): 16–18, 56–59.

Neuberger, Richard L., and Hardin Glascock. "Ah Wilderness." Transcript of a discussion moderated by Tom McCall. Broadcast on *Viewpoint*, KGW-TV, Portland, OR, 1958. Forest History Society, Durham, NC.

Norse, Elliott A. *Ancient Forests of the Pacific Northwest.* Washington, DC: Island Press, 1990.

North Cascades Study Team. *The North Cascades: A Report to the Secre-*

tary of the Interior and the Secretary of Agriculture. Washington, DC: U.S. Department of the Interior and U.S. Department of Agriculture, 1965.

Noyes, Winninette A. "French Pete: Lowland Valley in the Cascades," *Living Wilderness* 32, no. 104 (Winter 1968–69): 25–29.

Onthank, Karl. "Problems of Oregon's Central Cascades." *Sierra Club Bulletin* 44, no. 1 (January 1959): 4–6.

Outdoor Recreation Resources Review Commission. *ORRRC Study Report 3: Wilderness and Recreation—A Report on Resources, Values, and Problems.* Report to the Outdoor Recreation Resources Review Commission by the Wildland Research Center, University of California. Washington, DC: Government Printing Office, 1962.

———. *Outdoor Recreation for America: A Report to the President and to the Congress by the Outdoor Recreation Resources Review Commission.* Washington, DC: Government Printing Office, 1962.

Oelschlaeger, Max. *The Idea of Wilderness.* New Haven: Yale University Press, 1991.

Opie, John. *Nature's Nation: An Environmental History of the United States.* Fort Worth, TX: Harcourt Brace College Publishers, 1998.

Oregon Wild: Preserving Oregon's Legacy. Portland, OR: Oregon Natural Resources Council, 2001.

Orr, Elizabeth L., and William N. Orr. *Geology of Oregon.* 5th ed. Dubuque, IA: Kendall/Hunt Publishing Co., 1999.

O'Toole, Randal Lee. *An Economic View of RARE II.* Eugene, OR: Cascade Holistic Economic Consultants, 1978.

Patterson, James T. *Grand Expectations: The United States, 1945–1974.* New York: Oxford University Press, 1996.

Peattie, Roderick, ed. *The Cascades: Mountains of the Pacific Northwest.* New York: Vanguard Press, 1949.

Popovich, Luke. "Ah, Wilderness—an Admiring Look at the Alpine Lakes." *Journal of Forestry* 74, no. 11 (November 1976): 763–66.

———. "Forestry Today: The Endangered Wilderness Debate." *Journal of Forestry* 75, no. 6 (June 1977): 341–43.

Power, Thomas Michael. *Lost Landscapes and Failed Economies: The Search for a Value of Place.* Washington, DC: Island Press, 1996.

Price, Larry W. *Mountains and Man: A Study of Process and Environment.* Berkeley and Los Angeles: University of California Press, 1981.

Price, Tom. "From Hardware to Software: How the Wilderness Movement Got Its Start." *High Country News* 33, no. 2 (January 29, 2001): 20.

Pyles, Hamilton K. "Multiple Use of the National Forests." Interview by Susan R. Schrepfer, 1971. Forest History Society, Santa Cruz, CA, 1972.

Pyne, Stephen J. *Fire in America: A Cultural History of Wildland and Rural Fire*. Seattle: University of Washington Press, 1982.

Rakestraw, Lawrence. "Conservation Historiography: An Assessment." *Pacific Historical Review* 41, no. 3 (August 1972): 271–88.

———. "A History of Forest Conservation in the Pacific Northwest, 1891–1913." Ph.D. diss., University of Washington, 1955.

———. *A History of Forest Conservation in the Pacific Northwest, 1891–1913*. The Management of Public Lands in the United States, ed. Stuart Bruchey. New York: Arno Press, 1979.

———. "Sheep Grazing in the Cascade Range: John Minto vs. John Muir." *Pacific Historical Review* 27 (1958): 371–82.

Rakestraw, Lawrence, and Mary Rakestraw. *History of the Willamette National Forest*. Eugene, OR: Willamette National Forest, [1991].

Robbins, William G. *Colony and Empire: The Capitalist Transformation of the American West*. Lawrence: University Press of Kansas, 1994.

———. *The Early Conservation Movement in Oregon, 1890–1910*. Man's Activities as Related to Environmental Quality. Corvallis: Oregon State University, 1975.

———. *Landscapes of Conflict: The Oregon Story, 1940–2000*. Seattle: University of Washington Press, 2004.

———. *Landscapes of Promise: The Oregon Story, 1800–1940*. Seattle: University of Washington Press, 1997.

———. *The Oregon Environment: Development vs. Preservation, 1905–1950*. Man's Activities as Related to Environmental Quality. Corvallis: Oregon State University, 1975.

Robbins, William G., and James C. Foster, eds. *Land in the American West: Private Claims and the Common Good*. Seattle: University of Washington Press, 2000.

Roe, JoAnn. *The North Cascadians*. Seattle: Madrona Publishers, 1980.

Rome, Adam. "'Give Earth a Chance': The Environmental Movement and the Sixties," *Journal of American History* 90, no. 2 (September 2003): 525–54.

Roth, Dennis M. "The National Forests and the Campaign for Wilderness Legislation." Unpublished manuscript, n.d. U.S. Forest Service Historical

Collection. Folder: Wilderness: Laws and Legislation—Campaign for Wilderness Legislation. Forest History Society, Durham, NC.

———. *The Wilderness Movement and the National Forests*. College Station, TX: Intaglio Press, 1995.

———. *The Wilderness Movement and the National Forests, 1964–1980*. Washington, DC: USDA Forest Service, 1984.

———. *The Wilderness Movement and the National Forests, 1980–1984*. Washington, DC: USDA Forest Service, 1988.

Rothenberg, David, ed. *Wild Ideas*. Minneapolis: University of Minnesota Press, 1995.

Rothman, Hal K. *Devil's Bargains: Tourism in the Twentieth-Century American West*. Lawrence: University Press of Kansas, 1998.

———. *The Greening of a Nation? Environmentalism in the United States since 1945*. Fort Worth, TX: Harcourt Brace and Co., 1998.

———. "'A Regular Ding-Dong Fight': Agency Culture and Evolution in the NPS-USFS Dispute, 1916–1937." *Western Historical Quarterly* 2 (May 1989): 141–61.

———, ed. *Reopening the American West*. Tucson: University of Arizona Press, 1998.

Rudzitis, Gundars. *Wilderness and the Changing American West*. New York: John Wiley and Sons, 1996.

Runte, Alfred. *National Parks: The American Experience*. 3rd ed. Lincoln: University of Nebraska Press, 1997.

Sabatier, Paul A., and Hank C. Jenkins-Smith, eds. *Policy Change and Learning: An Advocacy Coalition Approach*. Boulder: Westview Press, 1993.

Sale, Kirkpatrick. *The Green Revolution: The American Environmental Movement, 1962–1992*. A Critical Issue Series, ed. Eric Foner. New York: Hill and Wang, 1993.

Schwantes, Carlos. *The Pacific Northwest: An Interpretive History*. Lincoln: University of Nebraska Press, 1996.

Schwartz, Susan. *Cascade Companion*. Seattle: Pacific Search Books, 1976.

Scott, Douglas W. "All of the 'Wild Skykomish Wilderness' Qualifies under the Wilderness Act." Research memorandum. Campaign for America's Wilderness. June 2003.

———. "Congress's Practical Criteria for Designating Wilderness." *Wild Earth* 11, no. 1 (Spring 2001): 28–32.

———. *The Enduring Wilderness*. Golden, CO: Fulcrum Publishing, 2004.

———. Interview by author, 29 April 2001, Eugene, OR. Tape recording in author's collection.

———. *A Wilderness-Forever Future: A Short History of the National Wilderness Preservation System*. A Pew Wilderness Center Research Report, 2001. Washington, DC: Pew Wilderness Center, 2001.

Scott, James C. *Seeing Like a State: How Certain Schemes to Improve the Human Condition Have Failed*. New Haven: Yale University Press, 1998.

Scott, John. "The Three Sisters Primitive Area." *Mazama* 33, no. 12 (December 1951): 53–54.

Seideman, David. *Showdown at Opal Creek: The Battle for America's Last Wilderness*. New York: Carroll and Graf Publishers, 1993.

Sierra Club, Pacific Northwest Chapter, comp. *Critique and Analysis of the USDA Draft Environmental Statement on Selection of Proposed New Study Areas from Roadless and Undeveloped Areas and Sierra Club Recommendations on Roadless and Undeveloped Areas in Region Six, U.S. Forest Service*. Eugene, OR: Sierra Club Pacific Northwest Chapter, 1973.

Simons, David R. *The Need for Scenic Resource Conservation in the Northern Cascades of Washington*. San Francisco: Sierra Club Conservation Committee, 1958.

———. "These Are the Shining Mountains." *Sierra Club Bulletin* 44, no. 7 (October 1959): 1–13.

Smith, Allan H. *Ethnography of the North Cascades*. Pullman: Center for Northwest Anthropology, Washington State University, 1987.

Smith, Frank E., comp. *Land and Water, 1900–1970*. Conservation in the United States: A Documentary History, vol. 2. New York: Chelsea House Publishers, 1971.

Snow, Donald. "A Politics Appropriate to Place." In *Writers on the Range: Western Writers Exploring the Changing Face of the American West*, ed. Karl Hess Jr. and John A. Baden. Boulder: University Press of Colorado, 1998.

Snyder, Gary. *The Practice of the Wild*. New York: North Point Press, 1990.

———. *Turtle Island*. New York: New Directions Books, 1974.

Society of American Foresters. *Converting the Old Growth Forest: Proceedings of the Society of American Foresters Annual Meeting, Held in Portland, Oregon, 1955*. Washington, DC: Society of American Foresters, 1956.

Sommarstrom, Allan Ralph. "Wild Land Preservation Crisis: The North Cascades Controversy." Ph.D. diss., University of Washington, 1970.

Soulé, Michael E., and Gary Lease. *Reinventing Nature? Reponses to Postmodern Deconstruction*. Washington, DC: Island Press, 1995.

Spagna, Ana Maria. *Now Go Home: Wilderness, Belonging, and the Crosscut Saw*. Corvallis: Oregon State University Press, 2004.

Steen, Harold K. *The U.S. Forest Service: A History*. Centennial ed. Seattle: University of Washington Press, 2004.

Stegner, Wallace Earle. "Coda: Wilderness Letter." In *The Sound of Mountain Water*, by Wallace Stegner. New York: Dutton, 1980.

———. *This Is Dinosaur: Echo Park Country and Its Magic Rivers*. New York: Knopf, 1955.

Stone, J. Herbert. "A Regional Forester's View of Multiple Use." Interview conducted by Elwood R. Maunder, 1971. Santa Cruz: Forest History Society, 1972.

Sutter, Paul Shriver. "'A Blank Spot on the Map': Aldo Leopold, Wilderness, and U.S. Forest Service Recreational Policy, 1909–1924." *Western Historical Quarterly* 29, no. 2 (Summer 1998): 187–213.

———. *Driven Wild: How the Fight against Automobiles Launched the Modern Wilderness Movement*. Seattle: University of Washington Press, 2002.

Tautges, Alan. "The Oregon Omnibus Wilderness Act of 1978 as a Component of the Endangered American Wilderness Act of 1978, Public Law 95-237." *Environmental Review* 13, no. 1 (Spring 1989): 43–61.

Turner, James Morton. "The Promise of Wilderness: A History of American Environmental Politics, 1964–1994." Ph.D. diss., Princeton University, 2004.

———. "Wilderness East: Reclaiming History." *Wild Earth* 11, no. 1 (Spring 2001): 19–27.

Turner, Tom. *Sierra Club: One Hundred Years of Protecting Nature*. New York: Harry N. Abrams, 1991.

U.S. Congress. House of Representatives. Committee on Agriculture and Committee on Interior and Insular Affairs. *Oregon RARE II Resolution Act of 1981: Joint Hearings before the Subcommittee on Forests, Family Farms, and Energy and the Subcommittee on Public Lands and National Parks on H.R. 1511*. 97th Cong., 1st sess., 19–21 February 1981.

U.S. Congress. House of Representatives. Committee on Resources. Subcommittee on Forests and Forest Health. *Oversight Hearing on Process Grid-lock on the National Forests.* 107th Cong., 2nd sess., 12 June 2002.

U.S. Congress. Public Land Law Review Commission (Paul W. Gates). *History of Public Land Law Development.* Washington, DC: Government Printing Office, 1968.

U.S. Congress. Senate. Committee on Energy and Natural Resources. *Oregon Wilderness Act of 1979: Hearings before the Subcommittee on Parks, Recreation, and Renewable Resources on S. 1384.* 96th Cong., 1st sess., 3 and 6 July and 27 September 1979.

U.S. Congress. Senate. Committee on Interior and Insular Affairs. *The North Cascades: Hearings before the Subcommittee on Parks and Recreation on S. 1321.* 90th Cong., 1st sess., 24 and 25 April and 25, 27, and 29 May 1967. Washington: Government Printing Office, 1967.

———. *Oregon Omnibus Wilderness Act: Hearing before the Subcommittee on the Environment and Land Resources on S. 812 and S. 1369.* 94th Cong., 2nd sess., 25 October 1976.

U.S. Department of Agriculture. Forest Service. *Final Environmental Impact Statement on a Recommended Land Use Plan for the Alpine Lakes Area of the State of Washington.* Washington, DC: USDA Forest Service, September 1974.

———. *In the Matter of: Mount Jefferson Wilderness Proposal.* Official transcript of proceedings before the USDA Forest Service. Salem, OR, 26 October 1966. Portland, OR: USDA Forest Service, Pacific Northwest Region, 1967.

———. *RARE II: Final Environmental Statement, Roadless Area Review and Evaluation.* Washington, DC: USDA Forest Service, January 1979.

———. *Roadless and Undeveloped Areas: Draft Environmental Statement.* Washington, DC: USDA Forest Service, 1973.

———. *Roadless Area Conservation Final Environmental Impact Statement Summary.* Washington, DC: USDA Forest Service, November 2000.

———. *Roadless Area Conservation Final Environmental Impact Statement.* Vol. 3, *Agency Responses to Public Comments.* Washington, DC: USDA Forest Service, November 2000.

———. *Summary, Final Environmental Statement: Roadless Area Review and Evaluation, RARE II.* Washington, DC: USDA Forest Service, January 1979.

———. *Wilderness: The National Forests . . . America's Playgrounds.* Washington, DC: USDA Forest Service, 1963.

U.S. Department of Agriculture. Forest Service. Department of the Secretary. "Special Areas; State Petitions for Inventoried Roadless Area Management, Final Rule and Decision Memo." *Federal Register* 70, no. 92 (13 May 2005): 25653–66.

U.S. Department of Agriculture. Forest Service. Mount Baker National Forest. "Historical Report, 1897–1950." Acc. 1525, v. f. 679. Manuscripts, Special Collections, University Archives. University of Washington Libraries, Seattle.

U.S. Department of Agriculture. Forest Service. Mount Baker and Wenatchee National Forests. *Glacier Peak Land Management Study.* Portland, OR: USDA Forest Service, Pacific Northwest Region, 1957.

U.S. Department of Agriculture. Forest Service. Pacific Northwest Region. *Draft Environmental Statement on a Recommended Land Use Plan for the Alpine Lakes Area in the State of Washington.* USDA-FS-DES-Adm 73-91. Portland, OR: USDA Forest Service, Pacific Northwest Region, July 1973.

———. *Report on the Proposed Alpine Lakes Wilderness, Mt. Baker–Snoqualmie and Wenatchee National Forests, Washington.* Portland, OR: USDA Forest Service, Pacific Northwest Region, 1975.

———. *State of Oregon Supplement to the USDA Forest Service Environmental Statement, Roadless Area Review and Evaluation II (RARE II).* Portland, OR: USDA Forest Service, Pacific Northwest Region, June 1978.

———. *State of Washington Supplement to the USDA Forest Service Environmental Statement, Roadless Area Review and Evaluation II (RARE II).* Portland, OR: USDA Forest Service, Pacific Northwest Region, June 1978.

U.S. Department of Agriculture. Office of Information. Motion Picture Service. *Wilderness Encampment.* 1961.

Vale, Thomas R. *The American Wilderness: Reflections on Nature Protection in the United States.* Charlottesville: University of Virginia Press, 2005.

Waldo, Judge John B. *Letters and Journals from the High Cascades of Oregon, 1877–1907.* Compiled and edited by Gerald W. Williams. Eugene, OR: USDA Forest Service, Umpqua and Willamette National Forests, 1992.

Walth, Brent. *Fire at Eden's Gate: Tom McCall and the Oregon Story.* Portland: Oregon Historical Society Press, 1994.

Warth, John. "Wilderness Is for Families, Too!" *Sierra Club Bulletin* 46, no. 4 (April 1961): 6–7.

Washington State Planning Council. *Cascade Mountains Study, State of Washington: An Inquiry into the Kind, Amount, and Utilization of the Resources of the Cascade Mountains of Washington as Delimited by the Boundaries of the Snoqualmie, Wenatchee, Columbia, Chelan, and Mount Baker National Forests.* Olympia: Washington State Planning Council, 1940.

———. *A Master Plan for Forestry in Washington.* Research Publication 4, December 1936.

Wayburn, Edgar. "Join the Glacier Peak Task Force." *Sierra Club Bulletin* 41, no. 3 (March 1956): 3.

———. *Your Land and Mine: Evolution of a Conservationist.* With Allison Alsup. San Francisco: Sierra Club Books, 2004.

Wazeka, Robert T. "Organizing for Wilderness: The Oregon Example." *Sierra Club Bulletin* 61, no. 9 (October 1976): 48–52.

Wengert, Norman. "The Ideological Basis of Conservation and Natural Resources Policies and Programs." *Annals of the American Academy of Political and Social Science* 344 (1962): 65–75.

Wilderness Alps of Stehekin. 30-minute, 16mm film, written and narrated by David Brower. 1958.

Wilkeson, Samuel. *Wilkeson's Notes on Puget Sound, Being Extracts from Notes by Samuel Wilkeson of a Reconnoissance of the Proposed Route of the Northern Pacific Ralroad Made in the Summer of 1869.* Seattle: Shorey Book Store, 1964.

"Will We Discover the North Cascades in Time?" *Sierra Club Bulletin* 42, no. 6 (June 1957): 12–16.

Willamette National Forest. "French Pete Creek." August 1973. Bound collection of documents obtained from the files of Gerald W. Williams, national historian, U.S. Forest Service.

Willers, Bill, ed. *Unmanaged Landscapes: Voices for Untamed Nature.* Washington, DC: Island Press, 1999.

Williams, Gerald W. "Creation of Wilderness in the Pacific Northwest: The Controversy Expands." Unpublished paper in author's possession. 25 November 1997.

———. "The French Pete Wilderness Controversy, 1937–1978: A Leadership Case Study." Unpublished paper in author's possession. N.d.

———. "Wilderness Act and the Roadless Area Reviews." Unpublished paper in author's possession. N.d.

———. "The Wilderness Controversy." Unpublished paper in author's possession. 9 May 2000.

Worf, Bill. Interview by Gerald Williams, 1 May 1990, Missoula, MT. Copy of transcript obtained from the files of Gerald Williams, chief historian, U.S. Forest Service.

Wyant, William. *Westward in Eden: The Public Lands and the Conservation Movement*. Berkeley and Los Angeles: University of California Press, 1982.

INDEX

In this index the use of *m* indicates that a map will be found in the text and the use of *n* indicates a note. Specific information regarding debates can be found by location.

listen) policy, 41, 80, 104; interwar era policies, 54; limited areas
designation, 27, 41, 80; local vs.
national concerns, responsiveness
to, 31; mining and road building
programs, 80, 163*n*50, 169*n*2;
National Park Service relationship, 45, 56–57; National Wilderness Preservation System and the,
5; post–WW II policies, 36, 45–
46, 52, 53; primitive areas, designation and regulation of, 23, 24,
25, 80; protected area designation, 5; roadless designation
defined, 110; roadless land,
public support for development
of, 126; wild area designation,
23–24; wilderness preservation
heritage, 10, 23, 36, 45–46, 72,
147, 168*n*31

Forest Service, autonomy over wilderness decisions: Alpine Lakes
debate and, 79, 95–97; citizen
influence on, 88–90; congressional oversight, 34–35, 59, 97;
conservation organizations influence, 58–60; culture supporting,
84–85; loss of, 12; post–Wilderness Act, 72, 82–85, 88–89;
RARE II attempt to regain,
124–127, 138–139; wilderness
advocates movement to limit,
34–35

Forest Service, multiple use management policy: defined, 106–107;
French Pete debate, 101, 106–
107; rhetorical strategy of, 45,

162*n*23, 171*n*17; Three Sisters
debate, 26; wilderness preservation vs., 44–47, 81

Forest Service, RARE I (Roadless
Area Review and Evaluation I):
Alpine Lakes debate, 93–94;
French Pete debate, 109–110;
wilderness areas identified by,
112–113

Forest Service, RARE II (Roadless
Area Review and Evaluation II):
failure/political insufficiency
of, 138–139; goal of, 124–125;
public input, 125, 126, 131;
roadless land inventory, 125–126,
181*n*3; timber industry reaction,
126; wilderness advocates challenge of, 129–130

Forest Service, RARE II final EIS:
California rejection of, 131–132,
134–135; EPA response to, 132;
judicial rulings regarding, 131–
132; land distribution recommendations, 127; ONRC lawsuit,
137; public response, 126–130;
timber industry response, 129–
131

Forest Service, RARE II, wilderness
bills post-: *1984* legislation, 138–
140; release language in debates
over, 132–135, 137–138, 140–
141, 185*n*52

Forest Service, timber sales and road
building programs: Alpine Lakes
Limited Area, 79–83, 86; Alpine
Lakes Wilderness Area, 169*n*2;
Cascades, 97; clear-cut logging

Forest Service *(continued)*
practices, 29–30; Cooper Lake
region, 81–85; Cooper Pass
region, 86; Dwyer decision, effect
on, 146; environmental movement to limit, 90; French Pete
Valley, 101, 102–103; Horse
Creek, 36, 101, 103; Jack Creek,
86; management policy, 133;
Mount Baker, 56; NEPA review
requirements, 89; Pelly moratorium proposal, 56; post–WW II
changes, 10–11; pressure to
expand, 105–106; road construction regulations, 80; Roadless
Initiative, 147–148; Skykomish
River valley, 121; Stevens Pass
region, 86; Three Sisters Primitive
Area, 101; Wenatchee National
Forests, 56; Whitewater Creek
valley, 63, 65, 67, 68, 70
Freeman, Orville L., 56, 66, 72, 82,
106
French Pete addition to Three Sisters
Wilderness Area, 100*m*
French Pete Creek: acreage, 112–
113; hiking in, 118; historical
overview, 102; map of, 20*m*,
100*m*; Three Sisters Primitive
Area, added to, 24; timber board
feet contained in, 105; timber
sales and road building programs
in, 101, 102–103
French Pete debate: citizen participation, 108, 111; compromise,
possibility of, 101, 106, 113,
117, 180*n*57; congressional

involvement, 108, 110; context
of, 101; mentioned, 124; Packwood legislation, 108, 111–113,
117, 179*n*44; timber industry
and, 104, 107, 117, 152,
180*n*57
French Pete debate, conservation
community in the: congressional
appeal, 108; divisions resulting
from, 116, 127–128, 144; intermediate recreation area proposal,
103, 104, 108, 111–112; Mazamas position, 116; OWC focus,
135–136; political influence, 116–
117; pressure tactics, 103; strategy of greater publicity, 104, 105,
111; student activism, 113–115;
wilderness designation attempt,
112–113
French Pete debate, Forest Service
plan: Endangered American
Wilderness Act effect on, 118,
119; Gibney position, 105–106;
NEPA effect on, 108–109; post-
EIS, 109; RARE I wilderness
recommendations, 109–110;
support for, 103–105, 116; timber management policy, role in,
133
French Pete Intermediate Recreation
Bill, 103, 104, 108, 111–112
Freyfogle, Eric, 15
Friends of the Three Sisters Wilderness, 27–28, 33, 36–37, 101, 102,
115
Frome, Michael, 39, 41
Frost, Robert, 14, 15

Mount Jefferson debate *(continued)*
position, 70–71; conservationists
proposals, 63–69; focus of, 8;
Forest Service proposals, 63–64,
67–72, 112; Glacier Peak debate
compared, 64; Marion Lake basin
inclusion, 74–76; recreation element in, 68; role of big trees in,
67–68, 74; timber industry position, 63, 69–70; wilderness advocates proposal, 72–73
Mount Jefferson Primitive Area:
boundaries, 61, 62m, 64, 68;
popularity for recreation, 64;
redesignation to Wilderness Area,
63–64, 66; timber sales and road
building programs in, 63
Mount Jefferson Wilderness Act,
12, 75
Mount Jefferson Wilderness Area:
boundaries, 61, 62m, 63–64;
congressional position on, 70;
described, 8; Marion Lake basin
inclusion, 74–76; Wilderness Act
effect on creating, 66
Mount Rainier, 8, 17
Mount Rainier National Park, 4m,
8, 45, 122m, 128
Mount Rainier Forest Reserve,
17, 45
Mount Stuart, 78m
Mount Thielsen, 4m, 123m
Mount Washington, 4m, 20m, 27,
123m
Mount Washington Wild Area, 20m,
26
Muir, John, 50

Multiple Use and Sustained Yield
Act of 1960, 45, 107
Murie, Olaus, 22
Murray, Patty, 142

Nash, Roderick, vii, 114
National Environmental Policy Act
(NEPA), 89, 93, 108–109, 132,
148
National Forest Management Act
(NFMA), 138, 146
National Forest Products Association (NFPA): Alpine Lakes debate,
involvement in, 90–92, 94, 96;
RARE II recommendations and,
130, 131, 133–135; as timber
industry lobby, 48
national forests: creation of, 17;
logging of, 10, 90, 101; price of
lumber in, 141; timber industry
position on, 46
National Forest Wild Areas Act, 112
National Forest Wilderness Areas,
4m
National Lumber Manufacturers
Association, 48
national parks, 45, 46, 52–60
National Park Service, 45; Forest Service relationship, 56–57; interwar-
era policies, 54; land control transfer from Forest Service jurisdiction, 52–60; National Wilderness
Preservation System and the, 5
National Recreation Area (NRA),
Alpine Lakes proposal, 90, 94
National Wilderness Preservation
System, 5, 55, 66, 73, 124

wilderness debates. *See also specific debates*: *1950s*, 25; *1960s* and *1970s*, 12–13, 99; citizen participation in, 12–13, 98, 99, 101; competing interests in, 11–12; lessons learned through, 143–144; post–WW II, 10, 13; role of big trees in, 64–65; twenty-first century, 145–151

wilderness movement. *See also* conservation community: *1950s*, 25; *1960s–1970s* social culture, effect on, 99, 114, 115–116; focus of, 11, 29, 99; forces shaping, 25; growth of, 34–35; internal divisions, 134–137; legacy of, 36; Northwest, 99, 113–114; political influence, 48–49, 116–117; post–WW II, 32; twenty-first century, 148–151, 169n1

wilderness movement, strategies used by: collaboration, 149–151; creating national parks, 11; greater publicity, 31, 49–52, 82, 92, 129; land control transfers, 52–60; lawsuits, 11, 12, 137, 171n37; letter writing, 31, 104, 129; photography books, 17; romanticization of the wilderness, 17; single-use rhetoric, 171n17

wilderness politics, 12–13, 36, 98. *See also* environmental politics

wilderness preservation: multiple use management policy vs., 44–47; pre vs. post–WW II, 17, 36

Wilderness Society, 29, 30, 50, 88–89, 169n1

wilderness system, acres in the, viii

Wild Sky Wilderness proposal, 142

Wild Sky Wilderness bill, 148–150

Wilkeson, Samuel, 9

Willamette National Forest, 29, 125

Willamette National Forest management: anti-logging moratorium demonstrations, 114; Horse Creek valley, 19; Mount Jefferson Wilderness debate, 70; timber sales and road building programs, 25–26, 65, 102, 105; timber volume, 105

Willamette Valley, 8

William O. Douglas Wilderness Area, 4m, 122m

Williams, Gerard, 119

Witter, Bob, 95

Woodpecker Ridge, 64, 68

Worf, Bill, 110

World War II, post-war years: environmental movement, 10–11, 41, 90; Forest Service wilderness protection, 45–46, 52; timber demand, 10, 46, 52, 53, 63; timber industry land-use practices, 77, 90

Wyden, Ron, 148

Yard, Robert Sterling, 52

Zahniser, Howard, 29, 30, 34, 35, 87–88, 124

Zalesky, Laura, 42

Zalesky, Philip, 42, 54

Native Seattle: Histories from the Crossing-Over Place
   by Coll Thrush
The Country in the City: The Greening
   of the San Francisco Bay Area by Richard Walker
Drawing Lines in the Forest: Creating Wilderness Areas
   in the Pacific Northwest by Kevin R. Marsh

WEYERHAEUSER ENVIRONMENTAL CLASSICS

The Great Columbia Plain: A Historical Geography,
   1805–1910 by D. W. Meinig
Mountain Gloom and Mountain Glory: The Development
   of the Aesthetics of the Infinite by Marjorie Hope Nicolson
Tutira: The Story of a New Zealand Sheep Station
   by Herbert Guthrie-Smith
A Symbol of Wilderness: Echo Park and the American
   Conservation Movement by Mark W. T. Harvey
Man and Nature: Or, Physical Geography as Modified
   by Human Action by George Perkins Marsh; edited and
   annotated by David Lowenthal
Conservation in the Progressive Era: Classic Texts
   edited by David Stradling

CYCLE OF FIRE BY STEPHEN J. PYNE

Fire: A Brief History
World Fire: The Culture of Fire on Earth
Vestal Fire: An Environmental History, Told through Fire,
   of Europe and Europe's Encounter with the World
Fire in America: A Cultural History of Wildland and Rural Fire
Burning Bush: A Fire History of Australia
The Ice: A Journey to Antarctica

Library of Congress Cataloging-in-Publication Data

Marsh, Kevin R.
Drawing lines in the forest : creating wilderness areas
in the Pacific Northwest / Kevin R. Marsh.
p. cm. — (Weyerhaeuser environmental books)
Includes bibliographical references and index.
ISBN-13: 978-0-295-98702-6 (hardback : alk. paper)
ISBN-10: 0-295-98702-2 (hardback : alk. paper)
1. Wilderness areas—Cascade Range—History. I. Title.
II. Title: Creating wilderness areas in the Pacific North-
west. III. Series: Weyerhaeuser environmental book.
QH76.5.C37.M37 2006   333.78'21609795—dc22
2006034210